Concealment of Politics,
Politics of Concealment

Concealment of Politics, Politics of Concealment

THE PRODUCTION OF "LITERATURE" IN MEIJI JAPAN

Atsuko Ueda

STANFORD UNIVERSITY PRESS
STANFORD, CALIFORNIA

Stanford University Press
Stanford, California

Printed in the United States of America on acid-free, archival-quality paper

Library of Congress Cataloging-in-Publication Data

Ueda, Atsuko.
  Concealment of politics, politics of concealment : the production of
"literature" in Meiji Japan / Atsuko Ueda.
      p. cm.
  Includes bibliographical references and index.
  ISBN 978-0-8047-5778-2 (cloth : alk. paper)
  1. Japanese fiction--Meiji period, 1868-1912--History and criticism. I.
Title.

PL747.6.U35 2007
895.6'34209--dc22

                         2007029929

Typeset by Bruce Lundquist in 10.5/14 Adobe Garamond Pro

For Makoto

Contents

Acknowledgments

It gives me great pleasure to finally be able to thank and acknowledge the many people who made this project possible. First, I would like to express my gratitude to my adviser, Ken Ito, for the unrelenting and tireless support he has given me throughout my graduate school years and beyond. He is my goal for what an adviser should be. I was also blessed to have Timothy Bahti, Ross Chambers, Jim Porter, and Esperanza Ramirez-Christensen on my dissertation committee, all of whom provided invaluable guidance at the dissertation stage.

On the other side of the Pacific, Professor Komori Yōichi of Tokyo University has been a tremendous mentor and a supporter, who so generously offered his time and expertise to this project. I am particularly indebted to writer and critic Mizumura Minae, who first inspired me to pursue this career when I was an undergraduate and has since been my guiding light.

Thanks are also due to Brett de Bary, who very generously read and commented on my dissertation even when I wasn't her student. Michael Bourdaghs and Thomas LaMarre were extremely helpful at the crucial stage when I was seeking a publisher; I thank them both for their support and friendship. I would also like to thank Naoki Sakai on the incisive comments he provided for the article that eventually turned into Chapter 4 of this book.

My former colleagues at the University of Illinois, Urbana-Champaign—Nancy Ablemann, Nancy Blake, Marilyn Booth, Kai-wing Chow, Kevin Doak (now Georgetown University), David Goodman, Rania Huntington, Lilia Kaganovsky, Alexander Mayer, Jerry Packard, Michael Palencia-Roth, Brian Ruppert, Robert Rushing, Ronald Toby, and Gary Xu—enriched my intellectual life while in Illinois. I am particularly grateful for the presence of

Simona Sawhney (now University of Minnesota), who helped not only intellectually but personally as I tried to keep my sanity as a beginning assistant professor. Ted Hughes (now Columbia University) was also a joy to be with, both as a talented scholar and good friend.

My colleagues at Princeton University have been a great inspiration, providing unwavering support to my personal and professional endeavors. I thank Amy Borovoy, Patrick Caddeau, Martin Collcutt, Benjamin Elman, Sheldon Garon, Tom Hare, Martin Kern, Perry Link, Seiichi Makino, Susan Naquin, and Willard Peterson. I am particularly indebted to Richard Okada for all the stimulating conversations and for sharing with me the love of Japanese *dorama* like no other, and also to David Howell, for not only being a careful reader of my manuscript but for offering his support as chair and valuable colleague. Young-ah Chung has also been a great presence at Princeton, as the discussions on Meiji texts I had with her often made me rethink about the arguments I presented in this book.

I also thank my colleagues in Japan: Andō Kyōko, Kanai Keiko, Kaneko Akio, Kōno Kensuke, Nakayama Akihiko, Ōno Ryōji, Takahashi Osamu, Yamamoto Yoshiaki, all of whom introduced me into the circle of Japanese *kokubungaku* when I initially began this project. It was with them that I learned to have scholarly discussions in Japanese and discovered that *real* discussions are done at *nomikais* held after official events.

I am extremely grateful for Yasuko Makino of Princeton University and Setsuko Noguchi of University of Illinois, Urbana-Champaign, two invaluable librarians without whom I could have never completed the project. I also thank Nobuko Toyosawa for assisting in the final preparation of the manuscript as she tirelessly checked the romanizations and citations in the book.

My friends continued to introduce joy and stimulation to my intellectual and personal life throughout the duration of this project: Mark Gibeau, Michele Mason, Miri Nakamura, Christopher Scott, Robert Tierney, and Leslie Winston. Tim Van Compernolle and David Rosenfeld diligently read versions of my chapters, offering thoughtful comments on how to improve my manuscript. Marcy Wheeler has been a friend and a model editor, whose comments much beyond mere editorial suggestions have contributed greatly as I struggled to clarify my too often cryptic arguments. Richi Sakakibara engaged with this project from its inception and has been an ideal friend and colleague who long shared with me the theoretical perspectives and the rigor by which to address reading and writing.

I am especially grateful to Christine Marran for her incisive and thoughtful comments on my manuscript; I am further deeply indebted to Jim Reichert, who offered timely suggestions and invaluable help throughout the process of writing this manuscript. I also thank Muriel Bell, Carolyn Brown, Cynthia Lindlof, Kirsten Oster, and Joa Suorez at Stanford University Press for making this project possible.

Funds from Horace H. Rackham Graduate School and from the Center for Japanese Studies at the University of Michigan supported much of my dissertation research and writing. The Center for Advanced Study at the University of Illinois, Urbana-Champaign, supported my leave when I made significant progress on revising the manuscript. Research funds from Princeton University have been invaluable in the final stages of revision. An earlier version of Chapter 3 appeared as "The Production of Literature and the Effaced Realm of the Political," in *Journal of Japanese Studies* 31, no. 1 (Winter 2005); and a version of Chapter 4 appeared as "The Colonial Ambivalence and the 'Modern Novel': De-Asianization in Tsubouchi Shōyō's 'The Essence of the Novel,'" in *TRACES: A Multilingual Series of Cultural Theory and Translation*, vol. 3 (Hong Kong: Hong Kong University Press, 2004).

My family has put up with a whole lot in the years I took to finish this project. I thank my parents, Naoharu and Yasuko Ueda, and my sister, Tomoko Ueda, for creating the very conditions from which my interest in Japanese literature grew and for providing continued support, both mentally and financially. Despite my being an oddball in the family, they never doubted me, even when my own confidence failed me. I am also grateful to the Hayashi family for quietly supporting my work and my way of life, welcoming me every summer despite the fact that I returned only for a very brief stay. My greatest debt goes to Makoto Hayashi, who has had to deal with my many tantrums throughout the years, especially as I tried to complete this project. I have been comforted by his presence; he offered not only tremendous emotional support but also material ones, as he took over the household chores when I was in a bind. Most of all, I thank him for letting me pursue my career, even when it meant living apart. And finally my sincere thanks to N for all the joy she brought to our lives, just by sitting by us and talking to us when she so chose.

Notes on Japanese Names and Terms

Japanese names, when cited in full, are written family name first. I have followed the Japanese convention by referring to writers by their pen names (e.g., Shōyō instead of Tsubouchi); for those writers who used their own names or those whose full names were pen names, I have referred to them by their family name (e.g., Fukuzawa for Fukuzawa Yukichi and Futabatei for Futabatei Shimei, a pen name for Hasegawa Tatsunosuke). For pre-Meiji writers, I have again followed the Japanese scholarly convention of referring to their given names (e.g., Akinari for Ueda Akinari). Names of writers of works in English, however, follow the order given in the publication. Japanese common nouns and proper nouns that appear in English-language dictionaries are rendered in roman type without macrons. All other Japanese terms are italicized with macrons used to indicate long vowels. All translations from the Japanese, unless otherwise noted, are mine.

Concealment of Politics,
Politics of Concealment

ONE

Introduction

Shōsetsu shinzui *as the Ideological Origin of Modern Japanese Literature*

No discussion of modern Japanese literary development is complete without references to Tsubouchi Shōyō's (1859–1935) *Shōsetsu shinzui* (*The Essence of the Novel*, 1885–86), which has consistently been designated as the origin of modern Japanese literature. Although literary historians have offered varying interpretations of *Shōsetsu shinzui* throughout the years, the rhetoric of "development" and "progress" that situates *Shōsetsu shinzui* at the originary point of modern literary reform and Shōyō as the founder of modern Japanese literature is ubiquitous.

This seminal text is one of the first comprehensive theories to be written on the *shōsetsu*.[1] As Kamei Hideo's "*Shōsetsu*"ron, a brilliant recent study of *Shōsetsu shinzui* has shown, much of *Shōsetsu shinzui*'s theoretical endeavors were on a par with, if not more advanced than, its Euro-American counterparts.[2] *Shōsetsu shinzui* is composed of two volumes, the first of which consists of six sections: "Shogen" (Introduction), "Shōsetsu sōron" (The Comprehensive Theory of the *Shōsetsu*), "Shōsetsu no hensen" (The Vicissitudes of the *Shōsetsu*), "Shōsetsu no shugan" (The Main Themes of the *Shōsetsu*), "Shōsetsu no shurui" (The Types of *Shōsetsu*), and "Shōsetsu no hieki" (The Benefits of the *Shōsetsu*). The second volume, which focuses on the methodological aspects of writing the *shōsetsu*, includes "Shōsetsu hōsoku sōron" (The Comprehensive Rules of the *Shōsetsu*), "Buntairon" (The Theory of Style), "Shōsetsu kyakushoku no hōsoku" (Principles of Construction in the *Shōsetsu*), "Jidai shōsetsu no kyakushoku" (The Configuration of the Historical *Shōsetsu*), "Shujinkō no setchi" (Configuring the Protagonist), and "Jojihō" (The Methods of Description). Just by the title of these sections, we can see the multiple perspectives from which *Shōsetsu shinzui* sought to theorize the *shōsetsu*.

Despite its multidimensionality, references to this seminal text are limited primarily to the first volume, and more narrowly to "The Main Themes of the *Shōsetsu*." Perhaps the most-often-quoted passage of *Shōsetsu shinzui* is the following from "The Main Themes of the *Shōsetsu*":

> A writer is like a psychologist. He must create his characters based on the principles of psychology. If he creates, by his own design, characters who deviate from human emotions (*ninjō*) or, worse, from the principles of psychology, those characters would merely be figments of the writer's imagination rather than those belonging to the human world. . . . The writer should therefore focus his talents on human psychology. Although the characters may be his own creation, he must not design them based on his ideas of good and bad or right and wrong. Instead, he must simply observe (*bōkan*) and depict (*mosha*) them as they are (*ari no mama*).[3]

It is not an exaggeration to say that this passage canonized *Shōsetsu shinzui* as the origin of modern Japanese literature. The focus on the apparent call for psychological realism, a *shōsetsu* that realistically portrays emotions (*ninjō*) and customs and manners (*fūzoku setai*), dominates the study of *Shōsetsu shinzui*, whereas discussions on the vicissitudes and benefits of the *shōsetsu*, not to mention the entire second volume, which theorizes the practice of writing a *shōsetsu*, are too often overlooked. Such a focalized, and as we shall see shortly, highly ideological view of *Shōsetsu shinzui* as the origin of modern Japanese literature can be traced back to the turn of the century.[4] Takayama Chogyū, for example, in his famous "Meiji no shōsetsu" (The *Shōsetsu* of Meiji, 1897) espouses Shōyō's position in the following manner:

> When Shōyō entered the scene, publishing *Shōsetsu shinzui* and *Tōsei shosei katagi* [*The Character of Modern Students*, 1885–86], he exposed the fallacy of didacticism (*kanzen chōaku*) and opened the path toward realistic *shōsetsu* (*shajitsushō setsu*);[5] everyone then began to pursue it, completely altering the literary attitude.[6]

Such narrative became even more dramatic with the advent of naturalism and the emergence of psychological realism as the primary theme of the *shōsetsu*.

Consider, for example, the following passage from Ikuta Chōkō's Meiji *jidai bunpan* (*A Guide to Meiji Letters*, 1907):

> *Shōsetsu shinzui* is truly a revolutionary (*kakumeiji*) of the world of the *shōsetsu*. The loud cry of this revolution—the loud cry that attempted to introduce a brand-new trend to our nation's literary world—woke up even the lifeless, old-fashioned writers of the time. The imprudent didacticism was defeated in the eyes of the public, and realism (*shajitsu*) was valued. Portraying the psychology (*shinri*) with emotions (*ninjō*) as the main aim of the *shōsetsu* became the general trend.[7]

Marking a transition from "old-fashioned" didacticism to psychological realism, *Shōsetsu shinzui* thus signified a break from "premodern" literary practices. Once such a narrative was established, *Shōsetsu shinzui* began to embody the criteria by which the *shōsetsu* was evaluated. It became a filter through which literary historians defined "premodern" and "modern" works. This narrative was reproduced throughout the twentieth century, and in different shape or form, *Shōsetsu shinzui* has since been an ideological site where modern Japanese literature was founded.[8] This is not to say, however, that there have been no scholars who questioned *Shōsetsu shinzui*'s status. Works by literary critics Maeda Ai and Kamei Hideo have, as early as the 1960s, questioned this sudden turn toward "the modern."[9] Asukai Masamichi, too, questioned the originary status of *Shōsetsu shinzui* and instead designated political *shōsetsu* as "the beginning of modern literature."[10] Peter Kornicki was similarly critical of *Shōsetsu shinzui*'s position as origin in his book, *Reform of Fiction in Meiji Japan*, where he discussed the varying forms of "reform" in the 1880s, highlighting the fact that Shōyō was by no means the first or the only critic to call for "literary reform." Yet for a long time these exceptions stood side by side with the many other narratives of literary histories that reinforced *Shōsetsu shinzui*'s ideological status. We have seen increasing efforts, especially in the 1990s and beyond, to critically examine the shifting categories of *shōsetsu* and *bungaku* (now a standard translation of "literature"), thereby questioning the basic assumptions of literary history that lie at the core of *Shōsetsu shinzui*'s status as the origin of modern Japanese literature: some such examples in addition to Kamei Hideo's "*Shōsetsu*"ron mentioned earlier are Fujii Sadakazu, *Nihon "shōsetsu" genshi* (*The Primal Origins of the Japanese* Shōsetsu, 1995); Noguchi Takeshiko, *Shōsetsu* (1996); and Suzuki Sadami, *Nihon no "bungaku" gainen* (*The Concept of "Literature" in Japan*, 1998).[11] These studies have given us means to question the ideological narrative that envelops *Shōsetsu shinzui*, to which this book is greatly indebted, but the fact remains that no other literary treatise has been as ideologically charged as *Shōsetsu shinzui*, as it was continually selected as a site of "literary modernity" that forms the institution of modern Japanese literature.

Interestingly, however, when we turn our attention to 1880s Japan, we find that *Shōsetsu shinzui* was not recognized by the literati immediately upon its publication nor did it gain its seminal status until later. Kōda Rohan (1867–1947) recounts in his "Meiji nijūnen zengo no nibunsei" (Two Literary Stars of the Late 1880s, 1925) that *Shōsetsu shinzui* neither moved many readers nor managed to garner a substantial response upon publication.[12] Peter Kornicki claims that he found "few trifling mentions" of *Shōsetsu shinzui* in the six years after its publication.[13] In fact, Shōyō's experimental fictional work, *Tōsei shosei katagi*, a text now considered to be a literary failure, was received with more immediate approval than *Shōsetsu shinzui*.

This initial obscurity is thought provoking in light of the repeated appearance of what literary critic Nakayama Akihiko calls the *Shōsetsu shinzui* clichés used in discussions of the *shōsetsu* around the time *Shōsetsu shinzui* was published.[14] By *Shōsetsu shinzui* clichés, I follow Nakayama's usage and refer to terms such as *ninjō*, *fūzoku*, and *setai* (emotions, customs, and manners) and *mosha* used to discuss the realm of the *shōsetsu* even when neither Shōyō nor *Shōsetsu shinzui* is directly mentioned.[15] Such clichés are called *Shōsetsu shinzui* clichés because they were retrospectively associated with *Shōsetsu shinzui*, but they began to be used in the early to mid-1880s independently of *Shōsetsu shinzui*. As early as 1881 and 1882, we see writers associating *shōsetsu* with "emotions" and "customs": Hattori Bushō (1842–1908) refers to emotions and customs as the main topic of *shōsetsu*; Nakajima Katsuyoshi (1858–1932) defines *shōsetsu*'s aim as the portrayal of emotions and customs.[16] Sakazaki Shiran's (1853–1913) "Shōsetsu haishi no honbun o ronzu" (On the Primary Role of *Shōsetsu Haishi*, 1885), published prior to *Shōsetsu shinzui*, also states, "What is *shōsetsu* after all? It is a medium that describes manners and emotions, and it is possible to call it a mirror of truthful depiction."[17] Such usages continue in the "debates on the decline of literature" (*bungaku kyokusui ronsō*) that occurred between 1889 and 1890, as the critics involved argue over whether the portrayal of emotions in *shōsetsu* is causing the deterioration of literature. In criticizing the contemporary *shōsetsu*, the writer of "Bungaku sekai no kinkyō" (Current Conditions of the World of Letters, 1890) states, "Writers of *shōsetsu* describe 'base emotions' and not 'correct emotions.'"[18] Uchida Roan (1868–1929), in response to such claims, asserts that "love is part of seven basic emotions, and it is not possible to portray 'emotions' without it," using phrases like "penetrate the depths of emotions" (*ninjō o ugatsu*) in the process.[19] Explicitly or implicitly, whether for or against it, these critics refer to "emotions, customs, and manners" in their discussions as if there is a naturalized association between such terms and the *shōsetsu*, which shows that there was a shift in literature that revolved around these terms.

In unraveling this shift in literature, "emotions, customs, and manners" must be putatively separated from *Shōsetsu shinzui* because *Shōsetsu shinzui* was merely one of the many texts that associated these terms with the *shōsetsu*, not the cause of the shift. Only retrospectively was *Shōsetsu shinzui* identified as the sole initiator of the shift to "emotions, customs, and manners." Positing *Shōsetsu shinzui* as the origin of the shift was thus not a descriptive act but an ideological one. With this act, *Shōsetsu shinzui* took on the role of the ideological origin of "literature." The designation "*Shōsetsu shinzui* clichés" manifests the uncritical association between *Shōsetsu shinzui* and "emotions, customs, and manners," which is at the core of the mechanism that supports and reinforces the ideological status of *Shōsetsu shinzui*. Despite the risk of misunderstanding, I chose to retain the designation as a constant reminder of this mechanism.

By methodologically separating "emotions, customs, and manners" from *Shōsetsu shinzui* and recasting them in the political and intellectual landscape of 1880s Japan, *Concealment of Politics, Politics of Concealment* highlights the moment when an epistemological shift occurred in the understanding of "literature," the moment that literature came into being as an ontologically independent category. When the *shōsetsu* found its raison d'être in "emotions, customs, and manners," it paved the way toward establishing the equation "*bungaku* = literature," an equation that was, as I will show shortly, yet to be established in the mid-1880s.

What then did "emotions, customs, and manners" constitute? It goes without saying that increased focalization on one theme cannot occur without simultaneous defocalization of another theme in the textual realm of representation. This book argues that the establishment of emotions, customs, and manners as the main theme of the *shōsetsu* is inextricably linked to the defocalization of "political" discourse. In the mid-1880s, emotions, customs, and manners appeared in direct opposition to a certain habitus that constituted the "political" at that particular historical juncture.[20]

Needless to say, texts and narratives that we now categorize under the rubric of literature were written long before this time. However, literature as category had yet to gain recognition, and at this particular historical moment, it did so by defining itself against the political. For literature to gain an independent identity, this political—posited in opposition to literature—had to be *produced*

as an object to be repressed. In other words, the production of "*bungaku* =
literature" occurred with the production *and* the repression of the political.
Despite the repression of the political, however, "*bungaku* = literature" is far
from apolitical; it embodies a new kind of politics that is manifested in the
concealment of politics.

Many politically oriented works continued to flourish, but once "literature"
was established, those works became part of a *literary* genre. The rubric *seiji
shōsetsu* is often used to categorize the politically oriented texts that proliferated in the 1880s. I will refer to many such works in the body of this book, but
I deliberately refrain from using this rubric based on my contention that *seiji
shōsetsu* had yet to become a genre at this historical juncture.[21] This is crucial
for my endeavor precisely because *seiji shōsetsu* is a *literary* genre that comes into
being along with "literature."

To elaborate on the methodology by which I examine this epistemological
shift, I will delineate the multiple significance of *Shōsetsu shinzui* in my project.
First and foremost, *Shōsetsu shinzui* is one of the many texts that featured the
association between emotions, customs, and manners and the *shōsetsu*. *Shōsetsu
shinzui* textually expresses the shift, sharing the space with the appearance of
the clichés in the 1880s to early 1890s. Accordingly, in reading *Shōsetsu shinzui*,
I closely analyze the textual positioning of key terms, focusing specifically on
what subsequently became *Shōsetsu shinzui* clichés, in order to decipher the
shift they embody. I not only offer a close reading of this text but examine how
the terms interact with various discourses that constitute it. In this respect,
this book is not a simple "historicization" or "contextualization" of *shōsetsu* and
"literature," which assumes a one-dimensional relationship between text and
context. This project is predicated on the idea that absence is inscribed in the
presence; that is to say, what appears on the textual surface shares its semantic economy with what is left out of the text, hence invalidating the artificial
boundaries often instituted between text and context. Reading the semantic
economy of *Shōsetsu shinzui* means reading the semantic distribution that com-
poses the very economy. I thus pay particular attention to the linguistic positioning of *Shōsetsu shinzui* clichés within this economy.

Shōsetsu shinzui is also an embodiment of the ideological category of literature. This raises an important methodological issue. Precisely because of the
originary status ascribed to *Shōsetsu shinzui*, the boundary of literature can be
deciphered by strategically treating *Shōsetsu shinzui* as a textual filter that includes as well as excludes certain writings in and from its discussion. In this
respect, I am unraveling the ideological frame that is projected onto *Shōsetsu*

shinzui. However, I recognize the logical inversion inscribed in this methodology. I treat *Shōsetsu shinzui* as a textual filter in order to derive the boundary of literature, but this should not be taken to mean that *Shōsetsu shinzui* prompted the production of literature. In fact, I argue against the idea that *Shōsetsu shinzui* effected the paradigm shift that brought ontological independence to the category of literature. So I am not arguing that the filter of *Shōsetsu shinzui* did establish the boundaries of literature. I am arguing that the exclusions *Shōsetsu shinzui* inscribes are crucial because those boundaries are what later scholars reinforced when they adopted *Shōsetsu shinzui* as an origin.

Not only is it historically flawed to claim that *Shōsetsu shinzui* initiated such change but it is theoretically invalid to say so. No single text can exert power upon the field of discourse to produce an epistemological shift. Modern Japanese literary history has overemphasized the role of *Shōsetsu shinzui* in narrativizing the development of modern Japanese literature. Accordingly, I seek to identify the varying discursive forces that, coincidentally or otherwise, facilitated the production of literature and ultimately endorsed the repression of politics and hence the ideological category itself. Because an epistemological shift cannot happen as the result of one text, we can understand the shift only by examining the larger discursive environment in which that shift took place. In this sense, the notion of linguistic economy is still quite restrictive in theme and in space; it narrows the discursive radar to what a given text—in all its presence and absence—engages, and as a result, does not do justice to the multiple levels of discourse that are set in motion when an epistemological shift occurs.[22] I have thus sought to locate parallel discursive movements that facilitate the paradigm shift central to my argument. This study extends itself to discursive realms that may, at first glance, appear wholly unconnected with the production of the *shōsetsu*, such as radical political activism that manifests in the many violent riots that occurred in the 1880s, the redefinition of "knowledge" (*gakumon*), educational reforms in the Meiji era, and the newly emergent geographical awareness. But such inquiries provide access to the forces that one way or another endorse the production of literature as an ontologically independent entity.

Finally, I examine *Shōsetsu shinzui* as a central site of the politics of concealment that has governed the institution of modern Japanese literature. As we will see in detail in Chapter 6, repeated designation of *Shōsetsu shinzui* as the origin of modern Japanese literature dissociated *Shōsetsu shinzui* from the specific condition in which it emerged. As literary histories of the later years overemphasized the role of *Shōsetsu shinzui* as the beginning of modern literary practices—based on the uncritical association between "emotions, customs, and manners" and *Shōsetsu shinzui*—they took for granted the existence of "literature" that had yet to take form in the 1880s. Naturally, an easy acceptance of *Shōsetsu shinzui*'s originary status also concealed the process through which literature came into being: through the concealment of politics. *Shōsetsu shinzui*, as ideological origin, thus embodies a double concealment. I seek to unravel the mechanism of this double concealment and challenge the very foundation of modern Japanese literary culture.

These multiple approaches to *Shōsetsu shinzui* are crucial to my effort to identify the epistemological shift and the effects it has on varying practices of "literature." As can be predicted, however, divisions between these realms are often not clear. These realms of inquiry thus appear in all of the chapters, sometimes feeding off one another and at other times producing friction with one another. Despite the apparent confusion such methodology may cause, I believe the differing yet interrelated realms of inquiry are crucial to the endeavor that constitutes this book.

The rest of the chapter is a prelude to the discussions that follow. To effectively highlight the processes through which literature gained ontological independence, I wish to first briefly discuss the categories of *bungaku* and *shōsetsu* and how they were mobilized among the literati of the time. I then inquire into the realm of "modern knowledge" and discuss the many contingencies with which the production of the *shōsetsu* engages, all the while demonstrating the power dynamics that govern the formation of modern knowledge. Finally, I examine the newly emergent geographical awareness and the ideological paradigm upon which it is founded. These discussions map out the important discursive tendencies that ultimately facilitated the production of the *shōsetsu*.

Bungaku ≠ *Literature and* Shōsetsu ≠ *Novel*

Prior to its coupling with literature, the term *bungaku* denoted "study" or "knowledge," and it primarily referred to writings of the *kangaku* classics.[23] Yet this should not be conflated with what we refer to as "scholarship" today. Until the Edo period, the definition of *bungaku* was "the study of *bun*"—a character that etymologically means "figure or pattern"—which meant "the reign of the country through means other than direct verbal orders and ordinances."[24] *Bungaku* referred not only to a paradigm of knowledge that had to be studied but also to the ideological forces that shaped the ordering system that was "lived" by people. Even in Meiji Japan, such a definition of *bungaku* remained. Nishi

Amane (1829–97), for example, says in the opening passage of *Hyakugaku ren-kan* (*Encyclopedia*, 1870): "*Bun* and 'the way' are two things that grew out of one; when *bungaku* flourishes, the way is bright. . . . If the *bun* does not flourish, then 'the way' will never be illuminated."[25] *Bungaku*, in other words, involved a definite moral element; it was a study of the "right" and "good" paths embodied by the *kangaku* classics.

These texts consisted of works such as *Chunqiu* (*Spring and Autumn Annals*), *Guoyu* (*Chronicles of States*), *Shiji* (*Records of the Grand Historian*), and *Hanshu* (*Book of Han*).[26] These are chronicles of the rise and fall of empires, histories of warfare, and the accomplishments and failures of leaders. In short, these classics were narratives about basic strategies of war, as well as the indispensable methods for building and ruling a nation. As such, politics, history, and literature were inextricably connected in the realm of *bungaku*, and this was a familiar framework for the members of the Meiji intelligentsia.[27]

The Sinitic Japanese compound *shōsetsu*, too, belonged to this discursive framework and had an entirely different signified compared to its current meaning.[28] Although *shōsetsu* were not regarded as highly as the official histories that constituted knowledge, the interrelatedness of politics, history, and literature was very much a part of this body of writing. *Shōsetsu* initially referred to writings by the low-ranking officials of the Chinese government who compiled information they gathered from the commoners. A dictionary entry usually quotes the following passage from *Hanshu*, one of the *kangaku* classics: "*Shōsetsu* writers and officials collected gossip from the local area by listening to rumors on the streets."[29] *Shōsetsu* was thus a collection of the "small talk" that derived from events occurring in the local community. In sharp contrast to the texts included in "official history" (*seishi*), *shōsetsu* referred to writings that had minimal importance. Accordingly, the term *shōsetsu* was often used by writers to diminish their own works.[30]

The meaning of *shōsetsu* began to change in the Edo period as *hakuwa shōsetsu* (Chinese vernacular fiction; *baihua xiaoshuo* in Chinese) started to be imported from China.[31] A form of narrative written in the vernacular style, this group of texts is said to have begun in the Sung dynasty (960–1279). In the Edo period, works such as *Sanguozhi yanyi* (*The Epoch of the Three Kingdoms*) and *Shuihu zhuan* (*The Water Margin*) became extremely popular; and adaptations of such narratives were produced by many *gesaku* writers, such as Kyokutei Bakin.[32] With the introduction of such narratives designated "*shōsetsu*," *shōsetsu* began to take on the meaning of fiction and was no longer simply limited to mere rumors and the "small talk" of commoners. However, even in the Edo period, *shōsetsu* did not signify a prescribed genre, and it retained the broad meaning "trivial writings" or "not-so-serious text."

The term *shōsetsu* was applied in various ways in the early years of Meiji. For instance, Nishi Amane in his *Hyakugaku renkan* uses *shōsetsu* to refer to fables, while adopting *haishi* for "romance," which he describes as "writings of ancient Rome . . . that are similar to history."[33] Kikuchi Dairoku (1855–1917), who translated Robert Chambers's (1800–1883) "Rhetoric and Belles-Lettres" (*Shūji oyobi kabun*, 1880), employs *shōsetsu* as a translation for "old romance," the category in which Chambers places the Arthurian legend.[34] Just two years prior to the publication of *Shōsetsu shinzui*, Nakae Chōmin (1847–1901) translated Eugene Veron's *L'esthetique* (*Aesthetics*, 1878; published in Japanese as *Ishi bigaku*, 1883) in which he introduced various literary genres of the West, including the novel, but he does not use the term *shōsetsu* at all. In fiction, Matsuura Shun'suke refers to his *Harusame bunko* (*Books of the Spring Rain*, 1876–82) as "*shōsetsu* of enlightenment" (*kaimei shōsetsu*), a work that he wrote specifically for "women and children."[35] Takabatake Ransen, in his preface to *Kōsetsu kono tegashiwa* (*Unreliable Talks on the Streets*, 1879), which features biographical sketches of people from the late Edo to early Meiji periods, states that the work that follows is "an inadequate *shōsetsu*."[36] Sakurada Momoe (1859–83) uses *shōsetsu* to refer to his *Nishi no umi chishio no saarashi* (*Tides of Blood and Small Storms in the Western Sea*, 1882), a translation of Alexandre Dumas's (1802–70) work on the French Revolution, whose target audience was the readers of *Jiyū shinbun*, hence the intelligentsia of the time.[37] Tōkai Sanshi, too, uses *shōsetsu* to refer to his *Kajin no kigū* (*Chance Meetings with Beautiful Women*, 1885–97), a best-selling work of political fiction among the literati of the time.[38] During this period, therefore, *shōsetsu* referred to everything from biography to children's fables, adventure stories to political fiction.

Despite the varying usage, however, the meaning of *shōsetsu* associated with the *hakuwa* tradition appears to be dominant, especially among the intelligentsia. Many featured heroic narratives with the plot structure of "encourage virtue, castigate vice" (*kanzen chōaku*), which typically featured the "good" heroes fighting against the "evil" figures. This may have been the most established meaning because works that adhered to the *hakuwa* lineage enjoyed a long history and were still being widely read and circulated. Kyokutei Bakin's works are the most well known of *hakuwa* adaptations, which were extremely popular among the Meiji literati. Moreover, *hakuwa* narratives grew in number and popularity between 1882 and 1885, roughly the time Shōyō conceptualized and wrote *Shōsetsu shinzui*.[39]

The linguistic style of the *hakuwa* adaptations was carried over to early Meiji fiction. Such stories often took the form of "translations" of European novels, which were very popular among *Shōsetsu shinzui*'s target audience, namely, "established and learned men" (*taijin gakusha*).[40] "Translation" took a variety of forms in early Meiji Japan, such as adaptation (*hon'an*) and content-oriented translation (*iyaku*).[41] Accordingly, there really was no clear boundary between the translated works and the original works produced by the writers; the distinction depended on whether the writer/translator would care to mention the presence of an "original" text from which he produced his own. The *hakuwa*-style works I mention later, therefore, include both "translations" and "non-translations."

What is important for our purposes is that these works expressed the political energy of the time. The country from which the writers picked the works often reflected their political stance. Members of the Jiyūtō (Liberal Party), such as Sakurada Momoe, Miyazaki Muryū (1855–89), and Sakazaki Shiran, translated French works that thematized the French Revolution to prefigure a revolution in Meiji Japan. Sakurada and Muryū translated Alexandre Dumas's *Mémoires d'un médicin: Joseph Balsamo* (*The Memoirs of a Physician*, 1846–48) and *Ange Pitou* (*Six Years Later; or, The Taking of the Bastille*, 1853), respectively, for such a purpose. A number of Victor Hugo works (1802–85) also circulated, especially after Itagaki Taisuke's (1837–1919) famous meeting with the writer during his trip to France in 1882. Itagaki, a well-known advocate of the Freedom and People's Rights Movement, asked Hugo about the effective ways to spread political awareness among the "uncivilized" people of Japan. Hugo told Itagaki to have them read novels such as his own. Itagaki accordingly returned to Japan with boxes of books, which resulted in a dramatic increase in translated fiction after 1882. Jiyūtō writers were also known for their fondness for the anarchists in Russia. Muryū's *Kishūshū* (*Lamenting Spirits*, 1884), an adaptation of *La Russia Sotteranea* (*Underground Russia*, 1882) by S. Stepniak (1851–95), is one such example.

Among the members of the Kaishintō (Constitutional Reform Party), Yano Ryūkei was perhaps the most popular writer. His publication *Keikoku bidan* (*Illustrious Tales of Statesmanship*, 1883), a work based on Greek history, became one of the best sellers of the time. The popularity of such fiction culminated with Tōkai Sanshi's *Kajin no kigū*, which began serialization the same year that *Shōsetsu shinzui* and *Tōsei shosei katagi* were published and, despite several lapses, continued publication until 1897.[42]

Many of these narratives, including Sakurada's and Muryū's translations of Dumas's texts, as well as *Keikoku bidan* and *Kajin no kigū*, feature heroes who seek to make right the wrongs done to them, clearly drawing on the *hakuwa* tradition in both linguistic style and theme. The popularity of these texts and their assimilation into the *hakuwa* tradition prove to be a large obstacle for *Shōsetsu shinzui* in its effort to dissociate *shōsetsu* from the *hakuwa* narratives. In order for the term *shōsetsu* to take on a new meaning, *Shōsetsu shinzui* had to first negotiate with the semantic economy that identified such works as "*shōsetsu*." Despite their popularity—or perhaps precisely because of it—these works are deliberately effaced from the textual surface of *Shōsetsu shinzui*. *Shōsetsu shinzui* attempts to sever the term *shōsetsu* from its previous semantic economy and forcefully connect it with the "novel."

"Novel" was an amorphous term for the Meiji readership. This is perhaps best illustrated by the preface to Oda Jun'ichirō's *Karyū shunwa* (*Romantic Stories of Blossoms*, 1879), an abridged translation of Edward Bulwer-Lytton's *Ernest Maltravers* (1837) and its sequel, *Alice* (1838), which was extremely popular among the youths of the time. Narushima Ryūhoku (1837–84), who wrote the preface to Oda Jun'ichirō's translation, has the following to say:

> Hard-headed scholars say, "People of Western countries are forever bound by practicality and preach the importance of profit but have no taste (*fūryū*) or emotions (*jōchi*)." This is a result of a complete blindness on the part of the scholars. I have traveled aboard a ship for a year and closely interacted with [people of Western countries] on deck. Their emotions were very much like mine.[43]

Ryūhoku ends the preface by saying *Karyū shunwa* will show precisely that. This preface allows us to discern the conditions under which *Karyū shunwa* was published. Western texts that had been translated previously had focused on "profit" and "practicality" to such an extent that the audience had conjured up the image of people in Western countries as lacking "taste or emotions." Until *Karyū shunwa*'s publication in 1879, works that fell under the rubric of "practical knowledge," such as political philosophy, economics, science, and geography, were given higher priority than fiction.[44] The Japanese readership that Ryūhoku addressed, in other words, was unfamiliar with the literary practices of the West; the novel was a vague concept, and its defining characteristics were far from clear to the readers.

Given the equation "*shōsetsu* = novel" that appears at the end of the introduction to *Shōsetsu shinzui*, we often forget that the equation itself was far from stabilized around the time *Shōsetsu shinzui* was written. Although the title of the work gives us the impression that it describes the essence of a preexisting entity called *shōsetsu*, *Shōsetsu shinzui* is not a descriptive piece but one better situated as a prescriptive piece. It is a text that attempted to *produce* a medium appropriate for the designation "artistic *shōsetsu*," which had yet to take form.

"Literature" as "Modern Knowledge"

In more ways than one, the production of the *shōsetsu* engages with the formation of "modern knowledge." First, disciplinary boundaries were changing: *bungaku* (later "literature") was clearly an amorphous entity, and so were other forms of knowledge. As I suggested earlier, boundaries between history, politics, and literature were far from established. Accordingly, *Shōsetsu shinzui* was governed by the need to sever *shōsetsu* from politics and history and establish *shōsetsu* as a legitimate form of knowledge in and of itself. Second, in the early Meiji period, what could qualify as "knowledge" was heavily contested. The value of *shōsetsu* was thus not a given; in fact, it was considered secondary to disciplines like history and politics, which were perceived to have a role in the nation-building process. The evaluative set of criteria for "knowledge" shifted throughout the first two decades of the Meiji period, and educational reforms were instituted accordingly.

Integral to such shifting paradigms of knowledge was a conflict between scholars of "Western learning" (*yōgaku*), "native learning" (*kokugaku*), and Confucian-based *kangaku*. Although a simplistic narrative of Japan's modernization typically discusses how Western learning gained prominence, slighting the "premodern" forms of learning in Japan's effort at modernization, such linear characterization does not do justice to the complex, often politically charged, processes involved in the development of modern knowledge.

Even among the advocates of Western learning, conflicts persisted. They played out in a struggle between government-sponsored and privately owned schools, which paralleled the struggle between the government officials and the Freedom and People's Rights activists. Hence these conflicts were directly related to the political debates over the legislative forms, judicial systems, and so on. Just like the novels that they translated, the Jiyūtō activists advocated the French system, and Kaishintō activists the British, whereas the central members of the government leaned primarily toward the Prussian system, especially for its constitution. The educational curriculum and reforms reinforced each party's beliefs. In short, they were far from uniform.

Such discord was further complicated as the Confucian scholars, whose study was deemed "old-fashioned" in the first decade of the Meiji period, began to reengage in the power struggle in the early 1880s. This was a part of the government-instituted reform, which sought to neutralize the Freedom and People's Rights Movement, that was considered to have been motivated by Western learning. Criticizing the scholars of Western learning for focusing only on "intellectual education" (*chiiku*), the Confucian scholars stressed the need for "moral education" (*tokuiku*) and argued for internal reform.

The power struggle between the various advocates of Western learning and Confucian scholars shapes *Shōsetsu shinzui* in varying ways, at first primarily as a force that labels *shōsetsu* as morally corrupt (by Confucian doctrine) and impractical (by the scholars of Western learning who espoused "practical knowledge"). *Shōsetsu shinzui* addresses these negative forces that shun *shōsetsu* as it tries to elevate the *shōsetsu* as a form of knowledge, a medium appropriate for "established and learned men."

The development of the university system and the institutionalization of "literature" are also of importance in examining the discursive forces that endorsed the production of literature. Literature entered the university within a few years of *Shōsetsu shinzui*'s publication, when Tokyo Imperial University established Kokubungakka (Department of National Letters) in 1889. Before this time, Tokyo University's Bungakubu (School of Letters) had included Wakan Bungakka (Department of Japanese and Chinese Letters) from 1877, but apparently it was very unpopular. In 1882, Katō Hiroyuki (1836–1916), then president of Tokyo University, established Koten Kōshūka (Program for Study in the Classics), separate from the already existing Department of Japanese and Chinese Letters. Such a reform marked the government's effort to gain control over opposition movements; it was an attempt to counter the Westernizing impulses that dominated the educational arena in the early years of the Meiji period.[45] In 1885, the Department of Japanese and Chinese Letters was split into Wabungakka (Department of Japanese Letters) and Kanbungakka (Department of Sino-Japanese Letters), and the Department of Japanese Letters was given the task to revive the study of Japanese classics. The Program for Study in the Classics was rather short-lived and closed in 1888, with only two classes of students graduating; interestingly, however, the graduates of this program and the students of the Department of Japanese Letters—renamed Kokubungakka (Department of National Letters) in 1889—contributed to the development of "national literature" within the university.[46]

Numerous literary histories (*bungakushi*) were produced within this academic arena. Literary histories, which embody an effort to demarcate disciplinary boundaries through the writing of its history, contain many *Shōsetsu shinzui* clichés. The actual link between *Shōsetsu shinzui* and national literature, however, is not easy to decipher. Given *Shōsetsu shinzui*'s initial obscurity, national literature appears to have discovered *Shōsetsu shinzui* clichés independently.[47] In response to the antiquarian studies of literature before them, the new scholars read texts as a reflection of the time and of the people's "inner spirit." Literary historians thus made many references to a "mirror of life" (*jinsei no kagami*) and "a reflective mirror of society" (*shakai no hansha kagami*) in situating works of literature as they linked the texts to people's "internal lives" (*shinteki seikatsu*) and "emotions and thoughts" (*kanjō shisō*).[48] Mikami Sanji and Takatsu Kuwasaburō's *Nihon bungakushi* (*History of Japanese Letters*, 1890), for example, claims that "literature is a reflection of people's heart/mind" (*jinshin*).[49] Regardless of the literary histories' actual connection to *Shōsetsu shinzui*, the academic national literature founded in 1889, four years after *Shōsetsu shinzui*'s publication, clearly embodies the discursive forces that facilitated the "inward" turn that ultimately endorsed the centrality of "emotions, customs, and manners" in the *shōsetsu*.

The appearance of the maxim "autonomy of knowledge" in the early to mid-1880s also adds critical dimension to my inquiry into the realm of knowledge. The autonomy of knowledge, which argued for depoliticization of knowledge, replicated the rejection of the political habitus, a central force that shapes the epistemological shift. It further sought to define knowledge as a "national" medium, rather than one divided by varying political agenda espoused by different factions, government or otherwise. As such, it engages with the government's objective to establish national literature in the academia to counter the Westernizing impulses: they both coincidentally facilitate the apparent nationalization of literature. National literature took form as the graduates of the Department of Japanese Letters and Program for Study in the Classics began to institutionalize the discipline through compilation of literary histories that, as mentioned earlier, defined the realm of literature with *Shōsetsu shinzui* clichés. Nationalization, depoliticization, and the inward turn in literature coalesce in the realm of knowledge. Accordingly, the reforms that shaped the realm of knowledge and the educational arena are of special interest to my project.

The Newfound Geographical and Historical Awareness: Ideology of Cofiguration

This project also examines the newly established geographical awareness and how it, too, facilitates the epistemological shift in literature. The category of literature came into being as the national and the global were being discovered. In exploring the new geographical paradigm, my primary focus is the ideological construction of "Asia" in early to mid-1880s Japan. The perspective I take draws from recent critical works that have given emphasis to the dialogue within nations in East Asia, which not only offset the imbalance apparent in the previous narratives of modernity that overemphasized the Western role but also recognize the importance of "Asia" in Japan's relationship vis-à-vis the West.[50]

In the early Meiji period, Asia was certainly not a stable or self-evident figure; it was still a contested site, both geographically and culturally. The manner in which Meiji Japan constructed the figure of Asia cannot be understood without the context of the newly found geographical awareness and the power politics that emerged along with it, which prompted a new set of negotiations within Asia.

I wish to examine the general paradigm that shapes this newly found "world" thematized by many writings of the time. Although this study focuses primarily on the new geographical awareness that appears in post-Meiji Restoration texts, the worldview began to shift long before the Restoration. As Yamamuro Shin'ichi and other scholars point out, this new worldview was one that the Japanese were familiar with through the maps and travel writings of the seventeenth century, such as Matteo Ricci's *Kon'yo bankoku zenzu* (The Comprehensive Map of All Countries of the World, composed in 1602 and taken to Japan in 1605).[51] Though certainly not accepted without controversy, the theories that the earth is in fact round and the world is divided into five continents (later amended to six) were disseminated. Because some Japanese intellectuals embraced it as a means to criticize Sinocentrism, the worldview inscribed in Matteo Ricci's map gained faster acceptance in Japan than in China. This is evident from the first world map composed in Japan in 1645, *Bankoku sōzu* (The Comprehensive Map of the World), which follows the oceanic line drawn in Matteo Ricci's map almost exactly. One of the works that had a tremendous impact upon the Edo intellectuals' geographical awareness, Nishikawa Joken's *Zōho kai tsūshō kō* (*On the Passage of Trade between China and Other Countries*, 1708) and its supplementary map, also traces the outline of Matteo Ricci's map. In the early Meiji years, works adopted as school textbooks in Japan, such as Fukuzawa Yukichi's *Sekai kunizukushi* (*The Countries of the World*, 1869) and Uchida Masao's *Yochi shiryaku* (*An Abridged Account of the World*, 1870), introduced the world of the five continents and disseminated such geography and the mode of categorization of the world inscribed within it.

This world order is complicated by the categories of the *seiyō* and *tōyō* and the various processes of negotiation these terms went through before they eventually came to signify "the West" (as Euro-America) and "the East" (as Asia). Just like "Asia," these categories were far from self-evident. The sinified compounds *seiyō* and *tōyō* are originally Chinese. They were situated within the Sinocentric worldview and the way in which trade was conducted in China: at the end of the Ming period, *seiyō* signified the sea located to the west of the trade line that ran from Canton, to Brunei, and then to Timor, and *tōyō* signified the sea east of the line. By the early eighteenth century, *tōyō* began to signify Japan: a small country in the Eastern Sea; and this use of *tōyō* continued well into the Meiji period, even in Japan.

The usages began to shift decidedly after the introduction of Matteo Ricci's map. His efforts to use *seiyō* and *tōyō* and all their variations in translating the maps he brought to China are often understood to be an attempt to negotiate with the world order already accepted by the Chinese. He portrayed China at the center of the map and used *taiseiyō* 大西洋 for the Atlantic Ocean, referring to himself as *taiseiyōjin* 大西洋人 (or a person from the Atlantic Ocean); *taiseiyō* thus also signified "the further West" relative to what the Chinese named the area west of China (which he referred to as *shōseiyō* 小西洋, denoting "the closer West"). At the same time, however, it is widely known that the maps were introduced to the Chinese with the intention of questioning the Sinocentric view.[52] In more ways than one, the new geography, in the use of terms and mode of categorization, grew out of incessant negotiations with a paradigm of power that shaped the struggle between European world order and Sinocentrism.

Japan also had to negotiate such a power struggle. Eventually, through re-naming and renegotiations at various levels, *seiyō* began to signify "the West" for the Japanese, referring to a region where the missionaries came from. Once the equation between the West and *seiyō* was established, it was very easy for the category *tōyō* to take on the meaning of Asia, "the East." Inoue Tetsujirō claims that the publication of Fukuzawa's *Seiyō jijō* (*The Condition of the West*) in 1866 stabilized the term *seiyō* as an equivalent of "Euro-America" in Japan. Moreover, as it did so, *seiyō* not only signified the geographical region but also its civilization and culture. Accordingly, *tōyō* also began to take on the meaning of civilization and culture, and as it did so, the awareness that countries within *tōyō* constituted a common collective began to take form. Many claims for *dōbun* (common language—referring to the use of *kanji* characters) and *dōkyō* (same teachings/religion—often referring to Buddhism and Confucianism) were also made. This was the basic premise that brought together the advocates of Asianism (*kōa*) who established Kōakai (The Society of Asianism, 1880), which subsequently became Ajia kyōkai (Asian Coalition, 1883).

The shifting worldview manifested in the terms *seiyō* and *tōyō* is much more complicated than what I briefly provide here; different maps named seas and regions differently, and political struggles led to a multitude of negotiations with newly imported maps and writings. I am clearly using my privileged perspective of retrospection to simplify this paradigm. But we must keep in mind that categories of *seiyō* and *tōyō* were contested and were deeply implicated in the struggle for power.

As a result of all the negotiations, *seiyō* and *tōyō* ultimately entered a "configurative" relationship, to borrow Naoki Sakai's term. Configuration is a mechanism of semantic correlation by which a collective represents itself vis-à-vis the other.[53] In effect, *seiyō* (as the West) and *tōyō* (as the East) entered a relationship of equivalence: characteristics attributed to each collective should and must correspond with each other. This configurative relationship is clearly ideological, one that reemerges constantly despite the obvious discrepancies that undermine equivalence.

Discussions that involve Russia often pose a problem to the configurative ideology; Russia occupied a very ambivalent position in this scheme. If "the West" was a distant and abstract figure that threatened to invade "the East," Japan was better off becoming allies with the neighboring countries, in which case Russia and China became logical allies. In 1857, for example, when a conflict arose between England and Russia, the rhetoric of "countries of symbiosis" (*shinshi no kuni*), one that we often see as Japanese intellectuals call for an Asian coalition, was used in relation to Russia.[54] Needless to say, however, Russia often took on the role of the "West," as it was included among the colonizing nations, especially with its invasion of the northeastern part of China.

The physical proximity to China was, in many ways, a source of fear and ambivalence that undercut the putative equivalence posited between the West and East. For Japan, the worst possible scenario was the West-China coalition. Accordingly, Japan sought to establish a stronger hold over the neighboring lands, specifically Korea, Ezo (present-day Hokkaidō), and Ryūkyū (present-day Okinawa), beginning as early as 1786.[55] The Sino-Japanese coalition was also conceptualized for similar reasons; as "countries of symbiosis," Qing China would help Japan ward off Western invasion of the East.[56] Yet the disintegration of Sinocentrism, a gradual process that in part began with the fall of the Ming dynasty in 1644 (and hence the defeat of the people of Han—*the* "Chinese"— by the Manchu) and more decisively with the consecutive losses in the Opium Wars (1840–42, 1856–58), had a strong effect on the Japanese views of China.[57] After Japanese intellectuals reported on Qing China's military forces in the two

Opium Wars, for example, the "incompetence" of the Chinese military had already become an accepted viewpoint among the Japanese. The first Opium War is often designated as one of the turning points of Japan's perception of China, but China's position was far from established in the new world order, and accordingly Japan had yet to be clear on the relationship it sought with China. At the conscious level, the Meiji intellectuals' relationship with China was at best ambivalent. For many, China, their long-term mentor, was still very much an object of respect and valorization. In the early Meiji years, it was not unusual for an individual to simultaneously have respect and contempt toward China. The idea that China and Japan belonged to the same collective called "the East" as compared to "the West" was certainly not a stable one.

The cofigurative relationship that lies at the core of the newly found worldview is further complicated by the social Darwinian formula based on the theory of evolution that proliferated in writings from the end of the Edo period to the Meiji period. Social Darwinism was a discourse of hierarchy that designated the West as *the* telos of evolution. Thus, the most civilized forms of society, culture, and so on were associated with the West. For example, Fukuzawa Yukichi's *Sekai kunizukushi* and Uchida Masao's *Yochi shiryaku*, the two texts used as school textbooks to teach world geography, relied heavily on Darwinian rhetoric, designating Europe as the center of enlightenment and the most "civilized" geographical region, while portraying Asian countries like India and Africa as full of ignorant, "barbaric" people. Such narratives clearly intersect with the idea of "the ages of civilization" (*bunmei no yowai*) that Fukuzawa further articulates in *Bunmeiron no gairyaku* (*An Outline of a Theory of Civilization*, 1875), which was modeled after Henry Thomas Buckle's *History of Civilization in England* and François Guizot's *General History of Civilization in Europe*. In it, he defines the stages of civilization in three categories—namely, "uncivilized" (*mikai*), "half-civilized" (*hankai*), and "civilized" (*bunmei*)—and situates Japan among the half-civilized. In effect, learning geography through these texts meant internalizing the social Darwinian hierarchy, setting the West as the goal and the model to follow.

Inscribed in this geographical awareness is a new model of desire that results from the intersection between the relationship of equivalence and the social Darwinian hierarchy. Equivalence cannot sustain itself and invariably produces "lack" and/or "excess." The standard of the "West-as-civilized or the West-as-modern" is used to "explain" this lack or excess. In other words, the West-as-civilized becomes the dominant regulative idea by which to measure the deviation.[58] In this paradigm, the lack (or excess) is inevitably attributed to the non-West, making the non-West strive harder to "Westernize."[59] Yet given that the West is inherently inaccessible, this new model of desire can be only *rhetorically* fulfilled; as such, Japan sought rhetorical equivalence with the West at various levels.

This model of desire governed practices of cross-cultural appropriation that proliferated in the early 1880s, which was inextricably linked to Japan's urge to situate itself within the new world order in which it found itself. The popularity of works such as Alexandre Dumas's and Victor Hugo's texts on the French Revolution clearly engaged with the newfound sense of history and world perspective. Using the images of the French Revolution to represent the struggles for liberty and rights against the Japanese government, writers—invariably the fighters of the Freedom and People's Rights Movement—clearly sought a *comparable* figure by which to *frame* Japan's own turmoil, producing, on the textual surface, a commensurate relationship between Japan and the West of revolutionary France. Cross-cultural appropriations, among other things, negotiate a ground for commensurability and rhetorically prefigure a relationship of equivalence.

The rhetorical effect of such appropriation does not stop here, because this relationship of equivalence is further governed by the social Darwinian discourse of "progress." In effect, the writers' effort to frame Japan's condition through cross-cultural appropriation can also be read as a way for Japan to insert itself in the social Darwinian formula of progress, a teleological path toward "civilization." For the advocates of the Freedom and People's Rights Movement, moreover, such appropriation prefigures "success" in their fight for liberty, because a revolution (technically) would manage to topple the existing establishment. The appropriations, therefore, tentatively and rhetorically fulfill the desire for equivalence and prefigure the eventual "progress."

Such a mimetic identification is, if achieved, only rhetorical and temporary; it is constantly threatened to being exposed as imaginary. These forms of cross-cultural appropriation incessantly reproduce the cofigurative desire, which is continually frustrated. This instability of rhetorical equivalence produces a chain of often conflicting reactions that manifest in desperate attempts to retain the equivalence, as well as many efforts to rewrite the rhetorical relationship. Furthermore, the energy that covets relief from the cofigurative model of desire seeks to channel the energy elsewhere to establish other forms of equivalence. In the years between 1882 and 1885, "Asia" was the most appropriate site for such an ideological mapping to take place. It is such an ideological mapping that facilitates a discursive movement that endorses the production of the *shōsetsu*.

An Overview

Several inquiries intersect in this book as I explore the emergence of literature as an ontological category. I inquire into the process through which the *shōsetsu*, whose textual space is demarcated around "emotions, customs, and manners," is posited through the concealment of the political. I seek out parallel discursive movements that facilitate this concealment and hence the epistemological shift. I further examine the boundaries of literature inscribed in *Shōsetsu shinzui* and explore what they suppress and, in turn, express in the historical moment of *Shōsetsu shinzui*'s production. I then show how twentieth-century appropriations of *Shōsetsu shinzui* as the origin of literature project their own meanings on the definitions *Shōsetsu shinzui* set, thereby repeating the concealment of politics *Shōsetsu shinzui* itself carries out.

Chapter 2 begins with an examination of the genealogy of the *shōsetsu* presented in the opening passage of *Shōsetsu shinzui*, as a product of multiple negotiations between the fluctuating terms that constitute it—such as *shōsetsu*, *monogatari* (tales), *haishi* (commoner's history), and *gesaku* (playful writings).[60] This genealogy of the *shōsetsu* provides us the most appropriate means to decipher what *Shōsetsu shinzui* includes and excludes from the textual realm of the *shōsetsu*. Many forces govern the filtering process. I discuss, for example, how new printing technology boosted the publishing industry and the shifting paradigms of knowledge that degraded the *shōsetsu* by designating it as a "morally corrupting" and/or "impractical" medium. This chapter thus engages with the numerous contingencies with which *Shōsetsu shinzui* negotiates in positing the equation "*shōsetsu* = novel."

What emerges through such an inquiry is that the *gesaku* line is set against the *hakuwa* tradition, which was inextricably connected to the political and translated fiction of the time. In *Shōsetsu shinzui*, *gesaku* is ultimately designated as the "natural" precursor to the *shōsetsu*. Among other things, this designation marks an attempt to sever the term *shōsetsu* from a group of texts associated with the political. Yet the choice of *gesaku* triggers a new set of issues given its degraded position in the shifting paradigms of knowledge within the post-Restoration world. As such, *Shōsetsu shinzui* makes many attempts to legitimize the *shōsetsu*, in and of itself, as a valid medium for "new" education. As the discourse on "human development" arose in mid-1880s Japan, the *shōsetsu* emerges as a potentially valid means to undertake development.

Chapter 3 begins by identifying the main constituents of the *shōsetsu* introduced in "The Main Themes of the *Shōsetsu*," the section that has been the most responsible for *Shōsetsu shinzui*'s status as the origin of modern Japanese literature. This section features what subsequently became the *Shōsetsu shinzui* clichés, such as *ari no mama* (literally "as it is" or "as things are") and "emotions, customs, and manners." In this chapter, I suspend the belief that *ari no mama* and "emotions" signify "mimesis" and "interiority," respectively, because such a reading can only reinforce the ideological boundaries of literature projected onto *Shōsetsu shinzui*. I instead focus on the textual positioning of these terms and show how these key constituents of the *shōsetsu* are posited through a chain of negation.

Shōsetsu shinzui's choice of Bakin's works as a negative embodiment of the *shōsetsu* is thus important. I explore Bakin's place within the discursive conditions of 1880s Japan and delineate what his works signified for *Shōsetsu shinzui*'s target audience. I contend that Bakin, known for his adaptation of *hakuwa* fiction, embodied the energy of the Freedom and People's Rights Movement and the language by which political aspirations were fostered and aroused. *Shōsetsu shinzui*'s rejection of Bakin and the *hakuwa* tradition extended far beyond the texts themselves; it signified, among other things, a rejection of a certain *physical* practice of reading that shaped the communal site, a habitus, in which participants felt a solidarity that was at the core of the energy that shaped the Freedom and People's Rights Movement. I supplement this inquiry with close textual analyses of fictional writings associated with the political movement, such as Sakurada Momoe's (1859–83) *Nishi no umi chishio no saarashi* (*Tides of Blood and Small Storms in the Western Sea*, 1882), Miyazaki Muryū's (1855–89) *Jiyū no kachidoki* (*Notes on the French Revolution: The Battle Cry of Liberty*, 1882–83), and Komuro Shinsuke's *Tōyō minken hyakkaden* (*One Hundred Biographies of Righteous Men*, 1883–84).[61] *Shōsetsu shinzui*'s criticisms of Bakin are in fact directed at these works, which are inextricably connected to the series of violent uprisings (*gekka jiken*) that swayed the nation from 1882 to 1885. *Shōsetsu shinzui* in effect embodies a rejection of such revolutionary politics.

The rejection of the political habitus, and hence the positing of the *shōsetsu* as an alternative medium to produce a new linguistic community, is further fostered by the general decline of the Freedom and People's Rights Movement, as well as the maxim "autonomy of knowledge"; this maxim calls for separation of knowledge and politics, which marks an attempt to politically "neutralize" the realm of knowledge. The political sanitation that occurs in the realm of knowledge curiously aligns itself with the rejection of the political habitus that occurs in the *shōsetsu*. I conclude this chapter by suggesting that the move away from the political habitus replicates the emergence of a new realm of politically neutralized knowledge.

In Chapter 4, I situate the production of the *shōsetsu* in a global context, within the cofigurative model of desire that shapes the newly found geographical awareness. I focus on the power struggle within East Asia played out in major newspapers of the time and examine Japan's mode of self-representation as it constructs "Asia" as the "barbaric other" from which Japan sought to differentiate itself. Asia, in other words, was (re)discovered as the "less civilized" other, a reference point used to express Japan's superiority and the desire to become the ever-inaccessible West. Forces that govern Japan's self-representation occupy an integral part of the discursive horizon that shaped the epistemological shift that I identify in "literature." The heightened debates for Asianism and de-Asianization, coincidentally or otherwise, played an integral part in what I refer to as "the repression of politics."

Specifically, I examine the various newspapers that report on three crucial events that occurred in the years between 1882 and 1885—the Imo Mutiny (1882), the Sino-Franco War (1884–85), and the Kapsin Incident (1884)—all of which intensified the power struggle in East Asia. I inquire into how Japan's self-representation, in all its variation, shifts as it responds to each crisis. I then offer a close textual analysis of Komuro Shinsuke's *Kōa kidan: Murenren* (*The Remarkable Story of Asianism: Dreams of Love*, 1884) and Fukuzawa Yukichi's "Datsu-aron" (On De-Asianization, 1885) and explore how they textually represent their anxiety and the kind of relief they seek.

This chapter in part constitutes my response to the *Shōsetsu shinzui* scholarship that has overemphasized the Westernizing aspects of the seminal work, often narrativized in terms of "influence." In such study, *Shōsetsu shinzui* has been understood as an attempt to institute a modern literary practice that emulates the Western novel, assuming that Western literary concepts were *imported* into *Shōsetsu shinzui*'s theorization of the *shōsetsu*, drastically *influencing* Japanese literary practice and causing it to abandon the premodern.[62] Such an understanding led critics to search for corresponding concepts in Western literary practice, as if *Shōsetsu shinzui* merely imported and deployed premade concepts from the West. The uncritical equation is drawn between the Western and the modern, which is accompanied by the critics' laborious, painstaking, almost obsessive search for the equivalent or corresponding terms and concepts in the West. The ideology of cofiguration clearly manifests in such practices.

The urge to focus on the positive definition of the *shōsetsu* has led critics to gloss over and hence endorse *Shōsetsu shinzui*'s urge to *produce* the more barbaric other. As Chapter 4 makes clear, the language of "good/bad and right/wrong" (*zen'aku jasei*), which links itself to the *hakuwa* tradition that formed the political habitus discussed in Chapter 3, was labeled "Asian" at this historic moment in time. In effect, along with depoliticizing forces, *Shōsetsu shinzui* embodies the notion of de-Asianization (the concept of *datsu-a*, or "leaving Asia behind") as it identifies this language as a "superficial language" that could represent only "uncivilized" emotions.

My focus on the power dynamics of Asia must not be interpreted as an effort to counter the Westernizing aspect of *Shōsetsu shinzui*. Such a reading merely reifies the division between the West and Asia, as if it were possible to institute a clean break between them. Asia, needless to say, does not exist without the West; they are always already implicated in the cofigurative relationship. I thus seek to situate the *shōsetsu* within the cofigurative schema that governs the geopolitical structure within which it was produced and examine how Japan's self-representation within such a structure facilitates the "repression of politics."

Chapter 5 conducts a close textual analysis of Shōyō's experimental work of fiction, *Tōsei shosei katagi* (*The Character of Modern Students*, 1885–86), to show how the *shōsetsu* textually manifests itself. Shōyō himself came to consider his experimental *shōsetsu* a failure, despite its popularity upon publication. In "Kai-oku mandan" (Remembering the Old Years, 1925), he claims the following:

> I wrote *Shōsetsu shinzui* to criticize Bakin's overly didactic tendency. However, having immersed myself in reading Bakin since childhood, I couldn't escape Bakinesque writing. My stories and style of writing so clearly had the markings of Bakin. . . . I had given my first work the title *Shosei katagi*, because I was beginning to prefer Jishō and Kiseki, but Kasei writings dominated within me, and I could not incorporate Genroku style.[63] As I became aware of this, I could see how disagreeable my style was, and although I disliked my own prose, I could not outgrow it. I had to struggle with it for years and years to come.[64]

Following Shōyō's evaluation of his own work, literary scholars believe that *Tōsei shosei katagi* is a failure, that Shōyō could not accomplish in practice what he was able to achieve in theory.[65] Many such critics refer to its *gesaku*-like prose, just as Shōyō did, as a cause of its failure. In effect, the narrative that emphasizes the rift between *Shōsetsu shinzui*'s alleged "success" and the experimental work's alleged "failure" has been very typical. However, the two texts, conceptualized and written concurrently, together configure the "civilized" textual realm; they are both implicated within the process of effacing the political. Perhaps the best way to characterize the two texts is that they are in a collaborative relationship; the dialogue between the two texts therefore is much more fruitful than situating one as an imperfect embodiment of the other.

The point of focus is on the text's urge to peripherize the political within the textual realm of the *shōsetsu*. Revolutionary politics, inextricably connected to the political habitus discussed in Chapter 3, was not the only domain of the political rejected in the configuration of the *shōsetsu*. The *shōsetsu*, I argue, also took a critical stance against a set of works that shared the plot structure with one of the best sellers of the time, *Karyū shunwa* (*Romantic Stories of Blossoms*), the abridged translation of Edward Bulwer-Lytton's works. The story is a bildungsroman that revolves around the personal development of Ernest Maltravers, who in the end gains professional success and consummates his love affair. Its impact on the Japanese literary scene is best described by the renowned writer and translator Morita Shiken (1861–97) in a preface he wrote for a translation of another of Bulwer-Lytton's works, *Night and Morning* (1841), published in 1890: "It was *Karyū shunwa*, a work translated by Oda, that incited the movement to dramatically change the practice of our *shōsetsu*."[66] For the students in Meiji who dreamed of "success and advancement" (*risshin shusse*) in the modernizing world, Ernest Maltravers's success story—which was inextricably connected with the consummation of love—was an embodiment of their ideal. Many works that reproduced such a plot structure followed. These stories feature a wealthy, beautiful woman who supports, both psychologically and financially, a poor but upright male political activist.[67] They typically end with the male protagonist's success and consummation of the love affair, a formula clearly drawn from *Karyū shunwa*. These are apparently the works that Tokutomi Sohō had in mind in writing his essay "Kinrai ryūkō no seiji shōsetsu o hyōsu" (On the Recently Popular Political *Shōsetsu*, 1887), where he criticizes them for being too "convenient."[68]

In *Tōsei shosei katagi*, the realm of the political that such works thematized is, though no means absent, peripherized. *Tōsei shosei katagi* deliberately dissociates its main story line from the political arena that undoubtedly governs the world in which the story is set. By situating *Shōsetsu shinzui* and experimental fiction as two collaborating texts, I seek to identify the dynamics of textual privileging that construct the story as a whole.

This chapter further explores the position of the protagonist, Komachida Sanji, a "nonpolitical" "knowing subject" (*gakusha*) whose supposed neutrality vis-à-vis the political arena is the locus of our inquiry. Sanji also has another crucial identity in *Tōsei shosei katagi*: he is given an interiority that struggles with love, one of the main themes of the modern canonical *shōsetsu*, defined retrospectively by the narrative that institutes *Shōsetsu shinzui* as their origin. Through Sanji we see how the protagonist begins to turn inward and finds his identity in love. The textual world he has access to embodies the boundaries of the "artistic" *shōsetsu*.

Finally, this project will not be complete without examining the manner in which the epistemological shift discussed in this book was in fact institutionalized. Chapter 6 traces the reception of *Shōsetsu shinzui* and its clichés and historicizes the narrative that designates *Shōsetsu shinzui* as the origin of modern Japanese literature. Up until this chapter, I focus, admittedly quite narrowly, on the first eighteen or so years of the Meiji period, and more specifically on the 1880s, in delineating the epistemological shift in "literature" as well as the discursive forces that endorsed it. Throughout the book, I suggest that such literature ultimately links itself to the production of "national" literature. However, I resist using the nation and nationalization as the essential pillar by which to narrativize the 1880s. The nation began to take institutional form soon after the time frame on which this book focuses; for example, the establishment of the imperial university system (1886), the promulgation of the constitution (1889), the founding of the Diet (1890), and the Imperial Rescript on Education (1890) are all decisive markers of nation formation. For our purposes, it is important to note that the Kokubungakka (Department of National Letters) was founded at Tokyo Imperial University in 1889, and many anthologies of Japanese literature began to be published soon thereafter. The notion of Japaneseness also emerged in national literature, especially in relation to the study of national language (*kokugo*). I do not doubt that what I discuss in this book, one way or another, link themselves to such institutional nationalization that occurred in the 1890s. However, I focus specifically on the years leading up to it in order to highlight the historical coincidences that coalesce amid the confusion of pre-institutionalization. This confusion is often concealed in scholarship that situates nation building as the primary cause of change—one that uses "nation" as a grammatical subject and hence the pillar by which a given imagined community is formed. The formulaic discussions that seemingly trace the nation-building process often end up in a self-fulfilling prophecy.

With Chapter 6, I leave the synchronic space I artificially create in this book and examine the historical development until the 1930s, with references to several discursive realms of interest, such as the development of national literature in the academy, the growing awareness of the Meiji period as history, and the role of the media, which changed dramatically at the turn of the century. My primary focus is on the literary histories produced throughout the years since their inception, as I trace how *Shōsetsu shinzui* was situated within these historical narratives. Specifically, I address two decisive phases that set the stage for

Shōsetsu shinzui's canonization. The turn of the century brings the first moment, as what literary critic Hibi Yoshitaka refers to as "self-portrayal" (*jiko hyōshō*) begins to take center stage in *shōsetsu*.[69] It is also accompanied by an establishment of a new mode of reading in which writers and readers publicly exchange information about fictional characters and their real-life models, dissolving the boundaries between reality and fiction.

The second moment of focus is the post–Great Kanto Earthquake era. The devastation and subsequent reconstruction brought about new technologies and new market strategies, as well as a renewed sense of history and historiography, all of which in some way shaped the discursive site that canonized *Shōsetsu shinzui*. Specifically, I discuss the emerging urge to document and hence create "the past" that arose after the earthquake, which featured a (re)discovery of Meiji. I also discuss, albeit briefly, the proletarian literary movement that reaches its height in the late 1920s and early 1930s. I focus specifically on the debates between politics and art that occurred between Marxist critics and proponents of art for art's sake and suggest how they intersect with the depoliticization of literature that I thematize in this book.

TWO

The Genealogy of the *Shōsetsu*

From Gesaku *to* "Shōsetsu = *Novel*"

The Constructed Linearity of Gesaku

This chapter analyzes the rhetorical strategies that make up the genealogy of the *shōsetsu* in the opening passage of *Shōsetsu shinzui*, particularly the way it focuses on "playful writings" (*gesaku*) as a precursor to the *shōsetsu*.[1] This discussion lays the groundwork for the subsequent chapters by identifying the forces that shape the genealogy of the *shōsetsu*, a genealogy that embodies the ideological gaze that designates *Shōsetsu shinzui* as the origin of modern Japanese literature. In effect, this chapter attempts to identify the many discursive fields that intersect with the epistemological shift in the understanding of literature thematized in the book.

The focus on *gesaku* as the precursor to the *shōsetsu* necessitated elevating *shōsetsu* into the realm of knowledge because the *shōsetsu* had to satisfy the eyes of "established and learned men," *Shōsetsu shinzui*'s target audience. However, "knowledge" was a contested field, being defined and redefined throughout the early years of the Meiji period. To complicate the matter, the new printing technology altered the ways in which such knowledge was circulated; these changes not only shaped the manner in which the readers accessed information but further shaped how the writers identified their roles in the distribution of knowledge in the new era. How the *shōsetsu* and *gesaku* were situated within such a complex network of shifting discourses clearly shapes the opening passage of *Shōsetsu shinzui*.

Gesaku embodies much of *Shōsetsu shinzui*'s rhetorical manipulation in the opening passage. The complex, diverse genre of the *gesaku* is reduced to an entity that becomes the negative precursor to the *shōsetsu*, defined as that which is not the *shōsetsu*. How *Shōsetsu shinzui* constructs the genealogical narrative vis-à-vis the category of *gesaku* will thus be a primary focus.

The following is the opening passage of *Shōsetsu shinzui* (the terms *monogatari* and *haishi* in the passage will be discussed later).

> How the *monogatari* has thrived in our country. Antiquity gave us *The Tale of Genji*, *The Tale of Sagoromo*, *The Tale of Hamamatsu*, and *The Tale of Sumiyoshi*, followed later by Ichijō Zenkō's *gesaku* and Ono no Otsū's *The Tale of Princess Jōruri*.[2] Closer to our own times, the fame enjoyed by such writers as Saikaku, Kishō, Fūrai, and Kyōden contributed still further to *shōsetsu*'s ever-increasing popularity, and thus literary talents of the day competed in producing *haishi*.[3] Ikku and Sanba gained popularity in "humorous stories" (*kokkeibon*) and "books of wit and fashion" (*sharebon*), and Shunsui's name is remembered for his "books of sentiment" (*ninjōbon*).[4] Tanehiko's fame derives from his *Rustic Genji* and Bakin's from *Hakkenden*.[5]
>
> Then the upheavals of the Restoration put a temporary stop to *gesaku* writers, and *shōsetsu* lost ground. Recently, however, it has made a very considerable comeback, the time being now propitious to the publication of *monogatari*. Everywhere we see all sorts of *haishi* and *monogatari*, each trying to outdo the others by simply seeking superficial novelty. Things have come to such a pass that even newspapers and magazines are publishing rehashings of threadbare old *shōsetsu*. As a result of this trend, there are innumerable *shōsetsu* and *haishi* of all varieties in circulation in our country—the sheer profusion defies description.[6]

Shōsetsu shinzui continues to criticize and lament the state of Meiji writings that focus on "encouraging virtue and castigating vice" (*kanzen chōaku*), a discussion to which I will later return. Condemning the "undiscriminating readers" and writers who are "slaves to public opinion," the introduction ends with the following:

> I hope that my theories will bring readers to their senses and at the same time enlighten writers, so that by henceforth planning the steady reform and improvement of *shōsetsu* we may finally bring it to the point where it surpasses the European *shōsetsu* = novel.[7] Our *monogatari* can then shine together with painting, music, and poetry on the altar of fine arts.[8]

One simple way of reading the opening passage is to say that it is an abridged history of Japanese literature that traces the development of the "*shōsetsu* = novel," as many critics have done. Nanette Twine, for example, translates the first sentence as, "How splendid has been the history of the novel in Japan" despite the fact that the words history, novel, and Japan are not present in the original text. I do not want to accuse her of mistranslation; rather, her translation is symptomatic of the manner in which *Shōsetsu shinzui* has been read. For such a reading to be viable, however, we must assume that "*shōsetsu* = novel" existed as an identifiable entity, one that could be traced in a continuous line in the history of Japanese writings. The novel was by no means a familiar literary medium in Meiji Japan, nor was it an established translation of the term *shōsetsu*. "Tracing" also presumes a smooth development from one literary configuration to the next, in this case from the representative *monogatari* to the Meiji adaptations of the late Edo *gesaku*. Yet such a smoothness or linearity of history cannot be assumed here. In fact, the use of the three terms *monogatari*, *haishi*, and *shōsetsu*, among other things, belies the fact that the works listed here do not have any causal or developmental relationship with one another.

At the risk of oversimplification, here are brief explanations of *monogatari* and *haishi* to supplement the definition of *shōsetsu* provided in the previous chapter. The meaning of *monogatari* is twofold. It refers to a genre of "tales" or prose fiction whose representative works are listed in the opening passage of *Shōsetsu shinzui*. The term *monogatari* is also a nominalized form of the verb *monogataru*, which refers to "the act of telling." The two characters that make up the word *monogatari* are *mono* (物), literally "thing" or "something," and *katari* (語), "to tell" or "to say." Even in the Heian period, when many of the representative *monogatari* were produced, for example, the term was often used simply to refer to the act of "recounting something."[9] Since then, the word has retained the meaning inscribed in its verbal form, referring to anything that is "narrated." *Monogataru* also had an oral component to it given that the act of recounting was associated with verbal retelling.[10]

Comparatively speaking, *haishi* (稗史) is a little more restrictive in its meaning. It derives from the Chinese system of classification in which *haishi* was defined against *seishi* (正史): the first character means "official" or "correct," and the second denotes "history."[11] *Haishi* thus refers to writings of historical events that were not included in "official history." Written by *haikan* officials—*haikan* being an official title in the Chinese political system given to those appointed to gather and compile stories of commoners—*haishi* focused on the lives of the "common" people. However, the criteria by which the boundary was drawn between official history and common history are difficult to determine. The dichotomy of the "official" and "popular-social" is not an accurate appraisal of this division; nor is "fiction" and "nonfiction." Perhaps the best way to classify these two is to say that what was endorsed officially by those who were in power as "history" was considered "official history," whereas other forms of historical writing—that is, the writing of past events—were referred to as *haishi*. It is easy to see that *haishi* and *shōsetsu* in many ways overlap; they were often used interchangeably, both in the Edo and the early Meiji periods.

The three terms, *monogatari*, *haishi*, and *shōsetsu*, intersect in many ways, but they are also rather disparate. For example, although the term *monogatari*, given its verbal form, could be used to refer to all the works listed in the opening passage, the terms *haishi* and *shōsetsu* cannot be applied to *Genji monogatari*, and not all the writers listed wrote *haishi*.[12] The term *haishi* was, in fact, mainly limited to the genre of historical fiction (*yomihon*, or "books for reading") that thematized the warriors of the past. The works of Saikaku were classified as "stories of the floating world" (*ukiyo zōshi*) and were not called *haishi* or *shōsetsu*. In the late Edo period, moreover, the specific names of *gesaku* subcategories such as *kokkeibon*, *sharebon*, and *yomihon* were used much more prevalently than *shōsetsu*. The rhetoric of linear development that appears to govern the opening passage becomes rather suspect when we consider that these three terms compose the lineage in question.

This lineage in *Shōsetsu shinzui*, however, is not completely arbitrary. It closely resembles the *gesaku* lineage that a representative *gesaku* writer, Kanagaki Robun (1829–94), included in his "Chosakudō kakiage" (The Way of Writing: A Humble Response). He and Sansantei Arindo (1832–1902) submitted this document in 1872 to the Ministry of Religious Instruction as a response to the Three Doctrines (*sanjō no kyōken*), passed by the government to "educate the masses," claiming that *gesaku* writers like themselves would do their best to adhere to the doctrines:

> *Gesaku* began as a medium that centers on "falsehood" (*kyo*) while placing "the real" (*jitsu*) secondary to it. Using real events and names, it took the basic skeleton of "official history." The examples are Luo Guanzhong [ca 1330–1400] and Li Yu [1611–80?] in China and our tales such as *Genji* and *Sagoromo*. Among the works that were produced, there were, of course, differences in loftiness and intellect, as well as in quality, but the later *gesaku* too had the same characteristics of the earlier ones. The later writers of western Japan, such as Ihara Saikaku and Hachimonjiya Jishō, produced *haishi* that mixed *monogatari* and Chinese *shōsetsu* (*kando no shōsetsu*); they nevertheless did not call their works *gesaku*. Later in the An'ei years [1772–80], Hiraga Gen'nai [1728–79], calling himself Fūrai Sanjin, appeared in the scene, and he was the first to use the term *gesaku*.[13] They were followed by a few works of Morishima Nagara, Tachikawa

Shibazenkō, Hōseidō Kisanji, and Tōrai San'na, but these were products of mere curiosity. However, with Santō Kyōden beginning to make a living with *gesaku* writing, Kyokutei Bakin, Shikitei Sanba, Ryūtei Tanehiko, Jippensha Ikku followed, allowing approximately ten to twenty writers to make a living in this profession since.[14]

The objective of Robun's description of history of *gesaku* is to legitimate the *gesaku* line, hence very different from that of *Shōsetsu shinzui*, which sought to produce a negative reference point by which to define the *shōsetsu*. But the similarity between the works and writers they take up is striking. Robun's "Humble Response" begins with the two representative *monogatari, Genji* and *Sagoromo*, and proceeds to works of Saikaku and Hiraga Gen'nai, all of which are included in *Shōsetsu shinzui*. After listing five mid-Edo *gesaku* writers (whom *Shōsetsu shinzui* skips but Robun's passage dismisses as rather minor anyway), it moves on to Kyōden, Bakin, Tanehiko, Sanba, and Ikku, the late Edo writers whose popularity was also noted in *Shōsetsu shinzui*. In constructing the lineage of the *shōsetsu*, therefore, *Shōsetsu shinzui* uses an accepted genealogy of the *gesaku*. As I will discuss in more detail later, the terms *shōsetsu, haishi*, and *monogatari*, which make up the opening passage, share the pretense that they are "secondary" to serious scholarship, an idea that is carried over from the accepted genealogy of the *gesaku*.

Yet the difference is also thought provoking, especially *Shōsetsu shinzui*'s omission of Luo Guanzhong and Li Yu, the renowned writers of the *hakuwa shōsetsu*, adaptations of which were produced by writers in Japan, most notably Bakin. This omission takes on additional significance because of *Shōsetsu shinzui*'s use of *shōsetsu* as a counterpart to the "novel." In early Meiji, the meaning of *shōsetsu* associated with the *hakuwa* tradition was the most dominant. Of course, *Shōsetsu shinzui* mentions Bakin, whose fame was based on his adaptations of the *hakuwa* fiction, but the deliberate omission of the two primary writers of *hakuwa shōsetsu* clearly results in the effacement of the *hakuwa* line from this *gesaku* lineage.

In effect, the *gesaku* lineage with which *Shōsetsu shinzui* opens should be read not as a "natural" precursor to the *shōsetsu* but as a constructed lineage that sets itself against the *hakuwa* tradition. Bakin is the sole embodiment of this lineage, and the literary tradition that his works carry is not given any consideration, here or elsewhere in *Shōsetsu shinzui*. I will discuss later in this chapter and the next what such a rhetorical strategy signifies. Here, I wish to touch upon *Shōsetsu shinzui*'s de-Asianizing impulses in producing a genealogy of *shōsetsu* of "our country," on a par with the movement to produce and retain what is "Japanese" as evidenced in the establishment of Koten Kōshūka (Program for Study in the Classics) in 1882. I do not wish to suggest an awareness of nationalism like that of Benedict Anderson's "imagined communities," in which the production of national literature plays a large part, as I believe such sentiment is still quite amorphous in mid-1880s Japan.[15] Yet efforts to isolate "Chinese literary tradition" as that which is *not* Japanese are apparent in *Shōsetsu shinzui*. This was especially true with the *hakuwa* tradition, despite its rich history in Japan and China. The deliberate omission of Luo Guanzhong and Li Yu in establishing the genealogy of the *shōsetsu* of "our country" is one indication. *Shōsetsu shinzui*'s discussion in "Principles of Construction in the *Shōsetsu*," which features a response to the famous "seven rules of the *shōsetsu*" that Bakin devised, also shows such de-Asianizing tendencies. Referring to tropes of "correspondence" (*shōō*) and "opposition" (*hantai*)—narrative devices that are similar to foreshadowing—*Shōsetsu shinzui* says, "These rules are specific to Chinese writers, who deem linguistic contrivance to be their primary objective, and thus not something to which our *shōsetsu* writers must adhere."[16] The "seven rules of the *shōsetsu*" were still a governing paradigm of literary analysis in 1880s Japan, and hence were by no means strictly "Chinese."[17] The distinction between "Japanese" and "Chinese" literary traditions was clearly ideological.

As Chapter 4 will show, the struggle for power in East Asia, especially vis-à-vis China, is everywhere apparent in major newspapers and hence within the discursive radar of the time. The urge to differentiate Japan from China—which was in many ways productive of "Japan" and "China"—permeates the discursive environment. I will return to this issue in Chapter 4 and further discuss how de-Asianizing impulses facilitate the definition of the *shōsetsu*.

Vicissitudes of Gesaku

Gesaku (戯作), a very amorphous category that appears to hold the lineage together, is one that warrants an extensive discussion. Here, with the ultimate objective of identifying the forces with which *Shōsetsu shinzui* engaged by designating *gesaku* as a precursor to the *shōsetsu*, I wish to provide a brief discussion of *gesaku*, what it signifies and what it constitutes, and further reflect upon how the category of *gesaku* intersects with *monogatari*, *haishi*, and *shōsetsu*. As Robun's "Humble Response" suggests, the history of *gesaku* features various breaks in literary practices that contest the seeming linearity that *Shōsetsu shinzui*'s opening passage presents.

The character 戲 (pronounced "ki," "ke," "gi," or "ge," meaning "playful") derives from the Chinese system of signification; the poetic collections of the Song and Tang dynasties embraced by the Edo literati include many uses of this character in sinified compounds, such as *kidai* (frivolous topics 戲題) and *kicho* (playful writings 戲著). These words were used to refer to verses that depicted lighthearted dialogues among friends, a poet's "love at first sight," or topics that were considered "better left unsaid."[18] When the character 戲 was first introduced to Japan is unclear, but we find the character beginning to appear frequently in the mid-eighteenth century in such occurrences as *gisho* (frivolous texts 戲書) and *gijutsu* (playful entries 戲述) referring to works that were written for entertainment and often objects of derision, especially from the perspective of the Confucian-educated literati. It was around this time that *hakuwa* narratives were imported in great number, and despite the stigma attached to producing such "secondary" writings, writers also felt justified in producing them as they saw the names of respectable scholars of China commenting on the brilliance of vernacular prose fiction.

Many adaptations of *gi* of course occurred prior to this time, but the use of the term increased in the mid- to late eighteenth century, when the first wave of *gesaku* writers (often referred to as *zenki gesakusha* or "early *gesaku* writers" in Japanese literary scholarship) began to write their *gesaku* or "secondary" works. Among the early wave of *gesaku* writers, Hiraga Gen'nai is included in the genealogy, both in Robun's "Humble Response" and *Shōsetsu shinzui*; many of them, like Gen'nai, were first-rate intellectuals, whether they were scholars of "native learning" (*kokugaku*) or of *kangaku*.[19] To retain their reputation as intellectuals, they needed to separate their "primary" work from their "frivolous" works, even if they enjoyed producing these writings. The more they produced secondary works, the more they needed to insist that they were *gesaku* and hence unrelated to their profession. This explains the increase in the use of *gi*, which distinctively separates *gesaku* production from production of primary scholastic work.

The early *gesaku* writers sometimes included the term *monogatari* in the title of their works, which gives us a good indication of the intersection between the two terms. On the one hand, by the Kamakura period (1185–1333), *monogatari*, as a genre of tales, had become mandatory knowledge for classical Japanese poetic composition (this was especially true for *Genji monogatari*); for example, the poet and scholar Fujiwara Shunzei (1114–1204), in his discussion of "allusive variation" (*honkadori*), identified the knowledge of tales as an indispensable subject for poetic composition. On the other hand, we should not forget that tales were considered a "secondary" medium, which was viewed as "women and children's reading." Tales were not included under the category of "knowledge" or *bungaku* prior to the Meiji period. Confucian scholars often derided *Genji monogatari* as "an immoral text," although there were many others who argued against such a view.[20] Despite the significant place that tales occupied in poetic composition, the *kangaku* classics as well as *kanshi* and *waka* poetry were deemed higher forms of knowledge. Furthermore, the representative *monogatari* included in the opening passage of *Shōsetsu shinzui* were all written by women in the late Heian to early Kamakura periods. Women's tales were narratives that could not enter the realm of *bungaku*, in which the primary and serious form of scholarship took place. Such secondary status linked *monogatari* with *gesaku*.[21]

The same can be said of writings categorized as *haishi* and *shōsetsu*. "Official history" (*seishi*) constituted knowledge in *kangaku*; and by definition, its opposite was everything but knowledge. Inscribed in the term *haishi*, therefore, was an implication of relative inferiority. *Shōsetsu*, from its first usage, signified "trivial writings" and "rumors in the streets." By the late Edo period, we also find interesting intersections between the three terms: although in many cases *haishi* and *shōsetsu* are used interchangeably, the characters for *haishi* are often glossed with *yomihon*; there is also an instance when the characters for *shōsetsu* are glossed with *monogatari*.[22] The proximity of these words is undoubtedly linked to their relatively inferior status.

In the mid- to late eighteenth century, the realm of *gesaku* expanded dramatically. With the development of the printing industry both in Edo (now Tokyo) and Keihan (Osaka and Kyoto) markets, by the time the late Edo *gesaku* writers entered the scene, representative writers such as Kyōden, Tanehiko, Bakin, Ikku, Shunsui, and Sanba were able to become professional writers. As Robun's "Humble Response" suggests, this clearly marks a break from previous writers.

The market expansion was accompanied by production of different subcategories of *gesaku*. At the risk of oversimplification, I provide here a brief description of each. "Books of wit and fashion" (*sharebon*) commonly tell stories of the pleasure quarters that celebrate the fashion and behavior of geisha and prostitutes. "Humorous stories" (*kokkeibon*) feature entertaining travel stories and parodies. Ikku and Sanba were famous for their *kokkeibon* and *sharebon*, such as *Tōkai dōchū hizakurige* (*By Shank's Mare through the West*, 1802–9) and *Ukiyoburo* (*Baths of the Floating World*, 1809), respectively. "Books of sentiments" (*ninjōbon*) feature stories of the pleasure quarters, with emphasis on the relationship between men and women, invariably a customer and geisha/prostitute. Shunsui is best known for his books of sentiments, his representative work being *Shunshoku umegoyomi* (*Colors of Spring: The Plum Calendar*, 1832–33).

"Books for reading" (*yomihon*) often dramatize historical events of the past. Bakin is the quintessential writer of *yomihon*. "Yellow-cover books" (*kibyōshi*) are considered the precursor to comic books—the illustrations are just as important as the stories themselves. "Bound books" (*gōkan*) are bound collections of three or four *kibyōshi*.

The subcategories are separated by criteria such as theme, narrative/linguistic style, and manner of compilation. For example, *yominhon*—unlike *kibyōshi* and *gōkan*—were written in a variety of sinified prose styles, though they were invariably "translated" with glosses (*rubi*).[23] At the same time, the thematic differences between these subcategories necessarily featured the use of different vocabulary. *Ninjōbon* and *sharebon*, for example, employed a variety of terms specific to the pleasure quarters, whereas *kokkeibon*, which often portrayed the lives of merchants, had their own economy of words.[24] The audience, too, differed depending on the medium; in fact, as contemporary literary critic Takada Mamoru suggests, the need to capture new audiences *produced* the new subcategories of *gesaku*.[25]

There was also a distinct difference in background between the early and late *gesaku* writers; high-class elite scholars, such as Gen'nai and Akinari, constituted the early writers, whereas the late Edo writers were mainly from the lower classes. The later writers Kyōden and Sanba were from the merchant class, and Ikku and Bakin were of the lower samurai class. Of course, "lower class" does not mean the bottom of the social strata; these writers were, after all, very literate (some more than others; Bakin, for example, was well known for his extensive knowledge in *kangaku* classics). A renowned scholar of Edo fiction, Nakamura Yukihiko, suggests that an interesting shift occurred in the use of the term *gesaku* with the advent of the late Edo *gesaku* writers: it became a means to gain entry to the literati. Use of the term *gesaku* was initially reserved for the high-class elites who also participated in "serious" work. Because they were engaged in serious scholastic work, they could use the term *gesaku* to designate their secondary works. By the use of the term, therefore, the later writers were able to become members of the literati by *claiming* that the texts they produced were *gesaku*, and hence "secondary," without necessarily having a primary scholastic work. When we consider these changes, the break between the early and later *gesaku* writers appears decisive.

There are at least three dimensions to the term *gesaku*.[26] First is the writing process; the writers allegedly wrote *gesaku* without any investment or seriousness. Second, the word refers to the end product of such endeavor, hence the common translation, "frivolous works." Despite the fact that *gesaku* itself experienced numerous changes, the very hierarchy that situated the works as secondary to the official and serious forms of knowledge was never reversed. Interestingly, the secondary status is what holds this disparate lineage together, producing a certain commonality that is invoked in the opening passage of *Shōsetsu shinzui*. Although Robun's "Humble Response" reconfirmed this secondary status by emphasizing *gesaku*'s ability to educate people with other forms of knowledge, *Shōsetsu shinzui* redefined this secondary status to produce a *shōsetsu* that is worthy of "established and learned men" in and of itself.

The third dimension is a product of a particular post-Meiji sentiment, one shared by *Shōsetsu shinzui* and the literary scholarship subsequent to it; this is the continuity between Edo and Meiji *gesaku*. Inscribed in the continuity is an assumption that *gesaku culminated* in the works of the late Edo *gesaku* writers. *Shōsetsu shinzui* clearly reproduces this assumption; all Meiji *gesaku* are "reworkings" and "rehashings" of the works written by Bakin, Shunsui, Ikku, Tanehiko, and Sanba. This is further reinforced by literary histories that simply consider Meiji *gesaku* as a continuation of Edo *gesaku*, which is more than apparent in the labels used to categorize these works, such as "Edo bungaku no zanshō" (the remains of Edo literature).[27]

The smooth continuity that *Shōsetsu shinzui* constructs between Meiji writings and late Edo *gesaku* is quite problematic. Meiji *gesaku* was very much a product of its time, a chaotic time of rapid change, and hence in many ways distinct from its Edo counterparts. The question, however, is not whether *Shōsetsu shinzui* presents a "correct" understanding of the *gesaku* but what it achieves by asserting such a continuity. First, it justifies the focus on late Edo *gesaku*. Many sections of *Shōsetsu shinzui* tend to focus on late Edo *gesaku* works, especially on Bakin, albeit negatively: "The Main Themes of the *Shōsetsu*" features the criticism of Bakin; "Principles of Construction in the *Shōsetsu*" discusses Bakin's famous "seven rules of *shōsetsu*"; and the examples used in the discussion of styles in "The Theory of Style" (Buntairon) are mainly of works written by Bakin, Tanehiko, and Shunsui. Second (and this is inextricably connected to the first), the assumed continuity allows *Shōsetsu shinzui* to evade discussions of Meiji texts. With very few exceptions, *Shōsetsu shinzui* rarely mentions Meiji works; when it does so, they are mentioned only in general terms and criticized as the "rehashing" of the old, for example. In this logic, Meiji *gesaku* is practically the same as Edo *gesaku*—if not its imperfect embodiment—and thus *Shōsetsu shinzui* can avoid any treatment of it. The works that are more directly linked to the *hakuwa* tradition—such as Yano Ryūkei's *Keikoku bidan* (*Illustrious Tales of Statesmanship*) and Miyazaki Muryū's *Jiyū no kachidoki* (*The Battle Cry of Liberty*)—which proliferated among the intelligentsia—can thus remain (rather conspicuously, given their popularity among *Shōsetsu shinzui*'s target audience) absent from *Shōsetsu shinzui*'s genealogy. The linguistic maneuvering that makes up *Shōsetsu shinzui* can be concealed only when we do not question the constructed linearity of the opening passage.

Denigrated Status of Gesaku*: The Advent of "Practical Knowledge" in the Meiji Era*

Before we turn to *Shōsetsu shinzui*'s discussion of Meiji discursive space, I wish to first explore the competing paradigms of knowledge specific to the post-Restoration era that ultimately interrupt the smooth linearity of the genealogical narrative. Such a discussion will allow us to identify some of the forces with which *Shōsetsu shinzui* negotiated as it designated *shōsetsu* as "learning" necessary in the post-Restoration world. The secondary status of *gesaku* and *shōsetsu* did not improve with the Meiji Restoration and the "new era"; in fact, it grew worse. Before the Restoration, the works called *shōsetsu*, *haishi*, and *monogatari* were deemed inferior primarily within the paradigm of *kangaku*; they were considered a means toward moral denigration, characterized as "writings that lure one to frivolity/desire" (*kai'in dōyoku no sho*). This sentiment was still so strong during the Meiji period that *Shōsetsu shinzui* argues directly against such characterization. For example, we see passages like the following: there are "some who censure the *shōsetsu* for teaching people to be lascivious and greedy. . . . Perhaps such condemnation by the Chinese is appropriate for works such as *Jin Ping Mei* [*The Plum in the Golden Vase*] and *Rouputuan* [*The Carnal Prayer Mat*] . . . but these are nothing but a spurious imitation of the true *shōsetsu*."[28] Throughout the text, *Shōsetsu shinzui* thus repeatedly defends the *shōsetsu* against criticisms that situate the *shōsetsu* as a vehicle for "moral corruption." However, Confucian thought upon which such criticism was based was not the only mode of learning against which *Shōsetsu shinzui* had to argue. The paradigm shift in the realm of knowledge that came with the new era produced another authority: that of "real" or "practical" knowledge (*jitsugaku*) as opposed to "false" or "impractical" knowledge (*kyogaku*); *shōsetsu* and *haishi* were quickly categorized among impractical knowledge.

The following is a famous passage from Fukuzawa Yukichi's *Gakumon no susume* (*Encouragement of Learning*, 1872–76), one of the best sellers of early Meiji. It defines the constituents of "real or practical learning."

> Being educated does not mean knowing difficult words or reading ancient texts or enjoying poetry and writing verse and other such accomplishments which

are of no practical use in the world. These accomplishments do give much plea-sure to the human mind, and they have their own values, but they are not to be esteemed and worshipped as much as the Confucian and Japanese scholars have tried to make them out to be. Since time immemorial, there have been very few scholars of the Chinese classics [*kangaku*] who were good household providers or merchants who were accomplished in poetry and yet clever in business. . . . Therefore, this kind of learning without real use should be left for another day, and one's best efforts should be given to an education that is rel-evant to everyday use—for instance, the 47 letters of the alphabet, correspon-dence, bookkeeping, the abacus and the use of scales. Advancing further, there will be many subjects to be taken up: geography is a sort of story and guide of Japan and all the countries of the world; natural philosophy is the knowledge of nature and function of all things under the heavens; history is a detailed chronology and studies the conditions of every country in the world past and present; economics explains the management of a household and of a country and of the world; ethics is concerned with the natural principles of a man's conduct, his relationship with his fellow men, and his behavior in society.[29]

"Practical knowledge" constitutes geography, natural philosophy, history, eco-nomics, and ethics; these are the forms of learning that must be pursued in order for a person to take part in the modernizing world. At the same time, *Gakumon no susume* rejects the study of *kangaku* classics, which was formerly considered the highest form of knowledge, as well as Japanese and Chinese poetry, the marks of erudition of the previous era.

In this long list of what constitutes learning, literary writings are not recog-nized as worthy of being pursued; in fact, they are clearly excluded as "having no practical use."[30] According to *Gakumon no susume*, "bookkeeping" or "the use of scales" has far more meaning than Japanese or Chinese poetry for the present. With the introduction of a new set of criteria (that is, practical knowl-edge), the representative literary traditions honored up until this point were denied their value.

Many embraced practical knowledge in the early years of Meiji, and the gov-ernment sponsored the move in that direction, evident from the implementa-tion of the Education Act (*gakusei*) in 1872, an educational system that leaned strongly toward "Western learning," much to the dismay of *kangaku* scholars.[31] Yet *kangaku* never disappeared from the scene; even after the Education Act was implemented, many former samurai and wealthy families educated their sons with *kangaku* at home.[32] The strength of *kangaku* and its primary principles are also apparent in the other best seller of the time, Nakamura Masanao's translation of Samuel Smiles's *Self-Help* (1859), entitled *Saigoku risshihen* (*Success in the West*, 1871). Nakamura, a famous *kangaku* sympathizer, deployed Confucian-based ethics in translating Smiles's text. In *Saigoku risshihen*, we thus see an interesting fusion of Smiles's Puritanism and Nakamura's *kangaku* philosophy. Here is a passage from *Saigoku risshihen*, a section entitled "The Harm Caused by *Shōsetsu*."

> *Shōsetsu* drives people to laughter, forcing them to deviate from their aims in life. Nothing else defiles knowledge as much as it does. It is sincerely regretful that there are many who write it, trying only to cater to public taste. The [writers] show no aversion to vulgarity nor to humor and break the laws of human ethics as well as those of the divine. Douglas Jerrold said, "People must not forget dignity in whatever they do. However, there are those who turn people and everything of the world into objects of laughter, producing *gibun* solely to desecrate the divine and infect society. It is extremely lamentable." John Sterling also said, "*Shōsetsu* is more harmful to the people—especially to those whose minds are still unformed—than diseases can ever be. It is just like the vermin that infects the water and makes sick those who drink it."[33]

Contrast Nakamura's version here with Smiles's text, which does not have any subheadings:

> There is almost a mania for frivolity and excitement, which exhibits itself in many forms in our popular literature. To meet the public taste, our books and periodicals must now be highly spiced, amusing and comic, not disdaining slang, and illustrative of breaches of all laws, human and divine. Douglas Jerrold once observed of this tendency: "I am convinced the world will get tired (at least I hope so) of this eternal guffaw about all things.". . . John Sterling, in like spirit, said: "Periodicals and novels are to all in this generation, but more especially to those whose minds are still unformed and in the process of formation, a new and more effectual substitute for the plagues of Egypt, vermin that corrupt the wholesome waters and infest our chambers."[34]

When Smiles refers to "popular literature," "periodicals," and "novels," Nakamura uses the terms *shōsetsu* and *gibun*. *Gibun* was a style of writing that provided entertainment for intellectuals. *Gi* here is the same character as the *ge* in *gesaku*; the secondary status attached to such style of language must therefore be clear. The value judgments inherent in these terms derive from the Confucian-based system. Nakamura, in the guise of translating Smiles, faithfully follows Confucian ethics, emphasizing how ethically corrupting *shōsetsu* and *gibun* can be. Not only are they useless for the new world but they also cause moral degeneration.

Gakumon no susume and *Saigoku risshihen* were best sellers for the youths in the early Meiji period who dreamed of independence and "success and advancement" (*risshin shusse*) in the new world, where people were allegedly considered "equal." The two different paradigms of knowledge upon which these works are based, namely, "practical knowledge" and *kangaku*, contest each other in early to mid-Meiji, a process I will discuss later.[35]

The secondary status of *shōsetsu* and *gesaku* was thus amplified with the advent of the new era; not only were they devalued by Confucian ethics but they were also considered useless by the paradigm of practical knowledge associated with "Westernizing" impulses. As a result, the very existence of these writings was threatened. Such sentiment was still strongly present in the early to mid-1880s. This is evident from the well-known anecdote about Fukuzawa's reaction to Shōyō's *Tōsei shosei katagi*. Upon hearing that Shōyō had written a *shōsetsu*, Fukuzawa became angry, saying that as a decent and educated man, Shōyō should not be immersing himself in something that frivolous.

Meiji Gesaku *and the Three Doctrines*

These different authorities of knowledge clearly shape the opening passage of *Shōsetsu shinzui*, especially its discussion of Meiji writings. Despite *Shōsetsu shinzui's* claims for the apparent seamlessness between Edo and Meiji *gesaku*, as well as the apparent homogeneity of Meiji *gesaku*, competing paradigms of knowledge produce changes that contest these claims. The following is a continuation of the opening passage.

> At the end of the Tokugawa period, the prolific output of *monogatari* by writers such as Bakin and Tanehiko led *shōsetsu* to prosper. Young and old, men and women, country and city dwellers alike, all pored eagerly over *haishi*, extolling them to the skies. Yet the popularity was still far from its present proportions because the readers of the Bunka [1804–17] and Bunsei [1818–29] periods were to some extent connoisseurs who purchased and read only works of outstanding quality. . . . Today, all that has changed. How extraordinary it is that every *shōsetsu* and *haishi* should enjoy the same popularity regardless of its quality, no matter how poor the *monogatari* or how vulgar the erotic stories, whether it be an adaptation, a translation, a reprint, or a new work. This is indeed a "golden age" of *shōsetsu*. There is certainly no shortage of *gesaku* writers, but most of them write adaptations. Not one can be called a writer in his own right. Every recently published *shōsetsu* and *haishi* has been a reworking of Bakin or Tanehiko, if not an imitation of Ikku or Shunsui. *Gesaku* writers of late have taken

to heart the words of Li Yu—they regard didacticism as the main purpose of *shōsetsu* and *haishi* and construct a moral framework within whose bounds they strive to devise a plot, with the result that even if they have not consciously set out to mimic earlier writers, the restricted scope of their *haishi* nevertheless forces them along already well-worn paths.[36]

Shōsetsu shinzui characterizes Meiji writings as mere adaptations and imitations of late Edo *gesaku*; to emphasize the continuity and the "already well-worn paths," the passage foregrounds the writers' deployment of didacticism as the main framework of *gesaku* fiction.

This opening passage has contributed to the widespread misunderstanding that didacticism is the primary characteristic of *gesaku*, which is certainly not the case for many works categorized as *gesaku*. It also ignores obvious disparities between Edo *gesaku* and the Meiji writings. First, early Meiji *gesaku* thematized the coming of the new era.[37] Some examples are Kanagaki Robun's *Seiyō dōchū hizakurige* (*By Shank's Mare through the West*, 1870), a humorous story of two heroes and the comical incidents that arise as they journey from Yokohama to London; and *Aguranabe* (*Around the Beef-Pots*, 1871–72), a narrative featuring a variety of characters talking about the new era as they sit around beef-pots (*gyūnabe*)—a symbol of enlightenment.

Second, Meiji writings were circulated through an entirely new configuration of the publishing industry, which had grown rapidly with the advent of new printing technology. The number of newspapers and magazines increased dramatically, as did individual publications by expanding publishing houses.[38] The first daily newspaper, *Yokohama mainichi shinbun*, began its circulation in 1871, and a number of other newspapers followed.[39] These were called "large" newspapers (*ōshinbun*) as opposed to "small" newspapers (*koshinbun*) that began circulation around 1875. Whereas the large newspapers published mainly political columns and debates written in difficult, sinified language—a language reserved for the intelligentsia—the small newspapers featured reports and rumors written in *kana* phonetic scripts with illustrations accompanying the text.[40] It is more convincing to think that these new media, given that they allowed more space for publication, produced "the golden age of *shōsetsu*" rather than the growth in the number of people with "less taste," as *Shōsetsu shinzui* would like us to believe.

The "golden age of *shōsetsu*" is also linked with the Three Doctrines (*sanjō no kyōken*) issued in April 1872, which gave the *gesaku* writers the best possible justification for their profession. Issued by the Ministry of Religious Instruction, this declaration consisted of three teachings: "(1) Respect for the gods and love of country should be embodied. (2) The ways of Heaven, Earth, and Man are to be elucidated. (3) Obedience to the Emperor and his Will should be inculcated."[41] The Ministry of Religious Instruction later issued sets of articles on how to preach these teachings, which included the need for compulsory education, virtues of conscription, and a call for a "wealthy nation and strong army" (*fukoku kyōhei*) and "civilization and enlightenment" (*bunmei kaika*).[42] Oral storytellers, as well as famous *gesaku* writers, were given the role of spreading this doctrine to the masses. At this time Robun officially published his response, entitled "The Way of Writing: A Humble Response," in which he discussed the *gesaku* lineage quoted earlier. He and many others welcomed the new role of publicizing this doctrine.[43]

Gesaku writers were thus given a social role to spread government-endorsed learning. The first decade of the Meiji period saw an increase in reportage and "documentary fiction" (*jitsuroku*), as well as "practical" works such as textbooks, many of which were produced by the *gesaku* writers. Robun, for example, reported on the Saga Rebellion (1874) in his *Saga denshinroku* (*Records of Saga Telegrams*, 1874) and also on the Seinan War (1877) in *Seinan chinseiroku* (*On Containing the Seinan War*, 1877). Somezaki Nobufusa (1823–86) wrote a history of late Edo to early Meiji entitled *Kinsei kibun* (*Stories of the Time Just Past*, 1873).[44] The small newspapers for which these writers wrote fulfilled the role of educating the readership with such contemporary events, as well as government proclamations and newly instituted laws, by printing explanations with *kana* phonetic scripts.

Not all *gesaku* writers wholeheartedly embraced the government-sponsored projects or practical knowledge; there were, in fact, many impulses of resistance. Despite the appearance of complete submission, there were times that small newspapers were censored for their antigovernment exposés. Mantei Ōga (1818–90), for example, resisted the wave of practical knowledge by writing parodies of the blind pursuit of the West. Baitei Kinga (1821–93), too, viewed forces of Westernization contemptuously. Other forms of playful writings also resisted the new era. Narushima Ryūhoku (1837–84), well known for his "*kanbun* chronicles of customs and mannerisms" (*kanbun fūzokushi*),[45] wrote *Ryūkyō shinshi* (*New Yanagibashi*), which became extremely popular in the first decade of the Meiji period.[46] *Ryūkyō shinshi* expressed Ryūhoku's ambivalence to the Meiji order through descriptions of the customs and manners of the Yanagibashi pleasure district, which had been the most prestigious quarter since the Edo period. Written in a highly sinified Japanese, the primary language of the intelligentsia, it mocks the unsophisticated attitudes of the new Meiji government officials, such as the low-ranking samurai from Satsuma and Chōshū who gained control after the Meiji Restoration. *Ryūkyō shinshi* became popular in the first decade of Meiji.

Despite the fact that the *Shōsetsu shinzui* leads us to believe that "encourage virtue, castigate vice" (*kanzen chōaku*) is one of the defining characteristics of *gesaku*, *kanzen chōaku* itself did not gain momentum in Meiji Japan until the late 1870s. The Three Doctrines and other regulations passed by the government, of course, called for *kanzen chōaku*, but it was not a dominant rhetorical form until "serialized fiction" (*tsuzukimono*), a new form of literary practice that grew out of small newspapers, began to flourish, taking up the language of *kanzen chōaku*. Taking *Shōsetsu shinzui*'s discussion of Meiji *gesaku* at face value can only blind us to the many rhetorical manipulations that compose it.

The Revival of Confucian Doctrines

Meiji *gesaku* saw further development in the late 1870s to early 1880s, but these changes are rarely emphasized in literary histories given the usual narrative that highlights 1885, the publication of *Shōsetsu shinzui*, as the turning point in modern Japanese literary history. *Kanzen chōaku* took center stage in the late 1870s and thus provides yet another context within which to situate *Shōsetsu shinzui*'s attack on *kanzen chōaku*.

As the increasing number of small newspapers began to make the market more competitive, individual papers naturally began to demand articles and columns that would attract a greater number of readers. This market principle fostered the birth of serialized fiction, a new form of practice that marks the late 1870s and the early 1880s.[47] What began as short entries of gossip from the pleasure quarters or mere reports of murder or theft were taken up as the most appropriate material for documentary fiction; a column was serialized for a longer period of time if it could attract readers (conversely, serialization was cut off if it could not attract readers). After eight years of non-*gesaku* writing, Robun, for example, came back to the *gesaku* scene with *Takahashi Oden yasha monogatari* (*The Tale of the She-Devil Takahashi Oden*, 1879), one of his most well-known works. Based on real accounts, *Takahashi Oden yasha monogatari* featured the life of a "poison woman" (*dokufu*) who made her way in life by manipulating men. Kubota Hikosaku's (1846–98) *Torioi Omatsu kaijō shinwa* (*A Story of Torioi Omatsu at Sea*, 1878) is another famous work thematizing the poison woman. In accordance with the formula of *kanzen chōaku*, in both these works the poison women were punished in the end for their foul deeds. Okamoto Kisen's (1853–82) *Sawamura Tanosuke akebono zōshi* (*A Story of Sawamura Tanosuke*, 1880), which thematized the life of a famous *kabuki* actor, was very popular upon its serialization; this story was also framed with the structure of *kanzen chōaku*.

When we focus our attention on the media in which the serialized fiction were published, namely, small newspapers, the commonality between serialized fiction and early writings by the *gesaku* writers tends to be emphasized. However, such characterization can easily blind us to yet another shift in the power dynamics of knowledge that had a great impact on *gesaku* writing of the second decade: the revival of Confucian doctrines. In fact, it may not be an exaggeration to say that the forces behind the resurgence of Confucian principles were what fostered the proliferation of serialized fiction.

The impulses toward "practical learning" had perhaps gone too far; in the process of defining and redefining imperial subjects, the issue of "moral education" was raised repeatedly. The problem was characterized in the dichotomy of "intellectual education" (*chiiku*) versus "moral education" (*tokuiku*). Motoda Eifu, a tutor to the emperor who had a profound impact on the emperor's vision in general, wrote "Kyōgaku seishi" (The Sacred Principles of Education, 1879), demanding that the policy of enlightenment education be modified in the name of the emperor.[48] In it, he criticized the overemphasis on intellectual education, which was, according to Motoda, being conducted at the expense of moral education. For Motoda, the "core of education" constituted "benevolence, justice, loyalty, and obedience" (*jingi chūkō*).[49] Motoda's call had a large impact on the educational reforms of the time, and as early as the following year, the Ministry of Education began to compile textbooks for ethical instruction.[50] Ethics instruction, which was last on the list of elementary school subjects in the 1879 draft of the Education Ordinance, moved to first on the list in the 1880 version.[51] "Shōgakkō kyōin kokoroe" (Guidelines for Elementary Schoolteachers), issued in 1881, first lists the need for moral education to implant "imperial loyalty," "love for the nation," and "respect for parents."[52] Recall that the Education Act passed in 1872 was oriented toward practical knowledge; the 1880 version thus signified a 180-degree turn.

One clear example of the revival of Confucian doctrines can be seen in Motoda Eifu's textbook *Yōgaku kōyō* (*Principles of Elementary Education*) published in 1881. It consists of six volumes and lists twenty "moral principles," including "filial piety" (*kōkō*), "loyalty" (*chūsetsu*), "friendship" (*yūai*), "courage" (*gōyū*), and "sharp intellect" (*binchi*). Each section begins with an explanation of a principle, followed by lists of entries from the *kangaku* classics, such as the *Analects*. They are then followed by specific examples from either Japanese or Chinese historical anecdotes. The textbook specifically excluded "foreign" examples, limiting the entries to the Sino-Japanese realm.[53] The textbooks that had been used previously, such as Fukuzawa's *Tsūzoku minkenron* (*On People's Rights*, 1878) and *Tsūzoku kokkenron* (*On National Rights*, 1878–79) and Katō Hiroyuki's *Kokutai shinron* (*A New Theory of the National Body*, 1875), were prohibited from use.[54] The movement to revive Confucian doctrines was sponsored by the government, and the study of *kangaku* classics that had been, for the past decade, considered "impractical" was revived, much to the joy of the *kangaku* scholars.

The emphasis on the need for moral instruction also refueled the language of "encourage virtue, castigate vice" (*kanzen chōaku*). Of course, the language of *kanzen chōaku* existed in Meiji prior to this revival. As Christine Marran points out, a small newspaper, *Kanayomi shinbun*, for example, deployed the language of *kanzen chōaku* while acknowledging the atmosphere that leaned toward practical knowledge. As she herself claims, however, the *kanzen chōaku* language was not at all the dominating style in small newspapers at the time. In fact, it was a distinct characteristic of *Kanayomi shinbun*, which leads Marran to conclude that the language was a way for the *Kanayomi shinbun* to produce a reading community of its own.[55]

The resurgence of Confucian doctrines in schools, the increase in the use of *kanzen chōaku* language, and the proliferation of serialized fiction were not unrelated occurrences. However, for serialized fiction to employ *kanzen chōaku* language was not simply to adhere to the need for ethical instruction espoused by the government; it provided the writers with a familiar form by which to frame a long story. For serialized fiction to take form, the *gesaku* writers had to find a literary schema that would allow them to write and shape a relatively long story. They needed a plot structure on which they could rely and shape the events they described. Inscribed in *kanzen chōaku* is a plot structure with a predetermined ending—the good wins out, and the bad is punished. *Kanzen chōaku* was thus an effective literary schema to which the writers of serialized fiction could turn.

Moral education was certainly not the only "educational" aspect of serialized fiction; taking as their theme the events that actually occurred, writers managed to educate the masses about the newly created laws (such as the criminal laws alluded to in Robun's *Takahashi Oden yasha monogatari* and Kubota's *Torioi Omatsu kaijō shinwa*), which are described and often implemented in punishing evil characters. In effect, serialized fiction could flourish with both tendencies of practical knowledge and the structure of *kanzen chōaku*.

If we take for granted *Shōsetsu shinzui*'s criticism of Meiji writings as hackneyed adaptations of Edo *gesaku*, following the "well-worn paths" of their predecessors named *kanzen chōaku*, we could only gloss over the varying shifts that shape the production of works we now categorize under the rubric "Meiji *gesaku*." If we take *Shōsetsu shinzui*'s criticism of "people's tastes" at face value, we also lose sight of the inextricable relationship between the newly assigned role of *gesaku* writers as educators within the competing discourse of practical knowledge and Confucianism, and the demands of print capitalism that inevitably shaped their works. The question is, what does *Shōsetsu shinzui* achieve by targeting *kanzen chōaku* as it also designates *kanzen chōaku* as the main thread that links Edo and Meiji *gesaku*?

Shōsetsu shinzui's selection of *kanzen chōaku* as the object of criticism signifies, in part, a rejection of the proliferating *kanzen chōaku* discourse deployed by writers of serialized fiction. It signified a rejection of *kanzen chōaku* plot structure, an alternative to which is discussed in the second volume of *Shōsetsu shinzui*. However, that would not completely explain *Shōsetsu shinzui*'s focalization on the late Edo *gesaku* writers, especially on Bakin, the quintessential writer of *kanzen chōaku* fiction. One explanation for this focus lies in the contemporaneous publishing conditions. The publishing houses were now equipped with new printing technology, and they set about reviving Confucian doctrines. For example, they began to reprint the classics, such as *Shiji* (*Records of the Grand Historian*).[56] With the success of reprints of the *kangaku* classics, prompted by the revival of *kangaku* scholarship, the publishing houses began reprinting Edo *gesaku*, led by Bakin's works—such as his most famous work, *Hakkenden*, and *Chinsetsu yumiharizuki* (*Strange Tales of the Crescent Moon*, 1806–10). Publishers saw a potential market for Bakin's works given that they relied heavily on the *kangaku* classics. Between 1882 and 1886, seven versions of *Hakkenden* were published by different publishers. In fact, just in the National Diet Library, there is a collection of ninety-one works by Bakin (albeit many overlaps, but reprinted by different publishers) published between 1882 and 1886; for comparison, thirty by Shunsui and twelve by Kyōden were reprinted during the same years. Bakin was by far the most popular writer whose works were reprinted during the time *Shōsetsu shinzui* was produced. Accordingly, *Hakkenden* was the embodiment of what a *shōsetsu* was for the Meiji readership.[57] In criticizing the great number of *shōsetsu* that are hackneyed adaptations of Edo writers, *Shōsetsu shinzui* is clearly addressing not only the writers who "imitate" Bakin but the omnipresence of Bakin's works.

Bakin's primary audience was not readers of small newspapers but the intellectuals, or perhaps more important, the "educated men" that *Shōsetsu shinzui* addresses. Many writers attest to Bakin's popularity in their memoirs and essays, reminiscing on how they engaged with Bakin's works. We know that Shōyō himself was an avid reader of Bakin's works, based on an essay he wrote in 1920, entitled "Kyokutei Bakin."[58] Ichishima Shunjō (1860–1944), Shōyō's friend and classmate, for example, claims that he had never encountered *shōsetsu* until he went to Tokyo where "Bakin's *shōsetsu*, *Hakkenden*, *Yumiharizuki*, and *Bishōneroku* [*Tales of Handsome Youths*, 1829–32, 1845–48] were popular in the student society of Tokyo."[59] Discussing the existence of "rental bookstores" (*kashihon'ya*), he mentions that he read through all of Bakin's works. Yoda Gakkai (1833–1909) and Aeba Kōson (1855–1922) were also defenders of Bakin's works.

Such popularity of Bakin's works in early Meiji clearly engaged with the energy of the Freedom and People's Rights Movement. As the contemporary literary critic Maeda Ai points out in "Meiji rekishi bungaku no genzō" (Images of Meiji Historical Literature), Bakin's narratives were very popular among participants of the movement precisely because they could be read as a "fulfillment" of the Meiji struggles and uprisings, written a hundred years or so before the actual occurrence. Describing how the eight warriors in *Hakkenden* recruit the help of peasants when fighting against the "brutal rulers" (*bōkun*) and "wicked officials" (*kanshin*), Maeda suggests that many such stories were read "as a literary embodiment of the riots that occurred during the height of the Freedom and People's Rights Movement."[60]

Although I will leave the detailed discussion of the works that specifically engaged with the Freedom and People's Rights Movement—and their inextricable link to Bakin's works—until the next chapter, it is worthwhile noting here that many such works deployed the language of *kanzen chōaku*: Sakurada Momoe's translation of Dumas's *Mémoires d'un médicin*, Miyazaki Muryū's translation of Dumas's *Ange Pitou*, and Yano Ryūkei's *Keikoku bidan* (*Illustrious Tales of Statesmanship*), to name a few. I contend that in many ways the existence of such writings played a large role in *Shōsetsu shinzui*'s choice to frame Bakin as a negative precursor to the *shōsetsu* and to target *kanzen chōaku* as a common ground upon which Edo and Meiji *gesaku* were produced.

The Shōsetsu *as a Means for "Human Development" versus the Endorsed Forms of "Knowledge"*

Shōsetsu shinzui's rejection of *kanzen chōaku* exhibits a clear stance against the revival of Confucianism and Motoda-led educational reforms. However, the forces behind the revival opened up new possibilities for *Shōsetsu shinzui* to legitimate the *shōsetsu*, which had been denigrated as "morally corrupt" and "impractical" in the new era. There was a need for "human development" (*jinbun hatsuiku*), which was one of the primary reasons that Confucian scholars, who argued for the importance of moral education (*tokuiku*), reemerged as central players of the Meiji educational system.

I must hasten to add, however, that the need for internal reform was widely discussed in the educational arena, and Confucian scholars were not the only group of intellectuals involved. Whether or not one agreed with the conservative scholars who sought to revive Confucianism, like Motoda Eifu, intellectuals agreed that "intellectual education" (*chiiku*) had to be supplemented by some kind of "internal" education. The rhetoric that was mobilized to accomplish this revolved around "the independent spirit" (*dokuritsu no seishin*), which was used equally among the Confucian scholars and those against the resurgence of Confucianism.[61] Motoda, in "Kyōgaku seishi," claimed that moral education centering on works of Confucius will ultimately produce men who would not deviate from "the independent spirit of our nation."[62] Likewise, Ono Azusa, a Kaishintō intellectual who gave a speech at the founding ceremony of Tokyo Senmon Gakkō (Tokyo Specialized School, the present-day Waseda University), said, "The autonomy of the nation depends on the autonomy of its people, and the autonomy of the people is rooted in the autonomy of their spirit (*seishin*). The autonomy of the spirit is, in fact, based on the autonomy of knowledge."[63] Despite the fact that these intellectuals were of an entirely different political faction, they mobilized the same rhetoric. As various literati promoted human development as a means of producing "civilized" humans capable of adapting to changes in the modernizing world, the educational arena began also to be associated with human development. *Shōsetsu shinzui*, in defining the *shōsetsu* as a means to foster human development, thus engaged with the shift in the educational arena, which ultimately constitutes yet another force that endorses the epistemological shift in literature.

Shōsetsu shinzui's effort to seek *shōsetsu*'s legitimacy in its ability to foster human development is first evident in the two sections of "The Benefits of the *Shōsetsu*," where *Shōsetsu shinzui* discusses "Hito no kikaku o kōshō ni nasu koto" (Ennoblement of Character) and "Hito o kanshō chōkai nasu koto" (Moral Instruction), both of which are on a par with the arguments for internal reform espoused by Confucian scholars who asserted the need for ethical instruction.[64] Here is a section from "Ennoblement of Character":

> The *shōsetsu* is not something to be used in the service of man's carnal passions. It aspires to entertain him by appealing to his more refined tastes. A taste for

elegance and an emotional sensitivity, however, are the most noble of attributes, to be found only in people of civilized, culturally advanced nations. . . .
The gentle medium of art is invoked to appeal to a man's aesthetic sensibilities,
to arouse his finer feelings, gradually to drive out lust and lure his thoughts
outside the everyday world, and to lead him to an awareness of the subtler kind
of beauty; then he will be uplifted in spite of himself and will soon escape from
the seas of passion. . . . Thus an art lover who indulges himself frequently will
develop more and more of a taste for elegance, and his character will become
increasingly finer.[65]

The *shōsetsu* as art thus takes on the role of refining "taste" and internal
"sensibilities," which are found only among "civilized and culturally advanced
nations," and promotes "elegance" and ennoblement of character. *Shōsetsu
shinzui* further defines *shōsetsu*'s objective as "criticism of life" (*jinsei no hihan*)
and designates *shōsetsu* as a vehicle for self-reflection (*hansei*): "Aspiring writers should always make criticism of life the primary objective of writing. The
shōsetsu, therefore, reveals what is hidden, defines what is indistinct, and brings
together all man's innumerable passions within the covers of a book, thereby
naturally stimulating the reader to self-reflection."[66] *Shōsetsu shinzui* thus clearly
deploys the discourse of human development in defining the *shōsetsu*'s validity
in the newly civilized world.

However, in order to establish the *shōsetsu* in and of itself, *Shōsetsu shinzui*
needs to make a slight alteration of surrounding discourse promoting such
reform. Just as *Shōsetsu shinzui*'s choice of *gesaku* as the precursor to the *shōsetsu*
prompted negotiations with the shifting paradigms of knowledge, *Shōsetsu
shinzui* encounters a new set of negotiations by seeking to validate the *shōsetsu*
through discourses of human development.

This is most apparent in "The Comprehensive Theory of the *Shōsetsu*," a section of *Shōsetsu shinzui* that immediately follows the introduction, which designates the *shōsetsu* as an art form. The section begins by quoting two authoritative
texts—Ernest Fenollosa's (1853–1908) *Bijutsu shinsetsu* (*The Truth of Fine Arts*,
1882) and the Buddhist scholar Ōuchi Seiran's editorials compiled in *Dainihon
bijutsu shinpō* (*The New Journal for Japanese Art*, 1883):[67]

Civilization is achieved entirely by the efforts of mankind. Human endeavor
bears two kinds of fruit—"functional" and "ornamental." The aim of the "functional" is to provide the necessities of life; while the aim of the "ornamental"
is to entertain the heart and eyes and ennoble the human character. . . . Is it
not a need of human society to entertain and enrich character (*kikaku o kōshō
ni suru*)? The difference [between the two] is that utilitarian labor is beautiful

because of its practical value (*jitsuyō*), while art has practical value because of its beauty. (Fenollosa)

Art is the mainspring of human development, because its aim is to give pleasure and ennoble character. Because it pleases, it creates a climate of friendship and warmth among men; because it has an ennobling effect on character (*kikaku o kōshō ni suru*), it subdues envy, greed, and cruelty. (Ōuchi)[68]

The focal point is clearly on the authoritative texts' emphasis on art's ability to "enrich" and "ennoble" character, associating the *shōsetsu* with such roles. Yet, after supporting their descriptions of art, *Shōsetsu shinzui* goes on to alter the definition by saying that "perhaps their logic is not entirely correct with regard to the principles that underlie them":

As art is not for practical use (*jitsuyō*), one expects its "aims" to be only to give pleasure and to achieve a transcendent beauty. Its perfection may inspire the beholder to forget greed and cruelty, and rejoice instead in nobler thoughts, but this is a natural side effect and not the "aim" of art. It is rather a chance product and not the ultimate goal. Were it not so, the artists of the world, painters and sculptors alike, would create a mold called "human development" and work within its confines. Surely this would be a grave mistake. . . . If the artist were to set his "aims" at human development, whether carving images of birds and animals or painting mountain scenery, he is bound to keep this aim always before him. Wouldn't this be a difficult task? It is difficult enough to seek perfection, designing and copying to produce a masterpiece, but for the artists' idea to be further manacled (*kubikase*) by a stipulation of this sort, the task would become even more difficult.[69]

"Human development" is here described as "a natural side effect" or a "chance product" of art and not the "aim." Moreover, the aim is identified as an impediment (*kubikase*) that interferes with the creation of a masterpiece. Why such logic? To sever "art"—the *shōsetsu*—from the notion that it is a *means* to a certain end and to establish its "perfection" as an end in itself.

This alteration is crucial given the status of *shōsetsu* in the early years of Meiji; whether in the context of practical knowledge or Confucian-based ethical instruction, it had been used as an educational medium, a *means* to some other end. As such, severing *shōsetsu* from other disciplines was an utmost necessity. Recall that the choice of *gesaku* lineage as the precursor of the *shōsetsu* reinforced the secondary status of the medium. *Shōsetsu shinzui* had other agendas in claiming such lineage (namely, to counter the *hakuwa* lineage inscribed in the term *shōsetsu*). However, it was necessary to claim a self-contained identity and discard *shōsetsu*'s secondary status to legitimate its own value.

The need for such a self-contained identity was particularly strong because two forms of disciplines—politics and history—ranked high in the hierarchy of knowledge sought to use *shōsetsu* for their purposes. Around the time *Shōsetsu shinzui* was written, we begin to see articles and columns in newspapers founded by Freedom and People's Rights activists arguing for the use of *shōsetsu* and *haishi* to spread political awareness among the readership. In 1883, an article entitled "Wagakuni ni jiyū no shushi o hanshoku suru ichi shudan wa haishi gikyoku tō no tagui o kairyō suru ni ari" (One Means to Sprout the Seed of Freedom in Our Country Is to Reform *Haishi* and Drama) is found in the large newspaper *Nihon rikken seitō shinbun*, designating *haishi* as a medium for building "civilized" masses that demand "equality and liberty."[70] The following year, we find "Seiji ni kansuru haishi shōsetsu no hitsuyō naru o ronzu" (On the Necessity of Political *Haishi* and *Shōsetsu*) published in the small newspaper *Eiri jiyū shinbun*, promoting the political uses of *shōsetsu* and *haishi* and claims that "without such means, it is not possible to spread political thoughts among the common people."[71] Participants in the Freedom and People's Rights Movement thus began to specifically identify *shōsetsu* and *haishi* as a means to implant political awareness among the readership. Such sentiment grew especially after Itagaki Taisuke's (1837–1919) famous meeting with Victor Hugo; the number of translated works of fiction grew dramatically as a result.

The increasing government crackdown on the Freedom and People's Rights Movement was one of the reasons behind the argument to use *shōsetsu* as a medium to propagate political awareness in the early 1880s. Numerous newspaper regulations were passed, along with the laws that restricted public meetings and speeches, making it more difficult to explicitly criticize the government. To counter such a move by the government, the activists began to produce *shōsetsu* to increase more awareness among the readership and to give themselves a medium to evade newspaper regulations and censorship.[72] *Shōsetsu* was thus beginning to take center stage in the political arena. It was vital that *Shōsetsu shinzui* sever *shōsetsu*'s connection with politics to establish *shōsetsu* as a medium with value in and of itself.

One other form of learning from which *shōsetsu* needed to be independent was history. What we may refer to as "fiction" today was inextricably connected to history in the early years of Meiji. In fact, *shōsetsu* and *haishi* were often categorized under "historical" writings. Nishi Amane's *Hyakugaku renkan* (*Encyclopedia*), for example, lists *shōsetsu* and *haishi* under "History," a category that also includes Biography, Chronology, and Synchronology.[73] Kikuchi Dairoku's "Shūji oyobi kabun" (a translation of Chambers's "Rhetoric and Belles-Lettres") classifies *shōsetsu* under historical poetry. Moreover, in sharp contrast to *shōsetsu*, which were denigrated by both *kangaku* and practical knowledge, history was endorsed by both. The importance of history did not need justification among the *kangaku*-educated intellectuals whose classics were primarily historical works. Even in the realm of practical knowledge, history was considered a necessity because no one contested the fact that a nation needed to have a history to legitimate its existence.

"The Comprehensive Theory of the *Shōsetsu*" has led many critics to assume that *Shōsetsu shinzui* argued for art for art's sake.[74] However, this is a reading that inevitably contradicts a section of *Shōsetsu shinzui* entitled "The Benefits of the *Shōsetsu*," in which *Shōsetsu shinzui* lays out the various benefits of the *shōsetsu*, including the sections "Ennoblement of Character" and "Moral Instruction" discussed earlier. Throughout *Shōsetsu shinzui*, there are two forces working simultaneously: *Shōsetsu shinzui* differentiates *shōsetsu* from other forms of learning while it defines *shōsetsu* as a new form of knowledge. The need to first disengage *shōsetsu* from other forms of learning is the underlying motive behind *Shōsetsu shinzui*'s definition of *shōsetsu* as "a form of art" that has value in itself. The benefits of *shōsetsu* discussed in "The Benefits of the *Shōsetsu*" then justify *shōsetsu* as a form of knowledge necessary for individuals in the post-Restoration world. We can locate a logical explanation within the historical contingencies that governed the writing process itself.

"The Vicissitudes of the Shōsetsu*": Shōsetsu* versus *History*

Leaving aside *Shōsetsu shinzui*'s engagement with politics until the next chapter, let us here take a close look at "Shōsetsu no hensen" (The Vicissitudes of the *Shōsetsu*), a section that immediately follows "The Comprehensive Theory of the *Shōsetsu*," which shows *Shōsetsu shinzui*'s attempt to sever the link between *shōsetsu* and history. In this section, *Shōsetsu shinzui*'s logic often falters, which makes *Shōsetsu shinzui*'s agenda to dissociate *shōsetsu* and history all the more apparent.

"The Vicissitudes of the *Shōsetsu*" first acknowledges that history and fiction share the same roots: they are traced to "antiquity" and to the development of "mythology" (*kishinshi*) that derives from the stories of warfare and struggles told by the ancients.

> In the barbaric age of fighting, there were many who rose precipitately in the savage wilderness to become heads of families and, soon after, clan leaders. . . . They told of the hardship they had endured and of their own exploits in battle. The

stories were true accounts of their own firsthand experiences and observations, but, in time, as they were passed on down the generations by word of mouth, faulty memories and exaggerations finally resulted in the loss of the original core of fact, and overdramatized versions, transmitted orally over long periods, eventually became the basis for mythology. . . . It seems quite certain that the myths of antiquity were the beginnings of the romance, and that many had been added to or falsified in the telling. . . . [The myths] are not completely true, but not all fictitious; they are facts dressed up with a combination of invention and misrepresentation to produce something in the style of history; it is partly history and partly *shōsetsu*. History and *shōsetsu* thus have a common source, their present dissimilarity being merely the result of their subsequent development.

Notice the use of the opposition truth/fiction to characterize the development of myths. This is soon accompanied by another dichotomy—writing/oration:

Through years of preliteracy, historical material was always passed on in song form. In the dark ages before the advent of writing, chants seemed the simplest and most convenient way of transmitting it with minimum of error. The orators, wanting to be able to memorize and recite easily, chose as smooth and fluid a diction as they could. Knowing that stylistic refinement and graceful circumlocution often catch the attention, they devoted much effort to clever phrasing. As the wording of those passages in chants that express emotion is usually full-bodied and elegant, the facts were often distorted for the sake of this effect. The chants thus became increasingly ostentatious and responsive to popular fancy, and in the process the veracity of their source material was much eroded, until little resemblance to the original remained. . . . Even after official history (*seishi*) appeared in the wake of cultural development and the dawn of literacy, chanted romances remained in vogue for a long time.[75]

The two oppositions, truth/fiction and writing/oration, clearly align themselves with one another. When initially told by tribal leaders, the stories of warfare and struggle are "true"—given that they are "accounts of their own firsthand experiences and observations." Yet once they begin to be passed down "by word of mouth," this "truth" is prone to be affected by memory lapses, the desire to exaggerate the accomplishment of ancestors, and the dramatic presentation of orators. The "true accounts" thus lose "the original core of fact." Oral transmission of historical materials continues until "official history" (*seishi*), the medium that represents "truth," appears with the dawn of literacy. Whereas the writing system allows truth to be fixed, oral presentation alters and transforms it, thereby producing fiction. With the advent of literacy, mythology splits in two: official history, a medium that faithfully passes "truth" on to descendants, and "romance" (*kiitan*), the prototype of *shōsetsu* that thematizes the fantastic (*kikai*).

By the use of two oppositions, *Shōsetsu shinzui* allocates truth to the realm of history and manages to sever the *shōsetsu* from the discipline of history. This is on a par with *Shōsetsu shinzui*'s later claim in "The Main Themes of the *Shōsetsu*" that *shōsetsu* is fiction: "There is, on the whole, no external difference at all between a *shōsetsu* and documentary writings (*jitsuroku*), but the hero of the *shōsetsu* is entirely a product of the writer's imagination."[76] Unlike documentary writings that grew out of newspaper reports of actual events, the *shōsetsu* thus thematizes entirely fictional characters.

However, in the process of deploying truth/fiction dichotomy to dissociate history and the *shōsetsu*, "The Vicissitudes of the *Shōsetsu*" perhaps inadvertently undermines the value of fiction, because fiction is produced by *falsifying* the "truth," which is attributed to a discipline that already has a place in the paradigm of learning. Moreover, the formula "truth = writing" also drew a parallel between fiction and oration. The *shōsetsu* must clearly be a written medium, not an oral one. *Shōsetsu shinzui* has found itself in a bind, unable to proceed with the two oppositions (truth/fiction and writing/oration). It is not a coincidence that this section ends with the following: "As civilization developed further, people grew tired of fantasy. Consequently the romance declined and the *shōsetsu* appeared. The steps in the development will be discussed later."[77]

Shōsetsu shinzui reorients the narrative and introduces a new paradigm with which to proceed. Tracing the development from romance, drama, and then to the *shōsetsu*, the narrative continues:

> With the development of a more advanced stage of civilization, drama gradually turned from the fantastic (*kikai*) and the supernatural (*kōtō mukei*) to ordinary subjects (*bonkin*) and then assumed didactic intent. . . . When then will the true *shōsetsu* appear? What will set it apart from romance (*kiitan*)? It will probably emerge when drama loses its popularity. In the dark ages, people enjoyed superficial novelty (*shinki*). Their outlook being limited, they were wont to take an interest in and lavish praise on anything singular that attracted their attention. . . . The emotions of those in such an age were so easy to see, allowing the contemporaneous romance to portray them, but there must have been many emotions and manners that the not very talented writers found it beyond their abilities to describe.[78]

The *shōsetsu*, as the most civilized form, will appear when the popularity of "superficial novelty" and the "fantastic" recedes. Two evolutionary formulae govern this narrative: one of emotions and manners that develop from the uncivilized to the more civilized, and the other of preferences that shift from the fantastic (*kikai*) to the ordinary (*bonkin*). As people evolved—and thus acquired more complex emotions—they grew fond of the ordinary and turned to drama, and ultimately the *shōsetsu*. By valorizing the "ordinary," the narrative solves the dilemma in which it found itself by the use of the truth/fiction dichotomy. If *Shōsetsu shinzui* was to simply denounce the fantastic (*kikai*) or the supernatural (*kōtō mukei*), which is the object of criticism in the above passage, it could have easily retained the idea of truth. To sustain its claim that *shōsetsu* is a form of fiction while introducing an alternative criterion by which to attach value to the realm of fiction, it valorizes the ordinary. The use of "ordinary" thus shows *Shōsetsu shinzui*'s negotiation with "history," an attempt to dissociate the value of fiction away from that of history. It marks a space that "supplements the many events that are left out of official history" and that offers "detailed portrayal of customs and manners that are not included in official history."[79] *Shōsetsu shinzui* further elaborates on this space in "Jidai shōsetsu no kyakushoku" (The Configuration of the Historical *Shōsetsu*), using Napoleon and Josephine as an example:

> The most important difference between official history and the *shōsetsu* is the ability of the *shōsetsu* to fill in gaps. I will explain this with an example. Let us assume that Emperor Napoleon I just finished his evening meal. This is undoubtedly a true event; no doubt he did finish it, and so he should have, but that point is far too trivial and uneventful to record in official history. Moreover, from the many histories of France, it is very easy to imagine that Napoleon had many heartbreaking conversations with Empress Josephine, but a portrayal of such in official history will be criticized for being unnecessarily detailed. However, such a scene can greatly appeal to people's hearts.[80]

Daily lives of characters, especially the struggle over the theme of love, most of which cannot be included in "official history," constitute the space of the *shōsetsu*. As I will elaborate in Chapter 5, this space of the "ordinary" is later renamed "the social" (*sewa*). The subsequent chapters will show that such a realm is necessarily divorced from the realm of the political.

Engaging quite extensively with the paradigm shifts in the realms of knowledge, *Shōsetsu shinzui*, at times clumsily and at times strategically, maneuvers its way in defining the role of the *shōsetsu* in the new world. The opening passage negotiated with and constructed the *gesaku* lineage as a "natural" precursor to the *shōsetsu*, thereby effacing the *hakuwa* line and evading a critical discussion of Meiji fiction, the full implication of which will be discussed in the next chapter. In response to the many criticisms of the *shōsetsu* by the two forms of learning, "The Comprehensive Theory of the *Shōsetsu*" designated *shōsetsu* as an art form and displaced the "benefits" and "aim" of *shōsetsu* to a "natural side effect" or "chance product." *Shōsetsu shinzui* then sought different criteria by which to establish the value of the *shōsetsu* so that it could posit the new space of *shōsetsu* away from disciplines of learning that already occupied a place in the realm of knowledge.

As we shall see in subsequent chapters, the realm of knowledge begins to assert its own autonomy by dissociating itself from politics. Such forces clearly endorse the *shōsetsu's* depoliticizing tendencies, which will be made apparent in the next chapter as we inquire into the reasons behind *Shōsetsu shinzui's* effort to "sanitize" *shōsetsu* of the *hakuwa* line and which appear most tellingly in the choice of Bakin as the negative embodiment of the *shōsetsu*.

THREE

The Main Constituents of the *Shōsetsu*

*Shōsetsu shinzui's Criticism of Bakin
and "Depoliticization"*

Criticisms of Kyokutei Bakin and His Literary Cosmos

This chapter offers a detailed discussion on how *Shōsetsu shinzui* articulates the concealment of politics. I begin with an analysis of "The Main Themes of the *Shōsetsu*," the most famous section of *Shōsetsu shinzui*, which is arguably the section that made *Shōsetsu shinzui* the origin of modern Japanese literature. Modern Japanese literary history, beginning around 1900, has equated its claim for "emotions" (*ninjō*) and "things as they are" (*ari no mama*) with psychological realism. As I argue extensively later, however, these constituents of the *shōsetsu* are not positively identified as such in *Shōsetsu shinzui*; instead, they are defined against the works of Bakin. Bakin was the quintessential writer of the *shōsetsu* in nineteenth-century Japan, that is, of the *shōsetsu* before its coupling with the novel; Bakin's works thus represent the *shōsetsu* before it was "sanitized" to take on the meaning of the novel. Yet in modern Japanese literary studies, Bakin's works have been evaluated by the criteria for literature established in *Shōsetsu shinzui* and confined to the realm of literature that had yet to exist in the nineteenth century. This is part and parcel of the mechanism of concealment.

This chapter then delineates the role that Bakin's works played in the political and intellectual currents of 1880s Japan; it shows how Bakin's works were revered by the advocates of the Freedom and People's Rights Movement and how they embodied the energy and solidarity essential to the movement. After I establish a firm link between political discourse and Bakin, I closely analyze this "political" discourse by taking up Sakurada Momoe's and Miyazaki Muryū's "content-oriented" translations of Alexandre Dumas's works and Komuro Shinsuke's *Tōyō minken hyakkaden* (*One Hundred Biographies of Fighters of People's Rights*, 1883–4), a collected biography of "righteous men." These texts were inextricably linked to the Fukushima Incident, one of the first violent uprisings (*gekka jiken*), which was prompted by the radical Jiyūtō activists involved in the Freedom and People's Rights Movement.

The examination of these texts demonstrates that *Shōsetsu shinzui*'s criticism of Bakin extends far beyond Bakin. In fact, when we examine the specific manner through which *Shōsetsu shinzui* rejects Bakin's works, we can see that it clearly targets the political writings of the time. What it rejected was a certain political *habitus* specifically linked with the forces behind the violent riots. This political *habitus* produced the image of a shared enemy and a sense of solidarity around it. Inscribed within this *habitus* was a certain *affect* that the participants shared through the *bodily* practice of reading. As such, the scope of the discussion extends to the varying ways in which the texts were disseminated and received.

"The Main Themes of the *Shōsetsu*" warrants particular attention because it is arguably the site of the ideological construction at the heart of modern Japanese literature. Literary critics Maeda Ai and Kamei Hideo, as well as many other scholars who followed their lead, have shown that it is important to suspend the belief that such terms as *mosha* and *ninjō* signify "mimesis" or "interiority." Consider, for example, Maeda's following comments:

> What Shōyō wanted to develop cannot be captured by the term "realism"; I think it was something much more broad. Take, for example, the term *mosha*. We often substitute this term with mimetic depiction (*shajitsu*), but in Shōyō's vocabulary, I think it was closer to the term *mosha* used by the painters of Edo to sign their paintings, which signified "so-and-so painted this." We have to remember that although we have a system of vocabulary to theorize literature, Shōyō had to first produce these words in order to discuss literature.[1]

Shōsetsu shinzui was thus constructing a new entity that had yet to take form. Despite its descriptive facade, *Shōsetsu shinzui* is a prescriptive piece that must be read accordingly. I thus refrain from equating *Shōsetsu shinzui*'s call for *mosha* or *ari no mama* with a call for mimetic realism.[2] Instead, I extract the textually specific meaning of terms in the text, provisionally treating terms as empty signs and finding what certain terms align themselves with or are defined against within the narrative itself. *Shōsetsu shinzui* often posits the key constituents of the *shōsetsu* through a chain of negation. For that reason, I wish to focus not so much on what it positively identifies as defining characteristics of shōsetsu but on what it rejects as that which is not *shōsetsu*.

As noted in Chapter 1, the following passage from "The Main Themes of the *Shōsetsu*" is often quoted to show that *Shōsetsu shinzui* argued for an objective portrayal of human emotions:

> A writer is like a psychologist. He must create his characters based on the principles of psychology. If he creates, by his own design, characters who deviate from human emotions (*ninjō*) or, worse, from the principles of psychology, those characters would merely be figments of the writer's imagination rather than those belonging to the human world. . . . The writer should therefore focus his talents on human psychology. Although the characters may be his own creation, he must not design them based on his ideas of good and bad or right and wrong (*zen'aku jasei*). Instead, he must simply observe (*bōkan*) and depict (*mosha*) them as they are (*ari no mama*).[3]

In reading this passage, it is easy to equate *ari no mama* and "an objective representation." However, the textual positioning of the key terms that are often extracted from *Shōsetsu shinzui* to support this line of argument—namely *ari no mama*, *bōkan*, and *mosha*—must be closely examined. These terms are used as *Shōsetsu shinzui* criticizes characters that are "designed" based on the writer's "ideas of good and bad or right and wrong" (*zen'aku jasei*). Strictly speaking, the only thing we know is that the notion of *ari no mama* is posited where the "writer's design" and *zen'aku jasei* are negated. In fact, throughout the text, *ari no mama* is never positively identified, only posited through such negation.

In order to further contextualize the criticism of *zen'aku jasei*, I quote *Shōsetsu shinzui*'s criticism of Bakin's most famous work, *Nansō Satomi hakkenden* (generally referred to as *Hakkenden, The Accounts of the Eight Dogs*, 1814–41):

> The eight heroes of Bakin's masterpiece *Hakkenden* are creatures of the eight Confucian virtues (*jingi hakkō*).[4] It is very difficult to describe them as human beings. Bakin set out to write a *shōsetsu* in which the characters, framed by the virtues, are perfect beings, using the theme of *kanzen chōaku* (encourage virtue, castigate evil). . . . The eight warriors are created based on Bakin's ideal and are not truthful depictions of humans of the present.[5]

What is being rejected here is *kanzen chōaku*, and Bakin's figuration of his characters is a prime example. Such criticism of *kanzen chōaku* has led critics to assume that *Shōsetsu shinzui* was against the educational use of *shōsetsu*, promoting, rather anachronistically, art for art's sake. However, such an argument can be made only with a great leap, disregarding many passages in the text where *Shōsetsu shinzui* makes claim for the *shōsetsu*'s educational value, not to mention an entire section entitled "The Benefits of the *Shōsetsu*" in which it discusses the numerous merits of the *shōsetsu*.

If *Shōsetsu shinzui* is not against the use of *shōsetsu* for educational means, what does it seek to reject in the name of *kanzen chōaku*? The criticism of Bakin's eight warriors is that they are "creatures of eight Confucian virtues" and hence "are created based on Bakin's ideal and are not truthful depictions of humans of the present." Let us leave aside the sudden appearance of the temporal framework "present" until a little later and note the alignment between "the ideal" and the eight Confucian virtues. This alignment appears again in the second volume of *Shōsetsu shinzui* as it discusses the creation of a protagonist. Bakin is categorized among the idealist writers who "apply the ready-made frames of benevolence, justice, courtesy, wisdom, loyalty, sincerity, filial piety, and obedience."[6] In other words, the ideal to which *Shōsetsu shinzui* refers is not just any ideal but the linguistic/value system of Confucian virtues, which constitutes and thereby shapes Bakin's literary cosmos.

The good/bad and right/wrong (*zen'aku jasei*) must also be contextualized within this literary cosmos shaped by central principles of Confucianism. Good and virtue clearly coincide with the eight virtues, and evil and vice are often expressed through the character *kan* (奸 or 姦), which creates compounds such as *kankei* (evil strategy 姦計・奸計), *kanshin* (evil official 奸臣), *kanpu* (evil woman 姦婦), *kanchi* (evil mind 奸智). This is, in effect, not only a value system but a style of language. The object of attack, then, is the ideal expressed through the deployment of such language.

Let us further explore the criticism of Bakin and inquire into *Shōsetsu shinzui*'s definition of *ari no mama*. In criticizing *Hakkenden*, it says: "As a didactic *shōsetsu*, *Hakkenden* is the greatest masterpiece; but as a narrative of human emotions, it is difficult to say the same. Look at the actions of the eight warriors. Not only their actions but even their deepest thoughts remain with the Way and not a hint of base desires can be seen in them."[7] The main criticism against the characters is that they are perfect beings who have no "base desires" and whose actions and inner thoughts are "with the Way." For *Shōsetsu shinzui*, in order for "things as they are" to be represented, *shōsetsu* must describe "the struggle between reason (*dōri*) and base desires (*retsujō*)."[8] This constitutes a methodological issue: two mutually opposing qualities must both be described, and the character must be torn between them for a given representation to appear "real."

Otherwise, the work can only be "superficial," which is, for *Shōsetsu shinzui*, the same as "uncivilized."[9]

It is important to remember that *Shōsetsu shinzui*'s criticism of Bakin's works is so reductive that it utterly fails to do justice to the complexity of Bakin's literary cosmos. As Takada Mamoru, Kamei Hideo, and others have shown, there is nothing simplistic about Bakin's portrayal of his characters.[10] His depictions are in incessant dialogue with the preceding configurations of the eight virtues, a knowledge of which Bakin's readers would have had. In rejecting the language of *zen'aku jasei* as superficial and uncivilized, *Shōsetsu shinzui* disregarded the entire literary tradition upon which Bakin's works were based.

Along with *zen'aku jasei*, *Shōsetsu shinzui* rejects "the writer's design" (*sakusha no ishō*). In fact, the writer's design and *zen'aku jasei* are always discussed together:

> [Characters that deviate from principles of psychology] are like marionettes. They seem at a quick glance just like a group of real people moving about, but the spell is instantly broken when closer inspection reveals the operator and the mechanism. Similarly, the *shōsetsu* at once loses its charm if it becomes obvious that the writer is behind each character pulling strings to direct his movements. Let me give an example of what I mean. The eight heroes of Bakin's masterpiece *Hakkenden* are creatures of the eight Confucian virtues.[11]

The association between the writer's design and Confucian virtues or *zen'aku jasei* language is not limited to "The Main Themes of the *Shōsetsu*" but appears again in "Shōsetsu kyakushoku no hōsoku" (Principles of Construction in the *Shōsetsu*), a section in the second volume of *Shōsetsu shinzui* that discusses what writers should *not* do. See, for example, "Kōzō henpa" (Favoritism):

> By favoritism, I refer to the writer's attitude toward his creations. . . . For example, a writer may unknowingly become attached to a virtuous and upright character; and as a result, even when the narrative progression calls for the character to act dishonorably, the writer may alter the story line and allow the character to act virtuously. Similarly, the writer may design the plot so that an evil character is made to take on all the evil deeds. . . . However, virtuous men also have base desires, and evil men too have conscience.[12]

Shōsetsu shinzui thus directly associates the writer's feelings toward a given character and the clear division between the good and bad. It goes without saying that "the writer's design" always exists; whether a given language foregrounds or effaces such design, and hence the manipulating hand, is entirely another issue. What is important then is the very fact that *Shōsetsu shinzui* identifies the writer's design in the use of the *zen'aku jasei* language. The dominant persona that controls the characters textually appears in the use of this language. We may deduce that the use of this language represents the writer's design. The association between the criticism of *zen'aku jasei* and the writer's design and the writer's thoughts and feelings will be made clearer when we turn our discussion to specific textual examples later in this chapter.

Let us return to the temporal framework introduced in the criticism of Bakin. When *Shōsetsu shinzui* characterized Bakin's creations as "not truthful depictions of humans of the present," it limited the time frame of the *shōsetsu* to the present. To supplement such an argument, there is a persistent renunciation of the "past" in *Shōsetsu shinzui*. One possible reason for this view of the past can be found in the need to sever *shōsetsu* from history; writing about the past is reserved for the realm of history, not for the *shōsetsu*. Yet this explanation is unsatisfactory. Sufficient differentiation between the two media can be provided by *Shōsetsu shinzui's* claim that the *shōsetsu* is not a representation of real events or real figures but a form of fiction that is a product of the writers' imagination; this is a dichotomy introduced in the preceding section, entitled "The Vicissitudes of the *Shōsetsu*," to dissociate the two realms. What then governs this rejection of the past?

"Shōsetsu no shurui" (The Types of *Shōsetsu*) classifies the *shōsetsu* into two categories, past (*ōseki*) and present (*gense*), promoting the latter as the artistic *shōsetsu*. The word *ō seki*, used here to denote "the past," will be our guiding thread to decipher the specific modality that structures *Shōsetsu shinzui's* view of the past. The two characters *ō* (往) and *seki* (昔) signify "bygone" and "past," respectively. *Seki* alone could have been enough to denote "past," but the first character adds the connotation that the past is no longer accessible. In other words, *Shōsetsu shinzui's* devaluing of the past is specific to the bygone past, a past that is discontinuous from the present. This clearly aligns with the criticism of Bakin's texts as historical works, a criticism from which *Genji monogatari* is exempt: Bakin's works, written in the late Edo period, are typically set in pre-Edo, that is, prior to the Tokugawa shogunate's establishment of a firm system of control.[13] Bakin's works thus *looked back* to the "inaccessible" past, to a time when the current regime had *yet* to be built. *Genji monogatari*, on the other hand, is set in the Heian imperial court, a system within which Murasaki Shikibu served.[14] The key to understanding *Shōsetsu shinzui's* repeated rejection of the past, then, lies in the rejection of the bygone past.

Let me briefly summarize what *Shōsetsu shinzui* rejects in positing the definition of the *shōsetsu*. It features a denigration of a certain kind of didacticism, one shaped by the Confucian linguistic/value system of eight Confucian virtues and the binarism of good/bad and right/wrong (*zen'aku jasei*), whose criticism aligns itself with a criticism of the ideal. The use of *zen'aku jasei*, moreover, is often connected with "superficial" representations (*hisō*), which are equated with "uncivilized" or "barbaric" representations. Inextricably linked to these characteristics are the rejection of the "writer's design," a manifestation of the writer's "thoughts and feelings" (*kanjō shisō*) that are made apparent in the language of *zen'aku jasei*. There is also a rejection of the "bygone past," thereby limiting the temporal framework of the *shōsetsu* to the "present." The main constituents of the *shōsetsu* are posited precisely where these constituents are negated; extrapolating from the series of negation, we understand the *shōsetsu* to be a medium that thematizes the "civilized emotions" in the "present" by way of *ari no mama* portrayal.

What I wish to do in the rest of this chapter is examine how the criticism of Bakin's works (and hence indirectly the definition of the *shōsetsu*) engages with the discursive currents of the time, especially with the Freedom and People's Rights Movement. We shall see how the Confucian linguistic/value system was inextricably linked to the works associated with the movement. Before I proceed, however, I wish to first examine Bakin's place in the second decade of Meiji and inquire into the reading experience through which Bakin's works were consumed within the discursive site of *Shōsetsu shinzui*'s production.

"Bakin" among the Freedom and People's Rights Activists

As Maeda Ai and others have argued, Bakin's historical fiction, especially *Hakkenden*, was particularly popular among the students of Meiji, many of whom were closely affiliated with the Freedom and People's Rights Movement. Maeda offers several thematic reasons for this popularity. First, he claims that "the students' passion for 'success and advancement' (*risshin shusse*)" in the new world was analogous to the passion of "the eight warriors who ultimately became the rightful retainers of the Satomi clan after their many adventures."[15] Maeda also sees a parallel in their lonely circumstances:

> The students could project their own loneliness—one that arose from leaving their hometowns to go to Tokyo—onto the lonely wanderings of the eight warriors. The warriors' pledge with one another was a symbol of their friendship that the students sought among themselves. . . . The eight warriors of *Hakkenden* . . . did not have any family ties; as such they fought a lonely battle against the strong forces of evil.[16]

From the students' perspective, therefore, the eight warriors of *Hakkenden* actualized "success and advancement" through a pledge of solidarity; the students projected themselves onto the warriors who, due to a lack of family ties, sought comrades with whom to fight a lonely battle against "forces of evil," which, for the advocates of Freedom and People's Rights Movement, signified the "oppressive government."

Maeda also suggests that Bakin's choice of the historical figures was at the core of Bakin's popularity among the People's Rights activists. Bakin often thematized not the victors of the political power struggle but those who suffered defeat, fictionally bringing to life alternative historical developments. Such stories, Maeda contends, were very appealing for those involved in the Freedom and People's Rights Movement, many of whom were defeated by the new Meiji leaders in their quest for power and remained dissatisfied with their positions in the new Meiji order. Maeda additionally points to the link between episodes in *Hakkenden* and Meiji uprisings that resulted from the collapsing economy. He refers to an episode in which Inuzuka Shino, one of the eight warriors, struggles against wicked and greedy officials who, during a famine, sought to monopolize the stocked provisions for themselves; Shino, with the help of local peasants, ultimately takes over the Isarago castle and distributes the provisions to the starving people. Maeda concludes, "The conflicts that take place in the Kantō region between [the oppressive leaders] and the eight warriors who are supported by the gallant men can be reread as a literary embodiment of the riots that occurred at the height of the Freedom and People's Rights Movement."[17] Bakin's stories could thus be transposed to the readers' Meiji present, allowing them to imagine and enact their own victory through their reading experience. Bakin's works captured the minds of many advocates because they spoke to the heroism sought in their People's Rights cause as well as the impending victory the stories promised.

The link between the political movement and Bakin was not limited to such a thematic level. Another, perhaps more significant point of intersection can be found in the practice of "communal recitation" through which the stories were "consumed." Many writers refer back to the early Meiji years, reminiscing on how they engaged with Bakin's works. Ichishima Shunjō (1860–1944), for example, discusses how popular the works of Bakin were among students of Tokyo: "We found the 7-5 rhythm so pleasurable, and many students memorized the famous passages in *Hakkenden*. If one couldn't recite a passage like Shino's parting with Hamaji, one had to feel rather inadequate among friends."[18] In writing an essay entitled "Kyokutei Bakin" in 1920, Shōyō claims, albeit self-critically,

"It was normal for many Bakin lovers to be able to recite his famous passages, but my ability was probably much above average. Even with my deteriorated memory, I can still remember some of the passages. How ridiculous it is."[19] Masamune Hakuchō (1879–1962), too, reminisces on his childhood years and says that he "found the rhythm of Bakin and Rai San'yō pleasurable," despite his insistence that his "youthful heart would not submit to their moral outlook."[20]

What is noteworthy here is that these writers all refer to the practice of memorizing and reciting aloud Bakin's works. In effect, what they shared in such practice is not only the content but the rhythm inscribed in the passages. The attention to sound and rhythm is a very important one because it makes reading a *physical* experience. Such linguistic engagement is consistent with the manner in which these men were educated in *kangaku* classics. *Sodoku* (literally, "raw reading") is a form of recitation that trained students to declaim and memorize *kangaku* classics through the rhythm and sounds of the sentences, whether or not the students understood their content.[21] For people who had such training in their youth, memorizing and reciting Sinitic verses were a form of recreation, and Bakin's works were often included in such practice. This produced a communal language that firmly shaped the students' psyche in early Meiji Japan.[22]

Communal recitation was further supported by the reading experience of *shōsetsu* many had at home. Customarily, the family enjoyed the work collectively; usually the father was a main reader, who read aloud to his family members. Yamakawa Hitoshi (1880–1958) recalls his father reading *Hakkenden* to his family after borrowing the work from a family friend. Ishikawa Sanshirō (1876–1956) recalls his father reading *The Epoch of the Three Kingdoms* to his brother.[23] In effect, *shōsetsu* was something that readers experienced orally and collectively—a practice that was continued by students after leaving their homes.

Communal recitation was precisely the site in which translated and political works of fiction were experienced. A scene from Tokutomi Roka's (1868–1921) *Omoide no ki* (*A Record of Reminiscence*, 1901) provides us with a compelling account of how youths engaged with the texts around them. Reminiscing on the general sentiments of the time and the excitement the word *freedom* had to the young protagonist, he claims:

> Change followed change, like the waves of an incoming tide. Two or three years before, we had been deep in *The Epoch of the Three Kingdoms*, thrilling to the tale of how Chang Fei destroyed the bridge of Chang Pau. Now, we pored as eagerly over current *shōsetsu* like *Nishi no umi chishio no saarashi* [*Tide of*

Blood and Small Storms in the Western Sea] and *Jiyū no gaika* [*The Battle Cry of Liberty*].[24] There was a student named Asai, and though he was seventeen years old, he only looked twelve or thirteen. When we made fun of him saying, "Why are you so small?" he would typically respond, "I can't grow taller because I am so oppressed by the despotic government that sits on my head. Just wait and see; I'll grow as soon as 1890 rolls around."[25] It was so uncharacteristic of him, but he had such a beautiful, musical voice, so fit for reciting. The instant the *Jiyū shinbun* arrived with the latest installment of *Jiyū no gaika*, we would look for him: "Asai, Asai, where is Asai?" He would then station himself by a dormitory window, and we'd gather around him, listening to him recite with that beautiful voice of his. Sometimes, with excitement we would cheer and applause. Then it was *Keikoku bidan*.[26]

At the center of their enthusiasm is Miyazaki Muryū's *Furansu kakumeiki: Jiyū no kachidoki*, a "content-oriented" translation (*iyaku*) of Dumas's *Ange Pitou*, to which we will turn later in this chapter. Along with Sakurada Momoe's *Nishi no umi chishio no saarashi*, which preceded Muryū's in the *Jiyū shinbun*, *Jiyū no kachidoki* was extremely popular in the early 1880s. Note that the excitement and enthusiasm with which *Jiyū no kachidoki* was received was shared through recitation. In communal recitation, a text is, in effect, a medium through which a shared sentiment is produced. The listeners, whose feelings toward liberty and freedom were particularly strong, were not passive participants but were actively involved, reciting and cheering along, identifying themselves with the characters in the stories; they were collectively and physically experiencing the rhythm of the recited passages. Writers, too, were conscious of their works being read aloud—they catered to that rhythm to produce and arouse a collective sentiment. Fundamentally, ideas alone are not powerful enough to produce a sentiment; in this case, the shared rhythm and sounds contributed significantly to the process.[27] The energy that ensued from the reading experience was apparently great. In reminiscing on his interaction with the participants of the uprisings, Itō Chiyū, a politician and oral performer, recalls that many of them decided to plan and participate in the uprisings after reading Muryū's *Jiyū no kachidoki* and Sakurada's *Nishi no umi chishio no saarashi*.

The works mentioned in the previous quotation are rather telling. They embody a genealogy of *shōsetsu* that traces itself back to the *hakuwa* tradition (such as *The Epoch of the Three Kingdoms*) of which Bakin was very much a part, followed by the two translated works by Sakurada and Muryū, and one of the most popular fictions of the time, Yano Ryūkei's *Keikoku bidan* (*Illustrious Tales of Statesmanship*). In effect, as we saw in Chapter 2, this is the genealogy of *shōsetsu* that *Shōsetsu shinzui* effaced in positing the *shōsetsu* by selecting the "sanitized" *gesaku* as its precursor. Such works of fiction and the communal practice of reading were inextricably connected to the Freedom and People's Rights Movement, and those who engaged in such practice were *Shōsetsu shinzui*'s target audience.

Shōsetsu shinzui ultimately rejects the Freedom and People's Rights Movement fought by the radical Jiyūtō activists, especially those involved in the violent incidents. It would be a practical impossibility to go into detail about *Shōsetsu shinzui*'s position vis-à-vis the works of *shōsetsu* produced by writers belonging to different factions or parties. I focus instead on the discourse mobilized by Jiyūtō figures who both indirectly and directly participated in promoting a worldview that ultimately led to the series of uprisings; these texts provide us with an insight into the link between radical activism and discursive trends we have discussed so far. By doing so, we will see a clear link between this discourse and the negative constituents of the *shōsetsu*, such as the writer's design and the language of *zen'aku jasei*.

Zen'aku jasei *Language and the French Revolution:* *The Radical Jiyūtō Leftists and* Gekka jiken

From the very founding of the newspaper in 1882, the Jiyūtō activists fully mobilized the images of the French Revolution in the *Jiyū shinbun*, both in newspaper columns and in fiction.[28] Sakurada Momoe's *Nishi no umi chishio no saarashi*, which thematized the French Revolution, began its serialization in the inaugural issue of *Jiyū shinbun* on June 25, 1882. A sequel to Sakurada's work, Miyazaki Muryū's *Jiyū no kachidoki*, which featured the fall of the Bastille, began on August 12, 1882. Overlapping with Sakurada's and Muryū's fiction was an essay entitled *Futsukoku kakumei giji nikki* (*Legislative Notes on the French Revolution*), which ran for approximately six months. Many Jiyūtō affiliates thus saw the spirit of freedom and equality in the French Revolution and valorized the people's uprising against the oppressive government. Even with the French setting, it is easy to see that these works featured the contemporaneous domestic condition, closely replicating the sentiments against the Meiji government.

The binarism of *zen'aku jasei* we identified earlier figures prominently in Sakurada's and Muryū's fiction: government officials are endowed with sinified compounds that include evil (*aku* and *kan*) and vice (*ja*), while the heroes embody courage (*yū*) and justice (*gi*). The dichotomy between oppressors and the oppressed is repeatedly emphasized, as the former are described as despotic and evil officials (*bōkun kanri* 暴君奸吏) and evil and cruel officials (*kansō kokuri* 奸相酷吏), and the latter as people of justice (*gijin* 義人) and an embodiment of just courage (*giyū* 義勇) and intelligence and courage (*chiyū* 知勇). Specifically, Marie Antoinette is characterized as a woman of "evil intellect" (*jachi* 邪智); and the keeper of the Bastille, de Launay, is described as "cruel and brutal" (*zan'nin kakoku* 残忍苛酷) and a man of "incomparable evil" (*kan'yū musō* 奸勇無雙). Governor Flesselles, who attempts to double-cross the people (*jinmin*), is identified as "a man of ill-will, malice, and vice with an evil mind and an instrument of government malevolence." In sharp contrast, the heroes (or the revolutionaries) of the works, Balsamo, Billot, Gilbert, and the "people," are "courageous and energetic" (*yūsō kappatsu* 勇壮活発) and are the "fighters of justice" (*gijin resshi* 義人烈士).[29]

Thematizing the Meiji present vis-à-vis their narratives of the French Revolution, these texts offer an exaggerated emphasis on the oppressive conditions experienced by the French people, as if to represent the inevitability of the eventual revolution. Because this eventual revolution is prefigured by the French Revolution, its "success" is predetermined. When we identify texts like these as objects of *Shōsetsu shinzui*'s criticism, the association made between "the writer's design" or "thoughts and feelings" and the uses of *zen'aku jasei* begins to fall into place. Sakurada and Muryū's use of *zen'aku jasei* is invariably connected to their political positions, as the central Confucian principles were embodied by the heroic characters who would lead the anticipated revolution. In effect, the language of *zen'aku jasei* was mobilized to disseminate the belief that revolution was an essential means to institute a political system based on civil rights and liberty. When we examine *Shōsetsu shinzui*'s criticism in this light, it makes all the more sense that the language of *zen'aku jasei* is precisely what represents the writer's design, the manipulating hand. Thus, it is not a coincidence that such a manipulating hand is directly tied to the writer's ideal and his "thoughts and feelings."

Such an equation becomes especially telling when we further decipher the connections between these texts and the Fukushima Incident. When the incident erupted at the end of November 1882, *Jiyū no kachidoki* was in the midst of its serialization and the last installment of *Nishi no umi chishio no saarashi* had just been published (November 16, 1882). As we shall see momentarily, these two fictional texts are closely linked to the incident.

Let me first briefly summarize the Fukushima Incident. Mishima Michitsune (1835–88) became the governor of Fukushima in February 1882 with the promise, "As long as I hold office, arsonists, thieves, and Jiyūtō members won't see the light of day."[30] The Fukushima Incident is said to have been triggered by Mishima Michitsune's notorious road construction project to connect the regions of Wakamatsu, Echigo, and Yonezawa, the burden of which fell on the local laborers, mainly the peasants. Despite the decision of the prefectural assembly (led by the Jiyūtō, which was headed by Kōno Hironaka, 1849–1923) to reject his proposal, Mishima, backed by the central government, forcefully went ahead anyway. Anticonstruction movements developed, but Mishima countered by arresting their leaders and the members of the Aizu Jiyūtō who legally represented more than eight thousand peasants who filed a lawsuit against Mishima's project. Upon hearing that their leaders were imprisoned, on November 28, 1882, the armed peasants gathered in the vicinity of the district jail in Kitakata where the leaders were incarcerated. The crowd dissipated after a confrontation with the police, leaving one demonstrator dead and several wounded. The following day, Mishima ordered massive arrests of the Jiyūtō members and peasants involved on the grounds that they conspired to "overthrow the government." Within a week, about one thousand men were arrested; many were tortured, and some died in prison.

The leaders of the incident were charged with treason, which was based only on the alleged existence of a "blood oath" signed by six members of the Jiyūtō. I here provide the Japanese version of the oath, followed by my translation.

第一　吾黨は自由の公敵たる擅制政府を顛覆し公儀政體を健立するを以て
　　　任となす

第二　吾黨は吾黨の目的を達するが爲め生命財産を抛ち恩愛の繋繩を絶ち
　　　事に臨みて一切顧慮する所なかるべし

第三　吾黨は吾黨の會議に於て議決せる憲法を遵守し倶に同心一體の働を
　　　なすべし

第四　吾黨は吾黨の志望を達せざる間は如何なる艱難に遭遇し又幾年月を
　　　経過するも必ず解散せざるべし

第五　吾黨員にして吾黨の密事を漏し及誓詞に背戻する者ある時には直に
　　　自刃せしむべし右五條の警約は吾黨の死を以て決行すべきもの也[31]

1.　Our party's mission is to overthrow the despotic government, the public enemy of freedom, and work toward establishing a political system for the people.

2.　In order to fulfill our goals, we relinquish our lives and wealth, sever our bonds of kindness and affection, and commit to our mission.

3.   We respectfully adhere to the constitution passed through our assembly;
      our body and mind are one with it.

4.   Our party will not disband until we fulfill our goals, even if we encoun-
      ter tremendous hardship.

5.   If our party members break the oath of secrecy or go against the words
      of the oath, they will be made to commit suicide. The five oaths will be
      fulfilled at the expense of our lives.

With this oath, we find the first compelling link between the Fukushima
Incident and Sakurada's *Nishi no umi chishio no saarashi*. Yanagida Izumi was
the first to notice the overwhelming resemblance between the blood oath of
the Fukushima Incident and the fictional oath that Balsamo, one of the main
characters of *Nishi no umi chishio no saarashi*, signs in the third chapter as his
faith to the cause is tested.[32] This third chapter was serialized on July 2, 1882;
and the blood oath was apparently drawn up sometime at the end of July or
early August. For comparison, I here provide the version in *Nishi no umi chishio
no saarashi* and its respective translation:

第一條○○○○○○○○○○○○○○○○○○○○○○○○○○○○○○○○○○
○○○○○○○○○○○○○○○○。

第二條吾黨ハ吾黨ノ志望ヲ達センガ爲メ生命財産ヲ抛ツベシ。

第三條吾黨ハ○○○○○○○○○○吾黨ノ會議ニテ織立タル眞誠ノ憲法ヲ遵
守スベシ。

第四條○○○○○○○○○○○○○○○○○○○○○○○○○○○○○○○○○
○○○○○○○○○○○○。

第五條苟モ吾黨員タル者ハ親子兄孫姉妹夫婦師弟朋友恩人等ノ俗縁ヲ断チ事
ニ臨テ一切顧慮スル所ナカルベシ。

第六條吾黨員ニシテ密事ヲ漏ス者アルトキハ直ニ斬ニ處スベシ。

第七條吾黨名ヲ鮮血革命黨ト稱ス。

第八條吾黨ハ如何ナル艱難ニ遭遇シ又幾百載ヲ経ルト雖モ上條ノ企望ヲ達セ
ザル以上ハ決シテ解散セザルベシ。[33]

1.   [censored]

2.   We will relinquish our lives and wealth to fulfill the goals of our party.

3.   We will respectfully adhere to the sacred constitution of our party
      established through our assembly.

4.   [censored]

5.   As members of our party, we will relinquish the mundane ties with our parents, brothers, sisters, wives, mentors, friends, and devote ourselves to the cause.

6.   Any member of our party who breaks the oath of secrecy will be killed immediately.

7.   Our party will be named "Bloodshed Revolutionary Party."

8.   Even if we continue to encounter hardship, we will not disband without fulfilling our goals.

Since the first and the fourth articles are censored out of the original publication, we have no way of knowing whether they completely match; the order of the articles is also different from the order of the actual oath. However, the resemblance in wording of what remains is indisputable. Moreover, the actual blood oath was never found and was reconstructed by the defendants in court during the trial.[34] We thus have no way of determining whether fiction prompted such action or the action was later reconstructed through "fictional" language. The issue, however, is not whether one influenced or motivated the other but rather that the same language is being used to represent both fiction and reality. For the participants, Sakurada's language undoubtedly had weight; it constituted a way to frame their own ambitions and goals. Clearly, the relationship between fact and fiction was much closer than our present imagination allows.[35]

Because of illness, Sakurada managed to publish only eighteen sections of *Nishi no umi chishio no saarashi.*[36] He was already dead by the time the fictional oath appeared in court, and hence he never lived to see the strange overlap between his fictional oath and the blood oath of the Fukushima Incident. Muryū was in a different situation. As Sakurada's serialization began to lapse, he was called on to succeed Sakurada as a primary fiction writer of the *Jiyū shinbun* with his *Jiyū no kachidoki*, a sequel to Sakurada's text that clearly glorifies the taking of the Bastille and the people's fight against the "oppressive government." In effect, Muryū's text presented itself as an actualization of Sakurada's text, whose oath, with its clear link to the actual incident, laid the foundation for the "revolution," transposed onto the Meiji present.

As Asukai Masamichi has speculated, perhaps this strong affinity between the Fukushima Incident and *Jiyū no kachidoki* is the reason behind its abrupt ending on February 7, 1883. Asukai suggests that there was pressure from the Jiyūtō headquarters, whose leaders wished to maintain distance from the actual participants in the incident to avoid the Jiyūtō party being held responsible for the attack itself.[37] To provide more proof to support Asukai's speculation, *Jiyū no kachidoki*'s serialization, which was quite steady at first, became irregular in December 1882. It lapsed from December 24 to January 13, 1883, and despite its return, the serialization became random; and after two days in February, it stopped all together. Whether pressure from the Jiyūtō headquarters in fact existed, in the last scenes that are translated, we find Billot, one of the heroes who brought about the fall of the Bastille, being disconcerted about how the revolution is proceeding and criticizing the unnecessary violence used by the members of the revolutionary party.

I wish to here provide a close textual reading of *Jiyū no kachidoki*, the longer of the two works, in an effort to identify the dynamic of such linguistic practice, and further examine how the text exemplifies *Shōsetsu shinzui*'s criticism of Bakin's works.

Zen'aku jasei *as a Marker of the Speaking Subject*

As Roka's *Omoide no ki* suggests, both *Nishi no umi chishio no saarashi* and *Jiyū no kachidoki* were two of the most popular fictions of the time.[38] Unlike Sakurada's work (which begins in 1770), Muryū's *Jiyū no kachidoki* goes right into the heart of the French Revolution, taking up the fall of the Bastille.[39] The plot is simple. Gilbert, who appeared in *Nishi no umi chishio no saarashi* as a servant whose favorite pastime was reading Rousseau, is now a doctor. At the beginning of the story, Dr. Gilbert is arrested and imprisoned at the Bastille for initially unknown reasons. Ange Pitou, the hero of this story, goes to Paris in an effort to save Gilbert, accompanied by Billot, a farmer and fighter for liberty. In their struggle to find Gilbert, Pitou and Billot encounter many self-serving aristocrats and malicious men of greed, such as the keeper of the Bastille, de Launay, and Governor Flesselles. It is not difficult to see the image of Governor Mishima in Flesselles and de Launay, the "evil" characters of *Jiyū no kachidoki*, who bring about pain and suffering to "innocent" men.

Supported by the people (*jinmin*) who, according to Muryū's translation, constitute the members of the revolutionary party (*kakumeitō*), they succeed in taking the Bastille and freeing Gilbert, killing de Launay and Flesselles in the process. After being freed, Gilbert becomes determined to track down the people behind his imprisonment and visits the director-general Necker and the king, and Gilbert eventually becomes the king's physician. Billot and Pitou remain in Paris as they continue their struggle with the revolutionary party to gain liberty and civil rights. In the meantime, we witness scenes from Gilbert's conversation with the king, Marie Antoinette's argument with Andrée over her jealousy of Charney, and much more. For reasons mentioned earlier, this text, like Sakurada's, is incomplete. Muryū translates a few more sections in another newspaper, the *Shinonome shinbun*, several years later. All the translated sections were compiled in book form in 1889, but the text was never completed.

Let us look at some of the passages closely. For the sake of comparison, I provide first the English version and then my translation of Muryū's text. I use the English version here, not only because it is convenient to do so but because there is every indication that Muryū used the English text and not the original French text.[40] For example, in the preface to *Jiyū no kachidoki*, Muryū refers to the original work as *Taking the Bastille* (rendered in *katakana* scripts) instead of *Ange Pitou*, the French title. In addition, all the characters' names follow the English pronunciation. Although it is difficult to determine which edition Muryū used, an English translation published in the late nineteenth century provides me with a suitable reference point by which to examine Muryū's translation.

The following is a description of the prison keeper de Launay waiting for assistance during the attack of the Bastille.

The English version:

> And, notwithstanding, this man was courageous.
>   From the previous evening the storm had been threatening around him. Since the previous evening, he perceived the waves of this great commotion, which was still ascending, beat against the walls.
>   And yet he was calm, though pale.[41]

Muryū's text:

> Typical of an evil man, de Launay was courageous. He would not be startled, even by the unexpected. Since the previous evening, Paris was in great commotion; the sound of the running horses echoed, gunshots approached, and the crowd, since that morning, gathered in fury in front of the prison. . . . Yet he showed no sign of anxiety, remaining extremely bold and fearless.[42]

Whereas the English text describes de Launay as simply "courageous," Muryū associates courage with de Launay's evil nature. Furthermore, the sense of fear represented by the phrase "though pale" in the English version is completely erased, or, rather, reversed in Muryū's text. If we consider *Shōsetsu shinzui*'s criticism against binarism, it would be easy to predict what its position would be; according to *Shōsetsu shinzui*, such suggestion of inner conflict evident in Dumas's text is the main theme of the *shōsetsu*, precisely because two opposing characteristics are being represented through the depiction of courage and calmness on the one hand and a sense of fear on the other. If *Jiyū no kachidoki* could have depicted such a conflict, it would have been a representation of the inner struggle appropriate for the *shōsetsu*. Muryū's translation, via the language of *zen'aku jasei*, erases the very ambivalence on which *Shōsetsu shinzui* focuses.

Such reading based on *Shōsetsu shinzui*'s claims does not do justice to Muryū's text; we must question what Muryū himself achieves by deploying this language and erasing such ambivalence. For him, the language of *zen'aku jasei* is a medium to produce division between the oppressor and the oppressed, and ultimately, a collective, that would constitute itself as a revolutionary subject, the "fighter of justice," and hence the embodiment of "the spirit of justice and courage."[43] In essence, the clear boundary produced by the language of *zen'aku jasei* would grant an identity to an indiscriminate group of people. One scene in particular makes this clear.

Before going to the Bastille, Billot and Pitou encounter a crowd demonstrating against the king's decision to dismiss Necker. Amid this demonstration, two men carrying Necker's wooden bust are shot to death. In the English version, the crowd dissipates in fear:

> All those who had formed the procession fled through the adjacent streets. The windows were instantly closed—a gloomy silence succeeds to the shouts of enthusiasm and cries of anger.[44]

The following is the corresponding section in Muryū's text:

> The death of the two men instilled rage among the revolutionary party. Carrying the corpses on their shoulders, they swore to bring about solidarity among the people with determination stronger than steel. "Instead of leaving our names in disgrace by living in deception, we would rather die and leave our names amid the fragrance of blossoming freedom. Now, proceed to take revenge for the two men!"[45]

Leaving aside the fact that Muryū completely reverses the situation, I wish to focus on the pseudospeech, of which there are many examples in the text, which is not attributed to any specific character. It is ascribed to a collective that suffers oppression, a group whose identity rests on "courage" and "virtue" and hence is clearly differentiated from the figures of evil. The language of *zen'aku jasei* gives the collective an identifiable form, and accordingly, "the crowd" becomes a group with an agency to fight for liberty at the expense of their lives.[46] Solidarity is further produced through anger against evil within such a collective, which constitutes itself as a speaking subject of sentences such as "we'd rather die as a creature of liberty than live a life as a debased citizen."[47] For Muryū, to blur that boundary between good and evil would mean losing the identity of the collective and hence the speaking subject. It is further noteworthy that the perspective of this collective often merges with that of the narrator, making it very difficult to separate the two (nor does the text try to keep that differentiation).

Anger against the evil and a sense of solidarity among the good both culminate in the taking of the Bastille. In the English version, one of the heroes, Gilbert, shows clear disapproval of the crowd that attacks de Launay and Flesselles; the crowd is, in effect, portrayed as an "uncontrolled mob," and Gilbert attempts to stop them from doing more violence. Such portrayal of Gilbert, though not completely absent, is perhaps understandably downplayed in Muryū's text. Instead, Flesselles's wickedness and the "justice" of the people's taking the Bastille are emphasized:

> [The men who] entered the local office soon found Flesselles. "Wicked and vicious-minded evil! You tried to deceive us into thinking that you're giving in, but you secretly corresponded with de Launay and double-crossed us. Even then the Bastille fell and de Launay lost his head. Now the life of the despotic government is nearing an end; you ought to wash your neck and take our sword!" Close by, de Losme was stabbed to death, and his head was placed on a pike, just like de Launay's. Voices then echoed, "Hail liberty!!" Flesselles too lost his life, and his head was displayed like the rest of them; the respect he enjoyed as the governor of Paris vanished like the dew of the River Seine.[48]

Notice the speech addressing Flesselles, which is again spoken by the indiscriminate "we," the "oppressed." Here and elsewhere, the collective pronoun used is *ware ware* (吾儕), whose utterance is not attributed to any of the heroes. In the English version, this utterance is not even represented as a speech. Instead we are given a description of a letter that de Launay had in his possession, proof that Flesselles did in fact try to double-cross the takers of the Bastille; and the main focus of the English narrative remains on Gilbert trying to stop the mob from murdering Flesselles. In contrast, Muryū's focus is clearly on the production of the speech by the nameless speaker. We are thus able to see that Muryū's use of *zen'aku jasei* is inextricably connected to the creation of this unidentified speaking subject. *Zen'aku jasei* is a language that allows him to produce and clearly demarcate the position from which to make the utterance. Within such a literary cosmos, for one character to have attributes of both good and evil is out of the question; such mixture could only erase the ground upon which the speaking subject and the utterance take form.

It is now worthwhile recalling how Meiji intellectuals read *Jiyū no kachidoki*. The utterances of the unidentified speaker, the oppressed people, were recited and shared among them, allowing them to identify themselves with the collective. As they actively recited the passages, experiencing the rhythm inscribed within them, the listeners became one with the represented collective. The recited passage ultimately became the textual embodiment of the communal sentiment. In criticizing Bakin, what *Shōsetsu shinzui* ultimately rejected was such shared sentiment and psyche, which often induced a strong resentment against the oppressors (that is, the authorities). Muryū, in writing (or translating) fiction, may not have intended to deliberately foster or promote violence like the Fukushima Incident. Yet this was precisely the language that was recited at the site of "communal recitation."

Imagine how the Fukushima Incident would have been received by the youths who had shivered with excitement reciting and listening to Muryū's *Jiyū no kachidoki*. The following passage from Roka's *Omoide no ki* shows how livid they became with the Fukushima Incident.

> Quite apart from textbooks and classroom lessons, a succession of dramatic events occurred in the world outside to widen our horizons further—and we don't know how often our blood boiled as we read the reports of these events. During the outcry of the Fukushima Incident, we fought each other for the papers to read the court proceedings, tearing the paper to shreds in the process.[49] We wept; tears fell down our cheeks as we thought about the hardships of Kōno, Aizawa, Hirashima, Hanaka, and Tamono.[50] If only we could fly to their side and kiss their wrists where the chains had bitten and stroke their backs where the police had struck them with their scabbards! How we longed to kick and thrash and trample under our avenging feet the bearded faces of the brutish magistrates and government officials who would defend the violence and injustice done by the local officials. And when we heard how the prisoners had been dragged barefoot through the snow, we went walking barefoot in the snow ourselves to test our strength of will, in case we had to follow in their footsteps.[51]

Anger against "the oppressors" and a rather emotional, if not overly exaggerated, identification with "the oppressed" clearly shape this passage. The shared excitement experienced in the reading of *Jiyū no kachidoki* produced a strong sense of resentment against the officials who defended the "violence and injustice" of those who violated rights and liberty. Through such a recitation, they shared not only the enemy but the anticipation of a revolution that *would* occur by continued oppression; and by extension, the readers internalized "the spirit of justice and courage" (*giyū no seishin*) as the most appropriate characteristic of the revolutionary subject. By identifying themselves as the "fighters of justice," they saw their role in the eventual revolution. In effect, when the youths partook in the communal experience of recitation, they collectively participated in the act of rhetorically prefiguring the revolution and ultimately *inscribed* themselves in the revolution.

Jiyū no kachidoki, just as many other texts that Muryū wrote and/or translated in early 1880s, is a text that prefigures a revolution. Such a position was on a par with Nakae Chōmin (1847–1901) and Kitamura Tōkoku (1868–1894), who had conceptualized the Freedom and People's Rights Movement as a vehicle to bring about a second revolution, one that would "complete" the Meiji Restoration, which was, as far as they were concerned, only an incomplete revolution.[52] In other words, for those who shared such a position, the Meiji government had prematurely put a stop to the revolutionary process that had yet to be completed. In effect, when the youths participated in the communal reading experience, they collectively participated in the act of rhetorically prefiguring the anticipated revolution and sought the moment of fulfillment.

The language of Muryū's narrative can thus be seen as a manifestation of the antigovernment discourse, produced and reproduced through a collective practice of recitation that disseminates the image of a shared enemy, resulting in a sense of solidarity and anger that precludes any critical thought.[53] It is further noteworthy that the *zen'aku jasei* language manages to paint a very similar textual world, whether the object of description is the French Revolution or the Russian nihilist movement. It regurgitates the structure of binarism, which schematizes the events being told, and erases the historicity of the events being portrayed. Instead, it produces solidarity and shared sentiment. It was such a site of communal recitation and the overly exaggerated sentiment produced through physical collectivity that *Shōsetsu shinzui* rejected in the production of the *shōsetsu*.

The antigovernment discourse exemplified by Muryū's text is one that is later associated with the language of "resentment and indignation" (commonly referred to as *hifun kōgai*).[54] This is a style that can already be identified in Muryū's text, evident in passages where it describes people's strong and exaggerated resentment against the oppressive government. Whether such language triggered the actual use of force and uprisings against the Meiji government is another issue. What is noteworthy is that the *use* of this language, inextricably connected to that of *zen'aku jasei*, began to signify an antigovernment stance at the height of the Freedom and People's Rights activism.[55]

In the following section, I continue with my inquiries into political discourse, this time with a specific focus on biographies of "good" and "righteous" men (*gijin*) and the new genre of "political oration" (*seiji kōdan*) that proliferated in the early to mid-1880s. The site of "political oration" is where the texts we have discussed intersect with stories of "good" and "righteous" men. An analysis of Komuro Shinsuke's *Tōyō minken hyakkaden* (*One Hundred Biographies of Fighters of People's Rights*), the main text of inquiry in the ensuing section that compiled stories of Edo *gijin*, allows us to examine one of the negative constituents of the *shōsetsu* that we have left untouched so far, namely, the "past." An inquiry into the manner in which Komuro Shinsuke and the reading/listening collective of political oration sought to discover and share the past will show us why *Shōsetsu shinzui*'s criticism of Bakin includes a rejection of the bygone past.

Seiji kōdan *and the "Past": Komuro Shinsuke and* Tōyō minken hyakkaden

Seiji kōdan is a subgenre of oral storytelling (*kōdan*), which initially featured oral readings and explanations of religious and edifying texts. It developed into a form of entertainment, covering a variety of topics such as historical chronicles, tales of vendettas and thieves, and stories of townspeople and common folk. In such practice, the storyteller would typically sit behind a desk and alternate between narrating the story and dramatizing different roles, all of which were punctuated by beats of a fan. In the Meiji period, many advocates of the Freedom and People's Rights Movement took on the role of oral storytellers (*kōdanshi*) and recited stories and tales to spread political awareness among the listeners by emulating the distinct practices of *kōdan*, hence giving birth to *seiji kōdan*, or "political oration."[56]

Political oration increased particularly after June 1882 with the amendment of the Public Ordinance Act (*shūkai jōrei*, first issued in April 1880), which increased government regulation over political speeches. According to the new policies, the meetings had to acquire prior authorization by submitting names, topics, and places. Police attended all the gatherings and disbanded them whenever the speaker allegedly deviated from the approved topic.[57] With government crackdowns increasing in severity against both writing and speech, the activists had to seek other venues to spread their philosophy and thoughts. Press laws and newspaper regulations restricted their writing, and hence we see an increase in *shōsetsu* that took the form of translations and adaptations. In public gatherings, many turned to political oration, which was performed not only at political rallies but also at banquets and teahouses. The audience accordingly varied: in addition to supporters of the political cause, listeners also included townspeople and prostitutes.[58]

The practices of political oration also played an important role in promoting solidarity among the supporters by fostering collective participation and disseminating the language that sought to prefigure a second revolution. The activists-turned-orators often chose to perform *Jiyū no kachidoki*, topics on the Fukushima Incident, and Russian nihilist–related subjects, hence continuing to mobilize and circulate the discourse we have discussed so far. Ogawa Jōmyō (a.k.a. Jiyūtei Kaishun, 1855–1919), for example, performed *Jiyū no kachidoki* along with *Furansu kakumeishi* (*The History of the French Revolution*).[59] An advertisement in the *Jiyū shinbun* shows that *Jiyū no kachidoki* was also selected by San'yūtei Enshū, who performed the text under the title *Jiyū kiwa* (*Strange Tales of Liberty*).[60] In a gathering held in September 1883, Okunomiya Kenshi (1857–1911), later involved in the Great Treason Incident of 1911, selected *Jiyū no kachidoki* and *Keikoku bidan*; and Watanabe Bunkyō (a.k.a. Hanagasa Bunkyō, 1857–1926) performed a story of Kōno Hironaka, the leader of the Fukushima Incident, entitled *Kōno Hironaka kun shōden* (*A Short Biography of Kōno Hironaka*), which was already in circulation in May 1883, four months before the High Court handed down the verdict.[61] The court proceedings from the Fukushima Incident were also performed by Okunomiya. Tatsuno Shūichirō (1846–1928), later arrested for his role in the Iida Incident in 1884, performed *Jiyū no kachidoki* in July 1884.[62] Despite government crackdowns, therefore, a community continued to be produced around these texts in the form of political oration, which evolved as a new site of communal practice that allowed the participants to *repeatedly* share the language of these texts.

Along with works that thematized the French Revolution and Russian nihilism, the orators also chose *gijinden*, or biographies of "righteous men," in their performance. For example, many references exist to the story of Sakura Sōgorō, one of the most famous *gijin* of the Edo period; Sakura Sōgorō was often considered the first figure to uphold values of "people's rights." Similarly, the orators showed much interest in Komuro Shinsuke's *Tōyō minken hyakkaden*, a text that features biographies of Edo *gijin*, which he set out to compile in search of "more men like Sakura Sōgorō" in Japan.[63] *Tōyō minken hyakkaden* was performed by orators soon after the publication of its first installment in August

1883; for example, Okunomiya performed it in September 1883.[64] In November 1883, Shōrin Hakuen, a well-known orator of the time, recited "Monju Kusuke den" (A Biography of Monju Kusuke) and "Totani Shin'emon den" (A Biography of Totani Shin'emon), taken from the first volume of Shinsuke's text.[65] Tatsuno, who was famous for his performance of *Jiyū no kachidoki*, was also well known for his oration of *Tōyō minken hyakkaden*. In August 1884, Tatsuno performed "A Biography of Totani Shin'emon," and in September he recited "Matsuki Shōzaemon chōsōden" (A Biography of Matsuki Shōzaemon), both of which were received with great enthusiasm.[66]

Perhaps predictably, *gijin* stories were inextricably linked to the series of uprisings as were *Jiyū no kachidoki* and other narratives at the center of the political habitus discussed earlier in this chapter. One ritualistic ceremony offers a compelling link between the two. Three *gijin* (Ishii Izaemon, Kaminaga Ichihei, and Sugama Sakujirō), biographies of whom were included in the third volume of *Tōyō minken hyakkaden*, were celebrated at a public gathering (*undōkai*) in the province of Mibu.[67] A report in the *Chōya shinbun* (August 25, 1883) shows that the gathering of over eight hundred people featured a ceremony by "stalwart youths equipped with spears" with Yokoyama Shinroku (later participant in the Kabasan Incident in 1884) stepping up to the altar to "celebrate the spirits" of those who were killed for "resisting official orders (*kanmei*)."[68] Also among the stalwart youths was Arai Shōgo, who was later arrested for his role in the Osaka Incident in 1885. Furthermore, Koinuma Kuhachirō, implicated in making explosives for the Kabasan Incident, contributed biographical materials of these "righteous" men to *Tōyō minken hyakkaden*. Participants in the uprisings were thus involved in celebrating and disseminating stories of *gijin* (Koinuma, Yokoyama, and Arai) and propagating them through political oration (Tatsuno).

Such a connection cannot be divorced from the political habitus that *gijin* stories and *Tōyō minken hyakkaden* inherited. The space of recitation clearly links the biographies to texts inextricably linked to the Fukushima Incident through repeated performances and continues to reproduce the political collective through the physical practice of reading. *Tōyō minken hyakkaden* features the often exaggerated oppression by evil officials that was also conspicuous in *Jiyū no kachidoki*; there are also several episodes in *Tōyō minken hyakkaden* in which the peasants gather to consider how to free the men who were "wrongly" incarcerated—like Gilbert and the leaders of the Fukushima Incident.[69]

Yet there is a crucial difference between *Jiyū no kachidoki* and *Tōyō minken hyakkaden*: the two texts mobilize the language of *zen'aku jasei* differently. On the one hand, the binarism of *zen'aku jasei* figures prominently in the biographies, clearly marking the good from the bad: the evil and greedy authorities who cruelly usurp their power and oppress the people are set against the righteous men of courage (*jinjin gishi, giyū* 仁人義士、義勇) who fight against them. On the other hand, such markings do not create an unidentified speaking collective as they did in *Jiyū no kachidoki*, which was a crucial component of the political habitus, and hence of "the affect" produced in the communal experience. This is, in part, a result of Shinsuke's choice to compile biographies, which necessarily focus on *identified* men of courage. Biographies thus inevitably preclude the production of the unidentified collective. This does not mean that this work lacks speeches in any way; in fact, as we shall see shortly, one of the dramatic moments of the narrative comes when the *gijin* make speeches immediately before they are put to death.[70]

Yet even without the production of the unidentified collective, *Tōyō minken hyakkaden* became a means to foster solidarity, reproducing the enthusiasm inscribed in the communal experience. This, I believe, is inextricably linked to Shinsuke's creation of the past vis-à-vis the Meiji present, the effect of which is, as we shall see momentarily, on a par with Muryū's position.

Let us now turn to the text, with a specific focus on its construction of the past and its relationship to the present. In the introduction to the first volume, Shinsuke states that men he honors and respects are

> the good and the righteous men who realize their goals without bending their ways against the oppressive authorities. The weight they put on their lives is lighter than dust, and they will sacrifice their pride, profit, wealth, and even their descendants as long as they are fighting for the province, for the people, and for reason; these are men who are now referred to as "fighters of people's rights" (*minkenka*).[71]

Shinsuke then claims that the reason he set out to compile their stories was to seek out more men like Sakura Sōgorō whose stories are undoubtedly buried throughout the country and "to make them known among the people so that the light of the peaceful world of Meiji will illuminate them, consoling their spirits that lay in the other world."[72] This act of reviving their existence in the world of Meiji and "consoling their spirits" is for Shinsuke equated with "promoting liberty and disseminating people's rights."[73]

There are two important rhetorical operations here. First, the righteous men who resisted oppression and fought for the people are renamed "fighters of people's rights" (*minkenka*), hence are made the historical predecessors of the advocates of the Freedom and People's Rights Movement. This, in effect, constitutes a gesture to seek the origin of the movement in the Edo *gijin*, constructing, as it were, a past that has a direct relationship to the present. Second, Shinsuke claims that *gijin*'s voices that are "buried" throughout the country need to be "consoled" by reviving them in this new world of Meiji; their voices, in other words, are designated as that which is waiting to be recovered. *Tōyō minken hyakkaden* thus produces a "past" that seeks something in the "present."

Let us look at the first biography of *Tōyō minken hyakkaden* and Shinsuke's attempt to restore *gijin*'s voices in the Meiji present. "Biography of Totani Shin'emon" tells of Shin'emon, a peasant who sacrificed himself for the people of Shimanomura and submitted a direct appeal (*jikiso*) to the Bakufu against the local officials (who oppressed the people by their own greed). The complaint is deemed legitimate, and the evil officials are punished for their deeds, but Shin'emon, as a peasant, is considered to have transgressed his class for submitting the complaint against the authorities in the first place; as a result, he is turned over to the provincial authorities, who put him to death. This is a very typical story line that frames the other biographies, one that in many ways inherits the structure of the Edo *gijin* stories.[74]

Often selected by orators of *seiji kōdan*, this episode in *Tōyō minken hyakkaden* has an appendix inserted by Shinsuke. It consists of a transcription of the speech he gave at Shin'emon's grave site. After he somewhat dramatically identifies Shin'emon as an "honorable fighter of people's rights" who embodies the "intellectual core of people's rights" by sacrificing himself for "liberty," he discusses the manner in which Shin'emon's name was not uttered even by the people whom he had protected, because they had "feared the officials." He continues, "If you had been born into today's world, you would have been valorized as a man of liberty and the polestar of People's Rights; you would have been the theme of speeches and newspapers. But you had been unfortunate to be born in an uncivilized world [of Edo]."[75]

In this speech, it is clear that Shinsuke institutes a break between the Edo and Meiji periods; comparatively, Meiji is a better place, a "civilized" world that is no longer bound by the laws that killed Shin'emon. Such contempt toward the Edo period is consistent throughout this text, which is also obvious from the negative characterization of Edo as "a world in which neither freedom nor rights existed" (*jiyū mo kenri mo naki yo*), a time when "meek or lowly people" (*hikutsu na jinmin*) quietly, though resentfully, submitted to the evil officials and followed their outrageous demands. The phrases clearly manifest the Meiji gaze by which Shinsuke frames the stories and hence the Edo period. This negative view of the Edo period also accounts for the lack of the unidentified speaking collective that constituted the agent of reform in *Jiyū no kachidoki*. The people in Edo had yet to become civilized enough to embody the concept of people's rights; the *gijin* are special people who, despite the fact that they were raised among the "lowly" people, gained the characteristics of "justice" and "courage." It naturally follows that the current fighters of people's rights are just as special, fighting for the right cause against those who wrongly oppress them.

This break instituted between the Edo and Meiji periods highlights Shinsuke's position, which is on a par with the stances taken by Muryū, Chōmin, and Tōkoku discussed earlier, namely, the view that the Meiji Restoration was a revolution, but merely an incomplete one. The Edo *gijin* had to die because of the "backward" system of Edo and the "lowly men" who could not do anything to help them. In the "enlightened Meiji," it is up to the people who can now understand and support the present-day righteous men to actualize a second revolution. Moreover, the Edo *gijin* may have been criminals in the Edo period under its law, but they would have been the "polestar of People's Rights" in the world of Meiji. This takes on an additional significance when we consider the activists in the Meiji period, such as the leaders of the Fukushima Incident. They may be "criminals against the nation" (*kokuzoku* or *kokujihan*) now, but in the subsequent world, that is, after the second revolution, they will eventually be heroes.

Despite the break instituted between Edo and Meiji, the two periods are not discontinuous in *Tōyō minken hyakkaden*. Quite the contrary, they are in direct relationship with one another as forces of Edo seek a moment of fulfillment in the Meiji present. The spirits that "lay in the other world," in order to be "consoled," await the second revolution. Let us examine one biography included in the second volume, "A Biography of Matsuki Shōzaemon," which ends with a speech made by the *gijin* before he was executed. A peasant by birth, Matsuki Shōzaemon lived in the province of Wakasa, known to pay its dues (taxes) with beans. Under the previous provincial lord, the equivalent of 1 *hyō* had been 4 *to* (1 *to* = 4.76 gallons), but with the arrival of the new lord, 1 *hyō* was increased by 5 *masu* (1 *masu* = .47 gallon). Needless to say, this created hardship for the peasants, who eventually decided to write a petitionary request. Shōzaemon was selected among the twenty men who were assigned to the task. Upon petitioning the authorities, the men were imprisoned and were told that they would be released if and when they apologized and retracted the petition; one by one they did so, and in the end, Shōzaemon remained in jail alone. After five long years of waiting, the authorities, fearing that rumors of Shōzaemon would spread to neighboring provinces, gave up and returned the dues to their prior rate.

However, to send a message to the peasants, the officials sentenced Shōzaemon to execution by crucifixion. Immediately before the spear pierced his body, he made the following speech addressing the "ten thousand brothers of Wakasa":

> On behalf of the ten thousand people, I have exchanged my life with your beans, your livelihood. You will from now on pay 4 *to* as your dues. The 5 *masu* of beans excluded from your dues constitute my flesh. The broth of beans is my blood. You will henceforth eat my flesh, drink my blood, and celebrate it amongst yourselves and your descendants . . . [Addressing the men who had left him behind in prison] If you feel any sense of shame seeing me today, reconsider your moral will and seek out your ambitions; devote yourself to the land. Let myself be your model![76]

In this textual world, such a spirit of the *gijin* inevitably lives on in the present, waiting for the moment of fulfillment. To console his spirit, the listeners must "reconsider" their "moral will" and hold him as a model and create a world in which he—and by extension all fighters of people's rights (the predecessors of Edo and the present activists alike)—can live as righteous men. Imagine such words, made effective through direct address, in political oration. The communal experience of this speech fosters collective participation in the movement to seek fulfillment in the present. Just as *Jiyū no kachidoki* prefigured a revolution, a moment of fulfillment, *Tōyō minken hyakkaden* produces a textual world that projects itself forward to a second revolution where the spirits of *gijin* will all be consoled.

Recall that *Shōsetsu shinzui*'s criticism of Bakin included a rejection of the "bygone past," specifically the act of looking back at the past. Not only does *Tōyō minken hyakkaden* look back at the Edo period but it seeks to revive it to foster a decisive change in the present; it seeks its energy in the past. *Tōyō minken hyakkaden* thus refuses to bury the past as a bygone past and instead offers a representation of a past that has yet to find its legitimate place in the present. It does not present a domesticated past that is already tamed by the present but a very threatening past that waits for the moment of fulfillment. *Shōsetsu shinzui*'s repeated rejection of the past, which accompanies its criticism against *zen'aku jasei* language, clearly targets such a textual world.

We have taken multiple steps to foreground the negative constituents of the *shōsetsu* and what they signify within the discursive condition within which *Shōsetsu shinzui* was produced. It is extremely important to keep in mind that the positive definition of the *shōsetsu*, namely "emotions, customs, and manners" and "things as they are" (*ari no mama*)—what subsequently became the

Shōsetsu shinzui clichés—are built upon the negation of the discursive space and its habitus examined in this chapter.

Shōsetsu shinzui thus rejected not only Bakin but what Bakin stood for in the early years of the Meiji period, especially among *Shōsetsu shinzui's* target audience. Bakin embodied the antigovernment stance represented by a special linguistic/value system of *zen'aku jasei,* as well as the view of the past that sought the moment of fulfillment, a second revolution. The renunciation of Bakin signified a renunciation of a worldview shared and continually reproduced through a communal and ritualized practice of reading and recitation that prefigured a revolution. This worldview was closely affiliated with a part of the movement that resorted to the use of force, especially in the years of decline, namely, the activists involved in the numerous uprisings that occurred between 1882 and 1885. *Shōsetsu shinzui's* stance vis-à-vis such an act will become even more evident in Chapter 5 when we examine its fictional counterpart, *Tōsei shosei katagi* (*The Character of Modern Students,* 1885), whose textual world is founded upon the "naturalized" present—which is completely cut off from the past—where none of the characters seek a revolutionary change nor question the basic paradigm that shapes the world within which they live.

"The Autonomy of Knowledge" and Political Neutrality

Shōsetsu shinzui's rejection of the political habitus, however, could not have exerted much influence on the discursive site in question without a general discursive trend to support it. The political movement was itself losing its steam; the Fukushima Incident of 1882 is said to be the beginning of the decline of the Freedom and People's Rights Movement, which largely disintegrated by 1885–86. It is not a coincidence that *Shōsetsu shinzui* took form during the movement's decline.

Shōsetsu shinzui was certainly not the only medium to reject such political discourse. The subsequent establishment of the journal *Kokumin no tomo* (*Nation's Friend*) in 1887 and Tokutomi Sohō's criticism of stalwart youth (*sōshi*) as "insensitive barbaric activists," calling for a more "civilized" and "internally sophisticated" subject as the basis for a national subject, also engaged with such a discursive trend. Just as *Shōsetsu shinzui* designated Bakin's creations—and by extension the radical activists—as "superficial" and hence "uncivilized," *Kokuminno tomo* characterized stalwart youth as a "barbaric" subject. *Kokumin no tomo* produced stalwart youth as the quintessential political figure of the Freedom and People's Rights Movement and rejected the figure on the basis of its being the uncivilized other, calling for a more civilized figure of *seinen*. Such rhetorical operation is described in great detail in Kimura Naoe's brilliant book *Seinen no tanjō* (*The Birth of Youth*, 1998). Stalwart youths were, according to Kimura, an embodiment of the discourse of "indignation and resentment" (*hifun kōgai*) and the bodily practice associated with it. In effect, both *Shōsetsu shinzui* and *Kokumin no tomo* eventually discovered the revolutionary fighters who were valorized through the use of *zen'aku jasei* discourse to be "barbaric."

As if to parallel such movement to produce the civilized subject, one other force endorsed *Shōsetsu shinzui*'s rejection of the political habitus, one that manifests in the maxim "autonomy of knowledge." In place of a conclusion, I wish to discuss the manner in which the realm of knowledge was being redefined as a politically neutral realm, which is especially important because it constitutes a force that endorsed the depoliticizing tendencies that *Shōsetsu shinzui* embodies.

In the years 1882–83, the rhetoric of "the autonomy of knowledge" appeared as one of the maxims linked to nation building. It is often considered to be a motto espoused by Tokyo Senmon Gakkō (Tokyo Specialized School, the present-day Waseda University), as evident in Ono Azusa's speech at the founding ceremony; but it is a maxim that Fukuzawa Yukichi also used in the serialized columns he wrote in *Jiji shinpō* initially entitled "Gakumon to seiji o bunri subeshi" (On the Need to Separate Knowledge and Politics), which was later republished under the title *Gakumon no dokuritsu* (*The Autonomy of Knowledge*, 1883).

In a speech he gave at Tokyo Senmon Gakkō, Ono made the following argument:

> I would like to make one desire known and demand such from this school and show how just and upright our school is. . . . Tokyo Senmon Gakkō is independent of political parties, and I demand that it be autonomous. (Huge applause). I am a member of this school and also a member of the Kaishintō party. As a Kaishintō member, I would like to lead you, the entire student body, toward the paths of reform [espoused by our party] and have you become our supporter. (Huge applause). However, as a member of this school, I would be embarrassed by the despicable act of luring students to my party in darkness. (Huge applause). The ultimate goal of our school is for you students to learn real knowledge (*shinsei no gakumon*) and use it in the real world. . . . Our school will never decide on how familiar we will be by asking you whether you'd enter Kaishintō, Jiyūtō, or Teiseitō [after your graduation].[77]

Similarly, Fukuzawa, in his *Gakumon no dokuritsu*, claims, "Since severing the connection between knowledge and politics is important for a nation, I pray that Japanese knowledge (*Nihon no gakumon*) would be separated from Japanese politics."[78]

> Fundamentally, "knowledge" is comparable to martial arts and fine arts in that it has no inherent relationship with politics. Regardless of a person's political inclinations, he should be qualified as a teacher if he has the ability to teach. To inquire into his political inclinations and to evaluate the good and bad of his political views in the process of hiring him have grave consequences. Of course, people may simply overlook it for now, but it is an augury of great disorder and chaos. I imagine the ways of the world in years to come and gravely worry that, if Japanese knowledge remains connected to politics, the degree of calamity may follow the disastrous precedents of the Song dynasty or the former Mito province.[79]

What Ono and Fukuzawa promoted in the name of "the autonomy of knowledge" was not universality or objectivity of knowledge. The maxim marked their effort to posit knowledge as a realm completely independent of politics and political parties.

Despite the apolitical facade, there is nothing apolitical about their claims: when Ono states that he would be "embarrassed by the despicable act of luring students" to his party, he clearly has in mind the other schools that do.[80] The same can be said of Fukuzawa, who takes a step further and criticizes the "connection" between politics and knowledge as "an augury of great disorder and chaos." His argument can be read as a direct criticism of the entire educational arena that was then governed by factional and party-driven divisions.

To clarify the link between the autonomy of knowledge and the production of the *shōsetsu*, let us examine the context in which such a maxim emerged, which is just as important as the maxim itself. The call for the autonomy of knowledge can be interpreted as a response to the political struggle within the educational arena that grew in intensity in the aftermath of the Meiji 14 Incident (1881), which set the date of the founding of the parliament in 1890. As the advocates of the Freedom and People's Rights Movement established political parties in preparation for the parliament, they also attempted to muster support among the voters by founding schools in which to train their supporters. In the opposing camp, government officials began to organize the public educational system with the imperial universities at the top in an effort to institute a system in which only the graduates of Tokyo Imperial University would gain access to government positions. Moreover, graduates of Tokyo Imperial University were given certain privileges, such as being exempt from exams to become government bureaucrats.[81]

In 1885, Tokyo Law School and Tokyo University merged, becoming a central school in which to educate future government officials. In effect, the government-implemented reforms in the educational system attempted to institutionally exclude nongovernment supporters from entering the government. This was on a par with the government-sponsored projects led by Motoda Eifu, which were instituted to oust the Freedom and People's Rights activists from the educational arena by emphasizing the importance of "moral instruction" (*tokuiku*) based on Confucian principles, thereby changing the curriculum and banning certain books from being taught in pre-university education.

It was in this context that Ono and Fukuzawa (both outside the government) called for "the autonomy of knowledge." Political neutrality of knowledge was, in effect, espoused by those who were being defeated in the struggle for power in the educational arena and hence losing the path toward the center of the government. Seen in this light, the autonomy of knowledge marks an effort to nullify the political struggle altogether. Note the will to power apparent here. It constitutes a desire to reclaim a position that stands outside the political struggle, but one that can coexist with those at the center. By positing a politically neutral realm, the agents of such knowledge dissociate themselves from the political movement that is clearly in its decline.

The advocates of the autonomy of knowledge also distance themselves from the political movement that resorted to the use of violence and claim their "civilized" status vis-à-vis the "barbarians" who participated in the uprisings. The realm of knowledge, then, becomes a domain where the agents can reinscribe themselves in the new institutional system with assumed neutrality to the political realm where they have already lost their battle. In the name of neutrality, the advocates of autonomy of knowledge, whether consciously or not, seek a new space in which their voices can be publicly inscribed.

This urge to create a new space endorses the textual boundaries of the *shōsetsu*, which, as a form of new knowledge, also embodies such a will to power. The *shōsetsu*, by demarcating a new space with "emotions, customs, and manners" becomes a realm where politically neutralized men, incapable of succeeding in the real world, get to play out their fantasy, their will to power. This is a topic reserved for Chapter 5. Before we discuss that topic, we turn in the next chapter to varying constructions of "Asia" and further examine the many forces that endorsed the textual boundaries of the *shōsetsu*.

FOUR

Constructing "Asia" and Imperial Longing

Basic Mechanism of Anxiety

Between 1882 and 1885, the years during which most of the violent riots led by the Freedom and People's Rights activists occurred, Japan's relationship to the rest of East Asia provoked extreme anxiety. This chapter situates the development of the *shōsetsu* in the context of this growing anxiety about Japan's position in East Asia and shows how this anxiety endorsed and facilitated the depoliticizing tendencies of the *shōsetsu*.

Within this globalizing context specific to the late nineteenth century, the *shōsetsu* engages with many of the anxieties associated with the cofigurative model of desire discussed in Chapter 1, which continually reproduces the desire to become the always inaccessible "West." The discussion of the cofigurative model of desire offers itself as a variation of Homi K. Bhabha's notion of "colonial mimicry," which has had tremendous influence on postcolonial studies. Bhabha delineates the manner in which the colonial discourse sustains its authoritative power through colonial mimicry, which is "a desire for a reformed, recognizable Other, *as a subject of a difference that is almost the same, but not quite*" (emphasis in original); it is a mechanism enveloped with ambivalence, as it "ruptures" colonial discourse by producing "its slippage, its excess, its difference."[1] Although Bhabha's primary focus is on a two-way relationship between the colonizer and the colonized—and how they sustain and destabilize each other through the mechanism of mimicry and ambivalence that is always already inscribed in their relationship—the cofigurative model of desire I underscore here is a three-way relationship: I seek to show how Japan's desire for authoritative power (the desire to become "the West") seeks out a more barbaric other (in this case "Asia"). Precisely because the desire can never be fulfilled, Japan searches for an other by which to *act* like the authoritative power and to establish a rhetorical (albeit temporary) equivalence with the West, enacting the mechanism of mimicry. Within this triangular relationship, Japan (vis-à-vis the West and Asia) produces for itself the position "that is almost the same, but not quite," which constantly reproduces imperial longing, the insatiable desire for equivalence.[2] How the forces that replicate such imperial longing facilitate the boundaries of the *shōsetsu* is the primary topic of this chapter.

I begin by revisiting the realm of knowledge in which Japan expressed such imperial longing that played an integral part in defining Japan as the leader of East Asia. Knowledge was a site where Japan, by asserting closer association with the West, claimed superiority over China, a clear contender to the position of leader in East Asia. Moreover, the anxiety over Japan's role in East Asia interacts with the debates on the maxim of "autonomy of knowledge" taken up in the last chapter. The point of focus here is the narrative technology of "neutrality" that is foregrounded when "knowledge of civilization" is posited in Japan's claims for superiority in East Asia. As we shall see, "knowledge," when rhetorically posited relative to "Asia," replicates the definition of *shōsetsu*, ultimately constituting it-self as a force that facilitates the production of the *shōsetsu*.

Anxiety was by no means limited to the realm of knowledge. A more general picture of how "Asia" was constructed in the early to mid-1880s will be made apparent by inquiring into arguments for Asianism (*kōa*) and de-Asianization (*datsu-a*) that proliferated in the early Meiji period. These arguments took on many forms, but it is perhaps helpful to briefly note four general tendencies in Japanese intellectuals' construction of "Asia" that an intellectual historian, Hashikawa Bunzō, introduces in his "Fukuzawa Yukichi no Chūgoku bunmeiron" (Fukuzawa Yukichi on Chinese Civilization, 1968): a call for Asian consolidation as a form of resistance based on the shared threat of Euro-America; an argument to "reform" China in an effort to promote Asianism, predicated on the understanding that China is incompetent; a call for de-Asianization based on the perspective that Japan has no time to wait for China to reform; and finally, a call for Asian invasion resulting from a strong identification with the Western imperial powers. As Hashikawa reminds us, moreover, these positions were not mutually exclusive; in fact, we see cases where a valorization and strong contempt for China coexist in an individual, despite their overtly contradictory characteristics.[3]

Such varied tendencies and their apparent opposing agendas have long concealed the basic mechanism of anxiety that Asianism and de-Asianization in fact share. As we shall see, inherent in the ambivalent constructions of "Asia" between 1882 and 1885—whether it be an argument for Asianism or de-Asianization—is the urge to conceal Japan's vulnerable status within East Asia, which is made apparent in the manner by which the proponents from both camps seek relief from "Asian anxiety."

Intellectuals defended their varying views on Asianism and de-Asianization through their major newspaper reports and columns; as such, the newspapers present themselves as the most appropriate means to examine the rhetorical operations of concealment. In particular, I focus on the reports covering three events that played a crucial role in defining and redefining the power dynamics of East Asia: the Imo Mutiny (July 1882), the Sino-Franco War (1884–85), and the Kapsin Incident (December 1884). Newspaper reports of these events allow us not only to see how arguments for Asianism and de-Asianization are mobilized in specific contexts but also to follow the daily reports of the incidents, from the initial reports to the intense discussions that ensue. Given that newspapers all represent different political factions and hence varying stances via Asia, they also give us a sense of the disparity and unity among the various parties.[4] We shall see how those with opposing political stances and agendas, which produce varied reactions to the Imo Mutiny, have come together by the time anxiety—which progressively intensifies throughout the years—reaches its peak with the Kapsin Incident. Detailed analyses of Asia produced in these reports, with specific attention to the changes it goes through, reveal the basic mechanism of anxiety and the manner in which it seeks relief.

I then take up two texts that espouse the opposing agendas—Asianism and de-Asianization—that were published during these turbulent years: Komuro Shinsuke's *Kōa kidan: Murenren* (*A Remarkable Story of Asianism: Dreams of Love*, 1884) serialized in *Jiyū shinbun*; and Fukuzawa Yukichi's article entitled "Datsu-aron" (On De-Asianization, 1885), published in *Jiji shinpō*. Published in the large newspapers, they were inevitably surrounded by the reports that covered the three crucial events that redefined the power dynamics in East Asia in the 1880s. These texts reproduce the surrounding anxiety and attempt, in varying ways, to offer much-needed relief, ultimately concealing, as it were, Japan's vulnerable status in East Asia. This rhetorical attempt to conceal Japan's geopolitical reality synchronizes with the forces that efface the political in the *shōsetsu*.

At the end of this chapter, I discuss the close link between the rhetorical practices of de-Asianization and those of depoliticization. The language by which Asia is constructed in arguments for de-Asianization closely resembles the political discourse embodied by Bakin in *Shōsetsu shinzui*, and hence is inextricably linked to the political habitus and the radical activism that translated to numerous uprisings. We will see that growing forces of de-Asianiziation that culminated with the Kapsin Incident not only attempted to sever ties between Japan and the rest of Asia but also sought to reject the violent domestic riots that marked the political movement in mid-1880s Japan.

The link between the production of the *shōsetsu* and "Asian anxiety" that I examine in this chapter is far from straightforward. There are some concrete links that I can establish between, for example, de-Asianization and depoliticization. However, there are other connections that I can only identify as a parallel discursive movement. My discussions on Japan's anxiety mark an attempt to decipher the multiple levels of discourses that are set in motion as an epistemological shift occurs in the understanding of literature. Japan's anxiety of its own position in East Asia may not have a direct causal link to the *shōsetsu*, but it constitutes one of the many forces that facilitate the paradigm shift I thematize in this book.

Mimicry and "Neutrality" of Knowledge

By 1881 or so, there was a rhetorically accepted notion that Japan was the most civilized nation in Asia, a sentiment that had gained widespread acceptance domestically and was shared among the major newspapers, despite their varying political stances.[5] I say "rhetorically" accepted because it had to be insisted on over and over again for it to be sustained. For example, Fukuzawa Yukichi's article "Chōsen no kōsai o ronzu" (On the Relationship with Korea) in *Jiji shinpō* argued that it was "Japan's responsibility" as the most civilized nation in East Asia to "help the neighboring countries" achieve enlightenment to protect them against Western invasion.[6] Similarly, an essay in *Yūbin hōchi shinbun* framed its arguments for Asianism in the following manner: "We must understand that our country has now progressed in the path of enlightenment, and this is accepted by others; who else can lead the mission of Asian consolidation?"[7] Ono Azusa, a Kaishintō affiliate, too, shared this sentiment, which is obvious from his "Gaikō o ronzu" (On Foreign Diplomacy, 1882), a famous speech in which he claimed, "Our country is the leader of Eastern civilization."[8] Such claims for superiority were often made in reference to Korea. In 1881, when the threat of Russian forces moving south to Korea became palpable, the progovernment newspaper *Tokyo nichi nichi shinbun* stated that Japan must stop Russian forces on behalf of Korea in order to display Japan's status as Korea's new suzerain state.[9] This rhetoric of superiority was thus very pervasive among the otherwise divided political factions.

As I will show in more detail in the next section, this rhetorical superiority was constantly questioned between 1882 and 1885, as Japan had to compete with China, Japan's long-term mentor and a natural contender for status of leader. To demonstrate Japan's leader status, it was vital for Japan to differentiate itself from China, especially on foreign policy over Korea. The realm of knowledge played an integral role in this process.

Expressions of superiority often took the form of a binary: Japan adopted the path toward enlightenment and reform, whereas China stubbornly stuck to the old-fashioned ways. *Yūbin hōchi shinbun* in 1884, for example, claimed: "Japan adopted Western materials (*bunbutsu*) and has reformed political and social institutions according to the best institutions of civilization. . . . Qing China, on the other hand, has been moved by the spirit to protect the old (*shukyū no seishin*) and has felt at ease in the old, uncultured ways."[10] Such a binary was mobilized as writers discussed the different means to bring reform to Korea: Fukuzawa's *Jiji shinpō*, for example, claims that whereas the Japanese could offer "enlightened" knowledge, China could only give the Koreans "the trifling teachings of old Confucian thought."[11] Japan, equipped with "materials and institutions" of civilization, is thus the more appropriate mentor to Korea. Emphasizing this position of "teacher" as a way to differentiate itself from China, *Chōya shinbun* states that Koreans with "a mind for reform" come to Japan rather than go to China even though "it is more dangerous to travel to Japan because they have to sail across the sea."[12] In effect, educating "uncivilized" people by giving them access to the Western materials and institutions that Japan had adopted since the Meiji Restoration became a means to substantiate Japan's claims for superiority. Notice the temporary fulfillment of the cofigurative model of desire, which strives for equivalence with the "civilized West": by discovering the more "barbaric" other by which to define Japan's superiority, Japan temporarily and rhetorically becomes the West.

The Japanese government supported such projects and sought Korean students to study in Japan. In 1877, Hanabusa Yoshimoto, the Japanese ambassador to Korea, sent an official letter to Korea stating that "[accepting students from Korea] would be an honor for Japan, and we could give you resources that allow your country to avoid foreign disdain."[13] Although Koreans did not respond to this entreaty until 1881, and not until after repeated requests from Japan, Korean students began to arrive; by 1883 there were about fifty students, many of whom enrolled in Keiō Gijuku (present-day Keiō University), founded by Fukuzawa Yukichi.[14] "Reforming the minds of men" (*jinshin kaikaku*) thus became one of the key issues inextricably linked to foreign relations in Asia.

Let us closely examine the mechanism of mimicry apparent in this "reform" of Korea. Fukuzawa, one of the devout supporters of Western knowledge, wrote "Gyūba Takuzō-kun Chōsen ni iku" (Gyūba Takuzō Goes to Korea) for *Jiji shinpō* in January 1883, which identifies Gyūba's role in Korea by addressing him in the following manner: "The primary objective is to transmit the teachings of Western knowledge (*yōgaku*) that you have learned and have their wise upper-class men voluntarily enlighten themselves."[15] Fukuzawa continues, "It is Japan's responsibility as the leader of Asia to bring about enlightenment in Korea by transmitting knowledge of civilization possessed by Japanese upper-class men."[16] The "knowledge of civilization" (*kinji bunmei no shisō*), which was earlier labeled "Western knowledge" (*yōgaku*), is renamed as "knowledge of civilization possessed by Japanese upper-class men."[17]

Notice the shift here that enacts mimicry: the act of "enlightening the Koreans" attributes the knowledge of civilization to the Japanese, as if it is *possessed* by the Japanese. The Japanese, who on the one hand needed to adopt Western knowledge—hence *internally* colonizing themselves—become an agent of enlightenment as they discover the "less civilized" other, in this case Koreans. In the process, specifically in the act of enlightening the "barbarians," the Western knowledge absorbed by the Japanese *becomes* Japanese knowledge. By having the "barbaric" other access not the West, but the West *through* Japan, the Japanese take on the role of the West. Accordingly, the subject "Japan" as an agent that possesses the knowledge of modern civilization comes into being. This is the subject of mimicry, a subject that *owns* "Japanese knowledge."

The speech Ono Azusa gave at the founding ceremony of Tokyo Senmon Gakkō that we examined toward the end of the last chapter further demonstrates this mimicry well. Ono makes this claim:

> This is what I wish to demand from this school: By continuing to reform our school for ten or more years, we should commit ourselves to developing the school that teaches our youth in our language (*hōgo*) and bring about the autonomy of our knowledge (*hōgakumon*). (Hear, hear, huge applause). The autonomy of the nation depends on the autonomy of its people, and the autonomy of the people is rooted in the autonomy of their spirit. (Hear, hear, applause). The autonomy of the spirit is, in fact, based on the autonomy of knowledge, and thus, if one desires the nation to achieve autonomy, its people must first attain autonomy. (Huge applause). If one desires for its people to

achieve autonomy, the spirit must first attain autonomy. And thus if one desires for the spirit to achieve autonomy, knowledge must first attain autonomy.
(Huge applause).[18]

Ono Azusa's call for "the autonomy of *our* knowledge" signifies teachings in "our
language." In interpreting his claim, we must not assume that Tokyo Senmon
Gakkō limited its textbooks to materials originally produced in Japanese or
by Japanese thinkers. The "table of textbooks and references" that lists the
primary texts used in the classes at Tokyo Senmon Gakkō consists of works by
Alexander Bain, Herbert Spencer, and John Stuart Mill, among other Western
writers.[19] It is clear, therefore, that "our knowledge" did not signify texts produced in Japan or in the Japanese language. Instead, it referred to a body of
works that was endorsed as knowledge necessary in the path toward modernization, and that, though originally written in a foreign language (primarily in
Western languages), were translated into a language to which the readership
had access; these texts were then distributed widely, to the extent that a certain
level of familiarity was achieved, a familiarity that granted them the status of
"*our* knowledge." Furthermore, in order to fulfill what Ono promoted as the
"autonomy of knowledge," the texts had to be commented on and talked about
in "our language." Such practice, according to Ono, was ultimately linked to
the autonomy of the national spirit. Note that in the process through which
foreign (Western) knowledge becomes *our* knowledge, the subject "we" is posited as one that *possesses* such knowledge. In effect, this body of knowledge, the
means to civilization, becomes that which belongs to "us." Furthermore, as the
"less civilized peoples" access not the Western texts but the translated Japanese
texts, the Japanese begin to *act* as the West and hence like an imperial power,
and Japan as the possessor of "knowledge of civilization" is essentialized.[20]

What complicates this issue is that such apparently international discussion has great domestic implications. Knowledge, as discussed in the last two
chapters, was a site of domestic political power struggle. In the early 1880s,
Motoda-led reforms had revived Confucianism and sidelined scholars of Western knowledge, who now sought ways to legitimate their learning. The advocates of Western knowledge found the most appropriate way to do so as they
sought to bring "Western reform" to Korea. Not only does this urge to bring
Western reform to Korea clearly manifest mimicry but it also shows a will to
power within the domestic circle.

To highlight the domestic implications, it is important to note that the
"knowledge of civilization," thus defined by the advocates of Western knowl-

edge, is posited specifically against Confucianism, which is equated with "old-fashioned Eastern ways." Take for example, *Yūbin hōchi shinbun*, which claims "Qing China leans toward the East and Japan toward the West" and emphasizes how Japan had led the path of reform based on sociopolitical systems of the West.[21] Fukuzawa's *Jiji shinpō* was much more direct, claiming that China can offer only "trifling teachings of old Confucian thought." In his "Gyūba Takuzō-kun Chōsen ni iku," he further elaborates on this opposition. Addressing Gyūba, Fukuzawa states, "You must neither carelessly interject yourself in their politics nor demand their custom to be destroyed. The primary objective is to transmit the teachings of Western knowledge that you have learned and have their wise upper-class men voluntarily enlighten themselves."[22]

According to this logic, China, because of its "old-fashioned ways," directly interferes with Korea's domestic and foreign policies; the Chinese thereby interject themselves in Korean politics, ultimately "destroying" their customs. This is set in opposition to the pseudo-egalitarian policies of the West (Japan) that "honor" Korea's independence because the West (Japan) only transmits the teachings and allows the Koreans to "voluntarily" enlighten themselves. Notice the neutrality that the knowledge of civilization embodies. In this scheme, Western knowledge automatically and "without design" enlightens its receiver, which logically precludes Japan's involvement in the process of "enlightening" the subjects. In direct contrast to China, equipped with "old-fashioned" Confucianism that represents interference, Japan, as the agent that offers Western knowledge, is given a "neutral" position in this conceptual scheme.

Such a definition of "knowledge of civilization" plays a crucial role in the domestic power struggle. Criticism against Confucian principles can be read as a criticism not only against China but against the Meiji government as well. Within this domestic power scheme, the government was presented as being *behind* Confucianism, trying to mold its subjects "with design." The neutrality of Western knowledge also finds its partner in the maxim "the autonomy of knowledge," because the maxim (which was in many ways antigovernment) posited knowledge as a neutral medium. Neutrality of knowledge is thus an expression of will to power, both in relation to China and Korea and in the domestic context.

The *shōsetsu* replicates the will to power of neutrality. The definition of Western knowledge that "naturally" leads men to reform—which is invariably posited in opposition to China's direct interference—brings to mind the definition of *shōsetsu* we saw in the last two chapters, where the benefits of the *shōsetsu* were defined as the "natural side effect." Recall also that *Shōsetsu shinzui* criticized the link between the language of good/bad and right/wrong (*zen'aku jasei*) and "the writer's design." In *Shōsetsu shinzui*, in other words, the linguistic/value system of Confucianism represents the writer's direct manipulation of the text. By contrast, the *shōsetsu* is supposedly free of the writer's design; the reader's mind is elevated because of the value inherent in the medium (the *shōsetsu*) itself.[23] *Shōsetsu shinzui* also argued that the *shōsetsu* is the most appropriate medium to promote "human development," a rhetoric mobilized not only domestically but internationally, especially vis-à-vis Korea in 1880s Japan. The *shōsetsu* can clearly claim a place within the surrounding discourse that defines knowledge as that which automatically and without design "reforms" the minds of men.

The manner in which the realm of knowledge is posited via Korea, inextricably linked to the domestic power struggle, thus constitutes a force that synchronizes with the definition of the *shōsetsu*. What is important to note is that this neutrality shared by knowledge and the *shōsetsu* engages with imperial longing. When the agent of knowledge gains an identity to transmit knowledge to the "uncivilized," he gains a place in the domestic power dynamic; but he must continue to reenact the mechanism of mimicry: mimicking the colonizer while he himself is colonized, which constantly reproduces the configurative model of desire that can only be frustrated. The claims for neutrality only conceal such a mechanism, and the *shōsetsu* thus becomes a site of concealment.

Intensifying Anxiety: The Imo Mutiny, the Sino-Franco War, and the Kapsin Incident

The anxiety regarding Japan's role in Asia did not take place exclusively within the realm of knowledge. The same anxiety appeared in newspaper reports on the Imo Mutiny, the Sino-Franco War, and the Kapsin Incident, all of which challenged Japan's superiority. By analyzing these newspaper discussions, I will show that Japan's anxiety intensified throughout the years and ultimately sought relief in "rhetorical fulfillment" that would conceal Japan's geopolitical reality. Ultimately, I suggest that this tendency to seek rhetorical fulfillment synchronized with the production of the *shōsetsu*, which sought to find its identity in the depoliticized arena.

The Imo Mutiny, which erupted in Korea in July 1882, was a revolt by the traditionalist troops of Korea resisting the Japanese-induced reforms of the Korean army. The tension between Japan and Korea (and by extension China, given its link to the traditionalists) intensified drastically as a result, and arguments for de-Asianization increased as anti-Korean and anti-Chinese sentiments grew among the newspapers. The newspapers, however, differed on how they proposed to approach Korea and China after the event. Even within one newspaper, several views might be presented. Consider, for example, the *Jiyū shinbun*: "Chōsen no henpō" (Reports on the Korean Uprising) argues that a victory against a small country like Korea is not going to bring merit to Japan because Korea's current state corresponds to approximately that of "the Tokugawa era," suggesting that the war with Korea is futile.[24] At the same time, Okunomiya Kenshi published his "Seikanron" (Korean Expedition)—which actually overlaps with "Chōsen no henpō" on the pages of the *Jiyū shinbun*—arguing that Japan ought to show force against the Korean government. There are other articles in the *Jiyū shinbun* that criticize, not so much the Korean traditionalists but China's role in the Imo Mutiny, highlighting China's interference with Korean affairs, which is characterized as an "attempt to humiliate our Imperial Japan."[25]

These varied reactions are shared by other newspapers as well. *Yūbin hōchi shinbun* called for the use of force to "erase the national embarrassment and regain national honor."[26] *Tokyo nichi nichi shinbun* criticized aggressive military policies advocated by *Yūbin hōchi shinbun* and stated that diplomatic negotiation was the most appropriate solution.[27] *Tokyo Yokohama mainichi shinbun* was generally against "interference" in Korean affairs, engaging in debates with other major newspapers, such as *Chōya shinbun*, that advocated the use of force.[28] Members of the Kōakai, a group founded in 1880 arguing for Asian consolidation, were also split in their reactions: while the leaders of the group (primarily those affiliated with the government) criticized China and supported the government policies, others severely criticized the government and its contempt toward China.[29]

In short, despite the common trope that situated Korea (and China) as inferior and Japan as the most advanced nation in East Asia, the newspapers were divided in the action they promoted, at least immediately following the Imo Mutiny. The anti-Korean and anti-Chinese sentiments had yet to consolidate the writers and activists as forcefully as they did two and a half years later, in the aftermath of the Kapsin Incident in December 1884.

This shift in the media sentiment between the Imo Mutiny and the Kapsin Incident cannot be understood without examining the role of the Sino-Franco War (1884–85), which erupted over competing claims to Annam (present-day Vietnam). The outcome of the conflict was an object of much interest for the Japanese given that the Sino-Franco disputes over Annam appeared to parallel those of Sino-Japanese relations over Korea. Or perhaps it is more accurate to say that Japanese intellectuals *preferred* to narrativize the relationship this way, in accordance with their claim that Japan was one of the leaders in East Asia, equal to (if not stronger than) China.

The major newspapers all covered the incident in depth, especially *Chōya shinbun* and *Jiyū shinbun*. *Jiyū shinbun*'s reports on the Sino-Franco conflicts are of particular interest to this chapter given that Komuro Shinsuke's *Murenren*, an object of inquiry in the next section in this chapter, was serialized in *Jiyū shinbun*. I wish to thus focus on the *Jiyū shinbun*'s reports and demonstrate how they reveal the basic mechanism of anxiety, which reached its peak with the Kapsin Incident as the rhetorically produced superiority was on the verge of being exposed as mere rhetoric.

At the outset of the Sino-Franco War, we see *Jiyū shinbun* being quite ambivalent in its position vis-à-vis France and China. On the one hand, given that Chinese forces appeared much more capable and better equipped in the initial stages of the conflict, the threat of China expanding its military power in East Asia became palpable; this led to an increase in anti-Chinese sentiments.[30] Speculating on the outcome of the conflict if China ends up victorious, some articles warn that if China wins, "it will necessarily turn its force to us."[31] This imminent Chinese threat provoked a trend in the *Jiyū shinbun* to side with France, and arguments for de-Asianization thus increased.[32] The threat of China in effect led to a strong resentment of China, which produced a sense of identification with France.

On the other hand, in 1883 *Jiyū shinbun* also calls attention to the larger implication of France's "policy of invasion" (*shinpan seiryaku*), which, as "Annan no senpō" (War Reports of Annam) claims, "would have an impact on policies that govern all of Asia."[33] Aida Aisaburō's article is another example where the writer warns against uncritical valorization of France. He fears that "Asian independence" will be jeopardized if France is victorious because of the possibility that France will monopolize the Asian market. Aida reminds the readers that France has already "taken away rich resources" and "took advantage of the uncivilized people" of China and India.[34] Such a sentiment no doubt was shared by many others. France's existence in East Asia was in itself a cause for concern. Despite the anti-Chinese sentiments, supporting France unconditionally was out of the question. In 1883, therefore, *Jiyū shinbun* remained ambivalent; voices that sought to assess France's threat in East Asia coexisted with those that identified themselves with France.

However, when China suffered an interim loss and was forced to sign the Tientsin Treaty in May 1884, *Jiyū shinbun*'s tone changes drastically as if it found the most fitting opportunity to devalue China. "Shinfutsu no wa" (Sino-

Franco Alliance), an article introducing the Tientsin Treaty to the readership, emphasizes Chinese incompetence in the following manner:

> A country large enough to have eighteen provinces and 400 million people surrendered to France, a country that brought merely thirteen to fourteen thousand men given the great length they had to travel. Deprived of their spirit, the many ministers [of China] were in utter confusion; those of high and low classes panicked and could not have thought to wait for the rightful am-bassador to appear . . . and ended up signing a humiliating treaty.[35]

After this decisive turn, the critical tone against China amplified, which was supplemented by an uncritical identification with France. With the unfounded superiority that came with a strong identification with France, supported by an even stronger contempt toward China, the very fact that Japan itself was being "internally colonized" as it was forced to internalize the gaze and principles that defined "civilized" conditions was concealed.

Jiyū shinbun was certainly not the only newspaper to enact mimicry this way; Ozaki Gakudō, who wrote for the *Yūbin hōchi shinbun*, also ridiculed China and Korea for "not knowing what international law is" in discussing how "international law does not recognize China and Korea."[36] Ozaki clearly meant to disparage China's and Korea's ignorance, but strictly speaking, international law did not recognize Japan until it successfully renegotiated the unequal trea-ties immediately before the Sino-Japanese War in 1894. In *Chōya shinbun* we find an article entitled "Waga hō no Shina ni taisuru seiryaku ikan" (On Our Policies against China, 1884) in which the writer argues for an alliance with France, one that the writer clearly conceptualizes based on equality, in the fight against China.[37]

This is not to say that there were no counterexamples to such arguments for de-Asianization and blind identification with France. In the same *Chōya shin-bun*, albeit in April 1884, an article expressed concern for the growing contempt against China as it argued for national expansion based on Asian consolida-tion.[38] In September of the same year, *Chōya shinbun* criticized the potential Japan-Franco alliance and argued for Japan's neutrality in the matter.[39] *Tokyo Yokohama mainichi shinbun* denounced Euro-American colonialist violence, specifically referring to the Sino-Franco War.[40] Yet the same newspaper pub-lished an article entitled "Shina no haiboku wa Nihon no sachi nari" (China's Loss Is Japan's Delight) in which hope was expressed that China would lose the battle to France.[41] The inconsistencies that permeate these reports are, in many ways, reflective of the increasing anxiety shaped by growing fear of the French presence in East Asia, the threat of China's military expansion, and the instability and unpredictability of Japan's status within such a power dynamic.

However, these varying positions virtually disappeared in December 1884 when Japan's rhetorical superiority via China (and by extension the rhetorical equivalence with France) was definitively questioned with the Kapsin Incident, a coup d'état organized by the pro-Japanese activists in Korea. Especially because China was still in the midst of a struggle with France, Korean activists like Kim Okkyun thought a coup d'état would be effortless. But given the swift response by the Chinese troops, the pro-Japanese activists were able to remain in power only three days. The Kapsin Incident showed, among other things, that Qing China was militarily stronger than Japan. Japan's claim to Korea was decisive in retaining its status as the leader of East Asia. If the claim was undermined by China, not only would Japan's "uncivilized position" be exposed but Japan would have to face its second-rate status within East Asia. Moreover, the same China, which supposedly had equipped itself with modern weaponry through its yangwu movement, had suffered a loss to France, a country that ten years before had suffered a huge loss to Prussia in the Franco-Prussian War, making it a second-rate European country. As Japan's self-definition as the leader of Asia was completely undermined, the fear of Euro-American power reached its peak.

It was with such intense anxiety that the newspapers practically united in their anti-Chinese, anti-Korean stance in the aftermath of the Kapsin Incident. In sharp contrast to the varying reactions to the Imo Mutiny, newspapers together called for a military confrontation, some arguing for the immediate dispatch of forces to Korea and others for an official alliance with France to seek military support. *Yūbin hōchi shinbun*, despite its earlier criticism against France and the Euro-American invasion of Asia in its reports on the Sino-Franco War,[42] called for a war with China to gain the status "the leader of Asia."[43] *Tokyo Yokohama mainichi shinbun*, known for its criticism against the war, also argued that there is much to be gained in war.[44] *Jiji shinpō* and Jiyūtō members, especially the radical left, were the most aggressive in their stance for military confrontation.[45] *Jiyū shinbun* specifically argued for the use of force against Korea and for a war with the Chinese forces: in the last issue it published on December 27, 1884, it claimed, "This is a great opportunity to display the strength of Japan's military power and surprise the conceited white race," exposing not only the anti-Chinese, anti-Korean sentiments but also a strong resentment toward the "white race" with whom Japan sought rhetorical equivalence.[46]

With anxiety at its peak, the call for an immediate military action was thus not too surprising. However, the aggressive rhetoric, all in favor of immediate military attack, should be read not as a means to protect Japan's position as the leader of Asia but as a desire to substantiate the claim itself.[47] It is as if the strong feeling of contempt toward China, coupled with the frustration that Japan could not be a "first-rate nation" even in East Asia, produced, as it were, a disturbed sense of consciousness that sought an outlet.

Despite such calls for aggressive military action, the Meiji government decided to solve the tension diplomatically. Whereas France secretly offered to form an alliance with Japan, the government accepted reparations and a formal apology from Korea with the Treaty of Seoul in January 1885. The Tientsin Treaty with Qing China was signed in April 1885, which stipulated that both parties simultaneously pull out military forces from Korea and inform one another beforehand if either decided to send troops to Korea in the future. The government's decision was, in part, a result of Japan's status vis-à-vis Euro-America: Japan had yet to successfully renegotiate the unequal treaties that the Tokugawa shogunate signed in 1858, hence was not recognized as a civilized country in the paradigm of the International Law of Sovereign States. Still subject to the treaties, Japan could rhetorically represent itself as a civilized nation but could not act with such agency. Perhaps it is more accurate to say that precisely because it could not *act* like a civilized nation, Japan repeatedly represented itself as such. Ten years later (1894), Japan entered the Sino-Japanese War immediately after its successful renegotiation of treaties with Great Britain that legally recognized Japan as a civilized country. To act like a civilized nation, it needed the official endorsement of Euro-American powers.

One other factor needs to be considered to understand the Meiji government's decision to take diplomatic measures to ease the tension with Qing China. With the Imo Mutiny in 1882, the future confrontation with Qing China began to appear unavoidable. The Meiji government thus saw the need to strengthen its national army and devised an eight-year plan, beginning with the issuance of the Imperial Rescript to Soldiers and Sailors (*gunjin chokuyu*) of 1882. However, when the Kapsin Incident erupted in Korea, the devised plan was only in its second year; the nation was in a recession because the Matsukata deflation policy had increased military spending. Japan was in no position to go to war, militarily or financially. Uprisings such as the Gunma Incident (May 1884) and the Chichibu Incident (October 1884) were carried out primarily because of financial hardships. Tokutomi Sohō, who was among the few to write against the immediate use of force (though it should not be valorized as an antiwar campaign), claimed that "people already suffer from the hardship imposed on them by the taxes, unable to eat day by day. From what pool are we going to pay for the war?"[48]

Yet Japanese intellectuals could not jettison the self-defined status as the leader of Asia, nor could they realistically act out the claim. To admit the emptiness of the rhetoric was completely out of the question. In short, rhetorical fulfillment was the only way to resolve their anxiety, which, as we shall see in the subsequent sections, shaped the calls for both Asianism and de-Asianization.

Asianism and Komuro Shinsuke's Kōa kidan: Murenren

Although de-Asianization is typically highlighted in discussions of early Meiji Japan, a call for Asianism still had a stronghold in the discursive space I take up in this book. Note that there was an association established to specifically promote Asian consolidation that was quite active during the years in question. Kōakai (Association for Asian Consolidation, which in 1883 became Ajia kyōkai, Association of Asia) was founded in 1880 to foster integration and solidarity among members of Asian countries to ward off Western imperialist threat. In a speech Watanabe Kōki (1847–1901) gave at the founding ceremony of Kōakai, he defines the purpose of Kōakai as "development of Asian civilization" and states, "Euro-American countries, despite their fierce competition with each other, benefit from their same race, same language, and same religion/teachings (*dōzoku, dōbun, dōkyō*)."[49] He then claims that Asian countries that also share the "same race, same language, and same religion/teachings" must also consolidate. Kōakai was quite active at its inception, establishing, for example, a Chinese language school (*shinago gakkō*) in which not only the language but political and military systems of China could be studied. *Tōyō gakkan* was also established in Shanghai in 1884 to promote the study of Qing China's politics and language and disseminate the ideals of Asianism.[50] Kōakai was thus the group most sympathetic in Asian affairs. However, it too could not escape the cofigurative model of desire, evident in the manner in which Watanabe defined Asia vis-à-vis Europe and the equivalence he sought in his claims for "same race, same language, and same religion/teachings." The group was also complicit in the claim that Japan was more advanced and hence the rightful leader in its efforts at Asian consolidation. Kōakai's suggested policies and measures thus revolved around how Japan could lead countries in Asia to unite.[51]

Although Komuro Shinsuke was not a member of the Kōakai, his fiction shares many ideals the group presented. With *Kōa kidan: Murenren* (*A Remarkable Story of Asianism: Dreams of Love*), Shinsuke arguably became the first to fictionalize the idea of Asianism in the post-Meiji Restoration world. The narrative was serialized in the *Jiyū shinbun* from April 6 to June 18, 1884, as the newspaper was, incidentally, filled with reports on the Sino-Franco War. Interestingly, as the serialization progresses, so do the anti-Chinese sentiments and aggressive stance against Qing China in favor of France in the news reports, creating, at least on the surface, a strange juxtaposition between the reports that propagate anti-Chinese sentiments and a work of fiction that apparently calls for Asian consolidation. The strange juxtaposition reveals just how complex "Asian anxiety" is. By creating a dialogue between *Murenren* and the reports that physically surround it, I will show that the fictional text enacts and attempts to relieve the anxiety about Asia expressed both in the news reports and in the fictional work.

The story of *Murenren* is set in China and begins around 1830 with the birth of the hero named Raishun (the characters signifying "lightning" and "spring," respectively, 雷春); he was born when lightning struck the tomb of a Japanese woman who drifted ashore on China's eastern coast after a shipwreck and died during the last days of her pregnancy. Raishun ultimately grows up to be a man whose natural grandeur and righteousness are revered by everyone—even by his adversaries. His training in the *kangaku* classics is recognized as he begins correspondence with Lin Zexu (Rin Sokujo in the Japanese rendering, 1785–1850), who is extremely impressed with Raishun's knowledge and intelligence. In the meantime, an American missionary who is appropriately impressed with Raishun's intelligence teaches him "Western learning." The main plot features a sort of adventure story that revolves around Raishun's trip as he sets out to visit Lin Zexu in Beijing.

At the beginning of the story, as Lin Zexu is introduced, the story revolves around the binary between Qing China and Britain; known for his valor and integrity, Lin Zexu is portrayed favorably as the righteous, well-educated man who fought against the wrongs of the British in fighting the Opium War. The binary therefore is the good Lin Zexu (for standing up for the country) and the evil British as colonial power. This binary shifts as the Taiping Rebellion and Hong Xiuquan (Kō Shūzen, in the Japanese rendering, 1814–64) appear in the story. The British are no longer evil; Hong Xiuquan now represents evil, and the emergence of the new evil is accompanied by the rhetoric of government corruption (*kan no fuhai*) and a representation of the people of China as those having the "tendency to be lowly and slavelike" (*hikutsu dorei no fūshū*). The underlying logic of the narrative is that the evil of Hong Xiuquan and the Taiping Rebellion cannot be put down because of government corruption and the lowliness of the people. As Raishun discusses the need for reform among his comrades, they have the perfect solution: Raishun should become the leader of their cause to suppress the Taiping Rebellion. Raishun is the one designated to correct the wrongs of the government and direct the people out of their slavelike existence.

What is extremely important is that Raishun is Japanese, and his natural leadership and nobility are tied to his Japanese identity. During Raishun's youth, the monk who raises him sees him grow up to be a skillful, courageous fighter and thinks, "I heard that Japan had long been a land that respects martial arts and upholds justice and courage (*giyū*). If a child of an unknown woman is this brave and heroic, a man born into a respected warrior family would be more so; it is no wonder that Japan produces courageous and intelligent men."[52] Raishun's natural splendor is thus attributed to his "Japanese heritage," making him the most appropriate leader to direct the Chinese to fight against the corrupt authorities of the Qing government.

Interestingly, the representation of the British as the colonizing agent disappears rather quickly. The enemy in this text is either government corruption or Hong Xiuquan. In fact, as the narrative progresses, we begin to get a rather favorable view of the British. In one of his many adventures, Raishun meets a pirate (named Sai Shiryō) who, like everyone else in this text, recognizes Raishun's intrinsic brilliance. Impressed by Raishun's grandeur, Sai decides to show him his treasures: military weapons from a British ship that he stole a few days before meeting Raishun. Raishun here describes Sai's success as "one great feat of justice" (*ichidai gikyo*).[53] Later on, however, the British come back to retaliate for the loss of the ship and capture Raishun. Upon his capture, even the British recognize his natural superiority (and they are more impressed when they discover that Raishun in fact speaks English). More important, Raishun is impressed with the new machinery he sees as well as the way he is treated by the British, and he begins to regret that he had evaluated Sai's act as "one great feat of justice." The British captain treats Raishun fairly, protects his rights, strictly adheres to the laws that bind him, and hands Raishun over to the Qing government. Raishun thus concludes that the British are more advanced not only in science but in their "emotions" as well. His shock is even greater after he is turned over to the Qing authorities, and they imprison him without much investigation. The difference between the two types of treatment is too great. Raishun says, "I see the clear discrepancy of the political and legal systems between the West and the East. I grieve over how flawed our political system is and am angered by how deficient our military capacity is."[54] Such identification with the British, coupled with the highly contemptuous attitude toward the Chinese, reiterates the discursive scheme of the reports on the Sino-Franco War. Incidentally, this section is serialized three days before "Shinfutsu no wa" (Sino-Franco Alliance), the article that showed a great tone of disdain toward the Chinese, which marked a decisive turn for the *Jiyū shinbun* in its treatment of the Chinese.

The story goes on a little longer, but it is incomplete. The story ends as Raishun finds a woman lying unconscious in a hot-air balloon; this is the woman destined to be Raishun's wife, his partner in his quest for reform in China. The narrator tells us that this woman is in fact a Chinese woman who was, at a young age, taken into slavery by foreign ships and ended up in France. She was saved by a French philanthropist and was educated there. Ultimately Raishun and his wife together "achieve a great feat by bringing success to Asia and warding off Europe."[55]

Murenren thus faithfully reiterates the discursive dynamic and anxiety that shape the reports that surround it. Raishun's initial skepticism of the British is on a par with *Jiyū shinbun*'s articles that warned against French presence in Asia. Raishun's increasing admiration for the British further coincides with *Jiyū shinbun*'s inclination to side with France, which replicates the desire for rhetorical equivalence that permeates the *Jiyū shinbun* reports we saw earlier. Perhaps most important, because he is Japanese, Raishun "naturally" embodies the disposition and skills necessary to be the "civilized" leader who would lead the "uncivilized" Chinese out of their "lowly" state. The figure of Raishun thus features a fulfillment of an ideal in which Japan rhetorically establishes equivalence with the "civilized" West, granting relief to the anxiety that arose with the Sino-Franco War.

It must be noted, however, that such rhetorical and temporary fulfillment is predicated upon concealment: the narrative does not question Japan's superiority, which is the pole by which Asianism is promoted.[56] Raishun alone embodies the potential of reform, and the narrative remains silent about what makes up the "natural" splendor Raishun possesses. Raishun himself never questions his Japanese origin (it is conspicuously present in the text as the narrative voice reminds us repeatedly, but it is not a topic that is discussed by the characters themselves). This is a topic that would have extended the discussion to the relationship between Qing China and Japan and Japan's position in the power politics of mid-nineteenth-century East Asia, but the narrative, as if deliberately, prevents the story from progressing in that direction. Instead, the historical lag is never foregrounded, and we get the silent alignment between Raishun's Japanese origin and the natural grandeur he embodies.[57]

Furthermore, the union between China and Japan is made in the form of love and potential marriage between Raishun and the Chinese woman, which appears to signify Asian consolidation in this text. This union not only feminizes China but further leaves ambiguous how Japan and China would consolidate given that the consolidation is figuratively made through marriage. In more ways than one, rhetorical fulfillment can be actualized only through multilayered concealment.

"Datsu-aron": Fukuzawa Yukichi and Jiji shinpō

The serialization of *Murenren* ended six months before the Kapsin Incident, and hence before Japan's anxiety vis-à-vis its position in East Asia reached its peak. In contrast, "Datsu-aron" (On De-Asianization, 1885) was published after the Kapsin Incident, after the tension between China and Japan had been tentatively resolved between the two governments. A textual analysis of "Datsu-aron" will identify yet another enactment of rhetorical fulfillment, which produces the figure of civilized Japan that retains rhetorical superiority over China.

Fukuzawa was deeply involved in the Kapsin coup, despite his criticism of direct interference in Korean affairs that he made as early as 1883.[58] Japan's foreign policy in East Asia was an issue that preoccupied Fukuzawa throughout the early Meiji years, which is clear from the great number of articles he wrote in *Jiji shinpō* on the topic since the newspaper's founding in 1882. He did much to "enlighten" Koreans, such as taking in Korean students at his own Keiō Gijuku and sending his students to Korea, and continued to argue that it was Japan's responsibility to protect Korea and ward off the Western imperialist threat. Accordingly, "Datsu-aron," which argues for immediate severance from the "barbarians" of East Asia, marks a turning point in Fukuzawa's position on Japan's foreign policy in East Asia. What is behind his call for severance, his change of heart, has been a topic of much debate, but I am not interested in ascertaining Fukuzawa's state of mind when he wrote the piece.[59] Instead, I am interested in how the text, taking the form of de-Asianization, seeks to renarrativize and reconfigure Japan's position vis-à-vis China and Korea, and hence expresses and finds relief for the growing anxiety, in light of all the events leading up to the Kapsin Incident.

After repeating what was by this time a clichéd narrative of how Japan embraced civilization and left the backward confines of Asia, "Datsu-aron" states the following:

> The most unfortunate is the existence of the two neighboring countries, one called China and the other Korea. . . . Men of these nations know nothing of progress or development, whether it be of an individual or of a nation. In this age of travel and mobility, it is not that they have not seen the things of civili-

zations, but what they see and hear is not enough to move their hearts. Their emotions simply choose to long for the old-fashioned ways, and they are no different from a hundred, a thousand years ago. . . . From the Westerners' perspective, the three countries are close in proximity; and because of that it is not without ground that the Westerners see the same in us and evaluate us as they do China and Korea.[60]

The narrative adopts the Westerners' gaze and claims that, despite the fact that Japan had left the backward confines of Asia, Japan is prone to be categorized among nations like China and Korea that "long for the old-fashioned ways" because of geographical proximity.

The following example is used to make this point: "If Koreans show cruelty in punishing their own people, the Japanese would also be considered to be lacking in compassion."[61] This reference clearly invokes the manner in which the pro-Japanese activists in Korea were executed in the aftermath of the Kapsin Incident. *Jiji shinpō* published an article entitled "Chōsen dokuritsutō no shokei" (On the Execution of the Independence Party in Korea) a month prior to the publication of "Datsu-aron." The execution, the article argued, was utterly "barbaric" and "inhumane" because not only the leaders but also their family members were executed: "From the perspective of one with civilized emotions, the cruelty displayed makes me shudder with fear, as I feel compassion for the ill-fated people."[62] Emphasizing that he belongs among the civilized people because of his civilized emotions, Fukuzawa states the following:

> Observing the emotions of those in Korea, it appears that, just like the Chinese, they are combative and hostile in nature, which is beyond our comprehension. I believe that we are equal by official treaty. But with regard to their emotions, if they do not leave the confines of the Chinese and learn the right way of civilization, and further attain the condition in which we could relate to each other without being completely taken aback, we can only categorize the Koreans in the same way as the Chinese.[63]

The typical narrative that situates Asia as "backward" and Euro-America (and Japan) as "civilized" here aligns with an evolutionary narrative of emotions, which identifies the use of force as manifestation of "combative," hence "barbaric," emotions. To validate the alignment, the narrative further takes up Saigō Tsugumichi as an example; it claims that even though Saigō Takamori was a "rebel against the nation" for bringing about the Seinan War in 1877, his brother Saigō Tsugumichi had been able to occupy a central place in the Meiji government. The following statement sums up the argument: "Once equipped with the power to kill, there is no need to kill. This is the strength of civilization."[64] The use of force, although necessary for any nation to have, should be controlled, and the ability to control force is equated with "the strength of enlightenment." In this rhetorical scheme, "barbaric emotions" are rendered visible in the use of force, whereas "civilized emotions" are represented by refraining from the use of force. Japan, which in reality does not have the means to use force, becomes a collective that possesses a heart and a mind of civilized men. In short, the rhetorical scheme of "Datsu-aron" produces both the civilized emotions that control the use of force and the barbaric "Asian" emotions that allegedly appear in the very use of force.

"Datsu-aron" ends in the following manner:

> To go about [our foreign relations], therefore, we have no time to wait for the neighboring countries to achieve enlightenment to develop Asia together. If anything, we need to transcend them and be with Euro-America in our endeavor. In dealing with China and Korea, no special consideration is necessary just because they are our neighbors. We should treat them the way Westerners would. If we affiliate ourselves with bad people, we cannot avoid bad names. In my heart (*kokoro*), I sever the ties with the evil people of East Asia.[65]

The rhetorical strategy I discussed earlier is again apparent: "We" will join Euro-America in the endeavor, because we are equal to them in our emotions, which are "civilized" enough to control the use of force and sever ties with the evil people, the barbarians who use that very force. The "heart" differentiates Japan from China and Korea, thereby securing for Japan the identity of "the most civilized nation in Asia." "Datsu-aron" thus produces a position that acts like (hence identifies with) Euro-America "internally," and the Japanese will further internally treat Koreans and Chinese as Euro-Americans do. It goes without saying that if Japan were to *internally* "sever the ties with the evil people" and join the "civilized countries of the West," it would be exempt from proving its civilized state by any type of action. In effect, it can find relief for the anxiety that intensified in the aftermath of the Kapsin Incident by naming *nonaction* as the civilized act. Positing the use of force as an act of a barbarian, the narrative of "Datsu-aron" conceals the reality Japan faced, the inability to take action as a civilized country, and succeeds in making the rhetorical link between "the leader of Asia" and Japan. In light of the unified call for aggression after the Kapsin Incident, coupled with the inability to protect national honor by the use of force, Fukuzawa had to rely on a new narrative technique to bring about rhetorical fulfillment and gain temporary relief.

In spite of the fact that *Murenren* and "Datsu-aron" argue for different goals (Asianism and de-Asianization), and in spite of the fact that they respond to slightly different historical events, they perform the same function—providing rhetorical resolution to Japan's anxiety via its position in East Asia. They clearly share the cofigurative model of desire that shapes the urge to conceal the geopolitical reality and seek rhetorical equivalence with the West. Yet precisely because the desire for equivalence is never satiated, it incessantly seeks a new narrative that rhetorically (and only temporarily) posits equivalence, which can only amplify the desire itself.

The textual realm of the *shōsetsu*, which is named the realm of "the social" (*sewa*), as we shall see in Chapter 5, is a realm in which such geopolitical reality does not become an issue. In other words, by adopting the narrative boundaries of the social, the *shōsetsu* does not allow such a vulnerable reality to enter the picture. I do not wish to claim that the realm of the *shōsetsu* logically (in the manner of cause and effect) engages with the narrative technology that we saw in either *Murenren* or "Datsu-aron." What I want to suggest is the possible synchrony between the urge to conceal the geopolitical reality and the coming into being of the textual boundary of the *shōsetsu*, both of which appeared at this particular historical juncture.

De-Asianization = Depoliticization?

Forms of rhetorical fulfillment we identified in *Murenren* continued to be reproduced through a group of texts later identified as *kokken shōsetsu* (translated as *shōsetsu* of "national rights").[66] Fujita Mokichi's *Saimin igyōroku* (*A Great Feat of a Savior*, 1886), for example, features a very similar hero: the savior, though born and raised in China, is in fact of Japanese descent. Sudō Nansui's *Chijin no yume* (*Dreams of Foolish Men*, 1887), an allegorical *shōsetsu*, posits Japan as the force of reform that ought to take an aggressive stance if necessary. Works such as these that thematized Japan's place in the new world order were numerous, especially in the decade following the time period on which this book focuses.[67] Although complicit with forces of concealment, works of *kokken shōsetsu* directly addressed the issues of national identity in the works. In this respect, the artistic *shōsetsu*, a site of depoliticization, engages more specifically with the narrative technology I identified in "Datsu-aron" because in "Datsu-aron," the rhetorical fulfillment is based on severance and the complete effacement of the geopolitical reality. In place of a conclusion, let us look at the rhetorical practices of "Datsu-aron" more closely in an effort to identify the manner in which they replicate the definition of the *shōsetsu*.

Recall that the logic of "Datsu-aron" designates the use of force as a barbaric act. Placed in the domestic context, such an assertion takes on additional meaning. Not only does it restrain the call for the immediate attack against China and Korea but it situates the radical activists who supported the antigovernment uprisings as those who had been driven to them by "barbaric Asian sentiments." The de-Asianizing impulses thus replicate the effacement of the *zen'aku jasei* discourse that is dramatized in the translated and political works of fiction.

This becomes especially apparent when we see that "Asia" of "Datsu-aron" is constructed primarily through the value/linguistic system of Confucian thought.[68]

> In this age of enlightenment, [Koreans and Chinese] uphold Confucianism for their education, and "compassion, righteousness, courtesy, and wisdom" (*jingi reichi*) as school doctrines, and only focus on the externals of things. Yet in reality, they are not only ignorant of fundamental rules but are morally corrupt and display tremendous cruelty, all the while showing no sense of remorse.[69]

The Asian emotions that appear in the use of force are attributed to "compassion, righteousness, courtesy, and wisdom," the main Confucian virtues, which shape Bakin's literary cosmos discussed in the previous chapter. This is a realm of the political discourse in which *zen'aku jasei* dominates the textual surface.

The alignment between "Asia" and domestic political uprisings is further apparent in *Kokumin no tomo*'s references to the Osaka Incident of November 1885, which was yet another failed uprising, led by a group of former Jiyūtō members who plotted to bring about another coup in Korea with the intention of bringing down the central (Meiji) government. For the leaders of the Osaka Incident, the idea was to develop a new international crisis with China—which would have surely absorbed much of the government's attention—and, using the opportunity, organize a number of uprisings to overthrow the government. Known for its criticism of "stalwart youth" (*sōshi*), *Kokumin no tomo* was predictably critical of the Osaka Incident. Condemning the leaders of the incident, it described the event as "a deliberate act to stage *The Water Margin* in present-day Japan."[70] The reference to *The Water Margin*, one of the classics of *hakuwa* fiction, is provocative here, especially because this is a time when the "Chineseness" of *hakuwa* fiction is being brought to the fore, which is apparent in the opening passage of *Shōsetsu shinzui*, which filtered out Luo Guanzhong and Li Yu from its *gesaku* genealogy of "our country." We can thus read *Kokumin no tomo*'s narrative as an attempt to condemn the leaders of the Osaka Incident as outlaws who were driven by Asian emotions represented in the "Chinese" classic *The Water Margin*. In such a discursive paradigm, the series of uprisings can only be deemed barbaric and hence manifestation of Asian emotions.

Kokumin no tomo's characterization of the Osaka Incident with the specific reference to *The Water Margin* compellingly links "Datsu-aron" and *Shōsetsu shinzui*'s rhetorical scheme. The linguistic tradition that can be traced back to *The Water Margin* makes up the *hakuwa* narratives, which, for *Shōsetsu shinzui*'s audience, was one that Bakin embodied. In effect, the linguistic system of *zen'aku jasei* that shaped didacticism, a language at the core of the discourse that constituted the imaginary revolution of the uprisings, was, at this moment in time, designated "Asian." Bakin's literary cosmos, and hence the language mobilized by the participants of the uprisings, becomes identified as "Asian" (and by extension "non-Japanese") and therefore "barbaric." Depoliticizing tendencies inscribed in *Shōsetsu shinzui* clearly had an ally in de-Asianizing impulses.

Yet I must hasten to add that Bakin was certainly not associated with the non-Japanese in the Edo period, let alone an Asia that needed to be left behind, in spite of the fact that Bakin's literary cosmos relied heavily on *hakuwa* fiction and the binaries tied to Confucian thought. Although the Confucian elements were (and are) often emphasized in discussions of Bakin's works, Bakin's literary cosmos also included elements of "native learning" (*kokugaku*), a form of study that developed in the Edo period in response to Sinocentric studies that sought to identify "Japan" through classical and philological studies. Moreover, among the group of critics who helped Bakin theorize his literary techniques were scholars of native learning, most notably Tonomura Jōsai (1778–1847), who was a student of Motoori Norinaga (1730–1801)—one of the "four great men" of native learning—and Ozu Keisō (1804–58), a student of Norinaga's son.[71] Hagiwara Hiromichi, also a scholar in native learning, was not shy about declaring his admiration of Bakin's works and agreed to write a sequel to Bakin's incomplete work, *Kyōkakuden* (*Tales of Chivalrous Men*, 1832–34) when commissioned to do so.[72] In other words, the association between Bakin and "Asia" as "non-Japan" is clearly a mid-1880s phenomenon, which arose within the dynamic of "Asian anxiety," constituting itself as one of the forces that replicated the de-politicization and de-Asianization of the *shōsetsu*.[73]

Furthermore, despite the fact that *Kokumin no tomo* undoubtedly shared the de-Asianizing impulses with *Shōsetsu shinzui*, their political outlooks differed significantly. They shared the rejection of the "barbaric" political subjects that embodied these Asian emotions, but they ultimately varied on the "civilized" figure they sought to promote. As Kimura Naoe has shown in her *Seinen no tanjō*, *Kokumin no tomo* rejected the embodiment of the *zen'aku jasei* discourse (the stalwart youth) and espoused an "internally sophisticated" figure of "the youth" (*seinen*) who would define a new political sphere as the "nation's friend."[74] In effect, "the youth" was very much a political figure. *Shōsetsu shinzui* sought instead to depoliticize the realm of the *shōsetsu*, and as Chapter 5 will make clear, the protagonist of the *shōsetsu* was a depoliticized figure. Of course, such a subject position is very political in itself, but it manifests in the form of the concealment of politics, which ought to be differentiated from the political stance of *Kokumin no tomo*'s "youth."

Constructions of "Asia" in early to mid-1880s Japan thus intersected with the *shōsetsu* in varying ways, at times as parallel discursive movements that synchronized with the definition of the *shōsetsu*, and at other times as a force that endorsed the boundaries of the *shōsetsu*. The *shōsetsu* locates its identity in the depoliticized figure that embodies "civilized" emotions, a figure liberated from the Asian, Bakinesque *zen'aku jasei* emotions. The textual boundaries of the *shōsetsu*, in which such a depoliticized figure lies, further engage with the forces that sought rhetorical and temporary relief by concealing the vulnerable geopolitical reality; the story line of the *shōsetsu*, as we shall see more clearly in the following chapter, develops in a realm in which such geopolitical reality is deliberately effaced. Because of such concealment, the *shōsetsu* becomes an ostensibly neutral medium, and, as a form of knowledge, a means to "naturally" elevate the mind of its readers. Inscribed in knowledge, however, are the forces of mimicry to which *shōsetsu* is complicit. This ideologically charged site of the *shōsetsu* thus enacts multiple levels of concealment and continually reenacts forces of imperial longing.

FIVE

Tōsei shosei katagi

The "Social" Shōsetsu

Jidai *(Historical)* / Sewa *(Social)*

The previous chapters discussed the various forces of depoliticization that form and endorse the boundaries of *shōsetsu*. We turn now to how such boundaries manifest in the *shōsetsu* and attempt to identify the textual realm where *shōsetsu* finds its raison d'être by taking up *Tōsei shosei katagi* (*The Character of Modern Students*, 1885), Tsubouchi Shōyō's experimental *shōsetsu* written concurrently with *Shōsetsu shinzui*. Despite the common understanding that *Tōsei shosei katagi* is a failed embodiment of *Shōsetsu shinzui*, *Tōsei shosei katagi* is worthwhile nevertheless for the way it works with *Shōsetsu shinzui* to produce the depoliticized textual space of *shōsetsu*. The dialogue between them will show that the "political" peripherized in the configuration of the *shōsetsu* was not limited to "revolutionary politics" but included the political arena of the Meiji elites as a whole.

To begin, let us briefly revisit *Shōsetsu shinzui* and examine how it expounds on the temporal framework of the *shōsetsu* in a section entitled "Shōsetsu no shurui" (The Types of *Shōsetsu*): "If we classify *shōsetsu* according to subject matter, *shōsetsu* falls into two categories—past (*jidai*, historical) and present (*sewa*, social). Tales of the bygone past (*ōseki monogatari*) are constructed around historical figures or real events of the past, and tales of the present (*gense monogatari*) around contemporary emotions and manners."[1] The English equivalents "historical" and "social" are provided parenthetically in *katakana* scripts. The latter dichotomy describes the types of *shōsetsu*: the historical portrays "historical figures or real events of the past," and the social portrays "the emotions and manners"—the social lives of the characters. Bakin's works, of course, fall into the category of the historical *shōsetsu*, whereas the *shōsetsu* that *Shōsetsu shinzui* promotes is the social.

Historical/social is not a self-evident dichotomy. The definitions of the respective types of *shōsetsu* do not oppose each other in any obvious way; if the social *shōsetsu* were to oppose the historical, the objects of description should have been "real events in the present" and/or "figures making history." Otherwise, the historical *shōsetsu* should have featured "emotions and manners of the past." What purpose, then, does this dichotomy serve? The binary does not describe the available types of *shōsetsu*, though the title of this section may lead us to think otherwise. Given that *Shōsetsu shinzui* is a prescriptive rather than descriptive text, the historical/social binary is better situated as yet another attempt by *Shōsetsu shinzui* to define the boundaries of the *shōsetsu*. From the apparent opposition between social and historical, we can deduce that the textual realm of the social logically precludes the defining constituents of the historical. That is to say, "figures making history" are excluded from the social. Moreover, a section entitled "Shujinkō no setchi" (Configuring the Protagonist) further elaborates on the social by saying, "*Shōsetsu*, being a medium that portrays human emotions, must thematize a love relationship between a man and a woman (*ome no sōshi*)."[2] Instead of a story in which "figures making history" are prominent, the social *shōsetsu* thus features a story of male-female romance in which figures making history do not take part.

Such a definition of the social *shōsetsu* constitutes a criticism of a set of works popular among the literati of the time, works that can be traced back to *Karyū shunwa* (*Romantic Stories of Blossoms*), an abridged translation of Bulwer-Lytton's *Ernest Maltravers* and *Alice*, featuring "a beautiful woman and a man of talent" (*kajin saishi*). The stories feature a poor but admirable political activist who meets an ideal partner in his quest for his political cause: a beautiful and wealthy woman who can support him materially and intellectually. The stories typically end with the protagonist's political success and consummation of love.[3] Invariably, such works focused on the political arena as they featured the love romance of figures making history. The social *shōsetsu* thus attempts to dissociate itself from such a set of works.

In accordance to the definition of the social *shōsetsu*, *Tōsei shosei katagi* constructs its main story away from the political sphere with which a beautiful woman and a man of talent were linked. The story line focuses mainly on a student named Komachida Sanji, who, despite his diligence and talent, has no chance of ever joining the ranks of figures making history. He falls in love with a geisha, Tanoji, who was once his own adopted sister. Although Sanji knows that an affair with a geisha can only be detrimental to his future, he nonetheless cannot sever his tie with her, and he "internally" struggles with his attachment to her. Later in the story, we find that Tanoji is in fact the long-lost sister of Moriyama Tomoyoshi, Sanji's good friend and classmate. This allows the story to conclude by raising the possibility of marriage between Sanji and Tanoji.[4]

It is important to note that they do not actualize their marriage. Such an ending marks an attempt to draw a line between *Tōsei shosei katagi* and *Karyū shunwa*–type narratives that ended in consummation of love between a beautiful woman and a man of talent. *Tōsei shosei katagi's* ending, in other words, resists the textual association with such a set of works and hence the textual arena in which figures making history took center stage.

Tōsei shosei katagi is full of such efforts to sever ties with "the historical" realm. As the narrative tries to demarcate the boundaries of the social and attempts to peripherize the historical, the tension is played out between the historical and the social realms. The historical realm is recognizable in the text, given that the figures making history govern the socioeconomic order in which the story of the social takes place. Yet "the social" tries desperately to efface "the historical," at times successfully and at others not so successfully. By identifying such tension between them, this chapter seeks to unravel the textual dynamic of the social, the space where the *shōsetsu* finds its identity.

The "Society of Students" and "the Competitive World of the Shizoku*": Socioeconomic Order of the "Present"*

From the onset of the narrative, *Tōsei shosei katagi* makes apparent its urge to peripherize figures making history by focalizing on the world of uncertainty. First we see students and rickshaw men presented as symbols of the new world, one group signifying "success" and the other "failure":

> The floating world changes in varying ways. When the *bakufu* prospered, only samurai succeeded in the grand city of Edo. The capital has now changed its name to Tokyo. Owing to the enlightenment, there is no discrimination now between the upper and lower classes; those with ability (*sai*) move up and become wealthy. While a son of a seaweed seller acquires a beard and rides a black-lacquered rickshaw, a former aristocrat runs through the street as a rickshaw man. In an unstable world, where there are varying kinds of prosperity and poverty, one must have intelligence to make ends meet.[5]

This passage features the rhetoric of "success and advancement" (*risshin shusse*), which was a pseudo-egalitarian dream specific to the post-Restoration era, based on the belief that education could lead one to success and wealth. In this narrative, students are the ones leading the path to success and advancement and are hence the ones with the potential for upward mobility.[6] In sharp contrast, rickshaw men embody downward mobility. Just as "a son of a seaweed seller" can attain wealth through education, a "former aristocrat" can end up pulling a rickshaw. Whether or not a former aristocrat in Meiji ever fell so low as to become a rickshaw man is another issue; the point is that becoming a rickshaw man signifies failure in this narrative. In the "unstable world," one must be equipped with "ability," or else one is destined to become a rickshaw man. Success and advancement are thus governed by the logic of the "survival of the fittest": in order to survive in this new world, one must have the "ability" to do so.

The view of this world soon grows even grimmer. After the contrast between success and failure in the new order is drawn, students and rickshaw men are equated in number:

> Given that this is a large city, people of all kinds come from all four directions. Among them, the largest in number are rickshaw men and students. They were both estimated at 60,000 seven years ago.[7] Now the number has even grown. There are rickshaw stands everywhere; wherever you go, you see students. When you see signs for student boardinghouses, you see paper lanterns for rickshaws. There are Western *shijuku* [private schools] down the alleys off the main streets, and there are rickshaws waiting for customers at intersections. . . . How extreme is the number of students and how excessive is the increasing number of rickshaws! . . . But with only a few customers, there are rickshaw men who go home empty-handed. And there are students—the same students who, upon leaving their hometown, were determined to kill themselves if they couldn't get the education they needed for success—changing immediately for the worse. They become delinquents, and very few actually graduate.[8]

In this unstable world, rickshaw men need to struggle to attract "a few customers," and "very few [students] actually graduate." The growing number of students and rickshaw men increases competition in the respective sectors, which are both governed by the same principle of prosperity and poverty.[9]

But why students and rickshaw men? On the one hand, these two groups were the symbols of society on the way toward "enlightenment": rickshaws were developed in 1869, a year after the Restoration, and students who dreamed of success and advancement were, of course, a product of the pseudo-egalitarian ideology of Meiji. On the other hand, we must not forget that these groups represent the two career paths that many former samurai (*shizoku*) had taken after the fall of the Tokugawa shogunate. The successful *shizoku* made sure that their sons led the way toward success and advancement, whereas the failed *shizoku* went into manual labor. Rickshaws, a newly established business, were a convenient means of eking out a livelihood.

The opening passage thus introduces the readers to the competitive world of the *shizoku*. These two realms, clearly separated by ability, do not intersect. Once a person is categorized among the "rickshaw men," the path toward success and advancement is forever closed. Even if one gains entry to the world of students, success and advancement are not guaranteed; one must compete and succeed among others with the ability to achieve success. With such a passage, *Tōsei shosei katagi* opens the door to "the society of students" who are trying desperately *not to fail*.[10]

One further note on the society of students taken up in *Tōsei shosei katagi*: the text focuses solely on private schools (*shijuku*) affiliated with the Freedom and People's Rights activists, as opposed to government-supported schools (*kanritsu gakkō*). Schools that were owned by government officials were in the process of being turned into state schools, whereas those run by the Freedom and People's Rights activists remained private. The main objective of the educational reforms enforced by the first minister of education, Mori Arinori (1847–89), was to produce supporters of the government. By 1885, when *Shōsetsu shinzui* and *Tōsei shosei katagi* were published, the Tokyo Law School had merged with Tokyo University, and this institution, which would later become Tokyo Imperial University, was slowly but surely becoming the elite establishment where future government leaders were trained. When it was officially founded in 1886, Tokyo Imperial University was placed under the direct control of the Ministry of Education, and its university president—who was in fact also the dean of its law school—took direct orders from Mori Arinori. Government policies on education were clearly driven by the effort to establish a firm system of control among the government elite and institutionally exclude those educated in private schools from entering the government. Precisely when *Shōsetsu shinzui* and *Tōsei shosei katagi* were written, an irreversible hierarchy was being instituted between state and private schools. The future of private-school students was grim: if the government were to succeed in its endeavor, they would have no hope of taking part in politics at the center. Not coincidentally, the intellectuals arguing for the "autonomy of knowledge," an expression of will to power that sought to sever knowledge from politics, were affiliated with private schools.

In the midst of such political/educational reforms, *Tōsei shosei katagi* focused on "the society of students" of private schools. Given that Tsubouchi Shōyō graduated from Tokyo University, coupled with the geographical setting of *Tōsei shosei katagi* (many events take place in Hongō, where Tokyo University is located), later critics were quick to assume that the student life portrayed in this work was that of Tokyo University students. However, the protagonist, Komachida Sanji, is clearly introduced as "a student left behind after a *shijuku's* public gathering,"[11] and all the other students that appear in this story are those attending private schools, whether it be a law or medical school. *Tōsei shosei katagi* thus features a life of uncertainty, the life of students who were on the verge of becoming excluded from the institutionally protected sphere of success.

This suggests that one important sphere remains effaced throughout *Tōsei shosei katagi*: the realm of utmost success controlled and governed by those at the center of the government. "Success" in *Tōsei shosei katagi* is represented by activists of the Freedom and People's Rights Movement, the members of the opposition parties. In this textual world, success is limited to those who are trying to gain control of the government and does not include those in control. The only government-affiliated character who appears in this work is the protagonist's father, Komachida Kōji, who, as we shall see shortly, epitomizes failure. Even the successful characters of this work are struggling not to fail. It is within such a competitive world that our protagonist, Komachida Sanji, strives to survive and locates a textual space in which the *shōsetsu* finds its identity.

As I will discuss in more detail later in this chapter, such space of the *shōsetsu* clearly embodies a will to power, one that is on a par with the advocates of the autonomy of knowledge. *Shōsetsu* is a space that gives the "life of uncertainty" a voice, one that excludes those in power.

The "Present": "Success" and "Failure" in Tōsei shosei katagi

The boundaries of the social *shōsetsu* are further complicated by the temporal setting of this world of uncertainty. The establishment of the temporal framework is always ideologically bound: "the present" is never a simple "here and now." It always involves selecting a beginning and an end; the beginning sets a break between the past and present, whereas the end sets the break between the present and the future. Such choices are inevitably ideological.

The Meiji Restoration was a dramatic event for many, but an event that had yet to be narrated as "history," which makes its portrayal in *Tōsei shosei katagi* all the more ideological. Since the Meiji Restoration was the foundation of the Meiji government, whether or not to unconditionally endorse it as the beginning of the present was clearly a political statement. The revolutionaries involved in the uprisings, for example, could only situate the Meiji present as a temporary setback. Although many such men welcomed the fall of the Tokugawa shogunate, the Meiji order was by no means their final answer, which is evident from the ways in which they prefigured the future and looked beyond the here and now by mobilizing images of the French Revolution and the histories of peasant uprisings. *Tōsei shosei katagi* is in clear dialogue with such a discursive environment. The configuration of the present—and in turn the past and the future—in the 1880s must be considered in this light.

The story in *Tōsei shosei katagi* takes place from 1881 to 1883, but with flashbacks and the narrations of the characters' background, the story goes back as far as the Battle of Ueno in May 1868—one of the battles of the Boshin War fought between the imperial army and the Tokugawa shogunate.[12] The story, in other words, begins when the Meiji period began, which is one clear indication that the text endorses the Meiji order.

Further implications of this designated beginning can be revealed by an analysis of the stories of "success" and "failure" in *Tōsei shosei katagi*, which feature another kind of comment on "beginnings" and "endings." Determining when and how the characters acquired their present socioeconomic positions will allow us to see the *shōsetsu*'s political stance vis-à-vis the new Meiji order.

Success in *Tōsei shosei katagi* is best represented by Moriyama Tomosada, the father of one of the main characters, and Miyoshi Shōemon, whom Tomosada befriends. Moriyama Tomosada and Miyoshi both belong to a generation that, prior to the Restoration, held political, economic, and social status within the Tokugawa system. In fact, they had once been on the side of the shogunate. Tomosada is a former samurai (*shizoku*) from Shizuoka, the region to which the last shogun, Tokugawa Yoshinobu (1837–1913), retreated during the Battle of Ueno. At one point in the narrative, Tomosada explicitly states that he was in fact "serving by the shogun" (*ohizamoto ni tsukaete*, or literally, "by his knees") upon the breakout of the war.[13] Yet after the Restoration, Tomosada had become extremely successful "by immersing himself in various businesses, changing his ways *in accordance with the passage of time*" (emphasis mine).[14] He begins to work at an export company and "succeeds in acquiring tremendous wealth."[15] Miyoshi similarly achieves success in the new world of Meiji.

Prior to the Restoration, he was an owner of a long-standing sword shop, a business very much tied to the *bakufu* system.[16] "His family business deteriorated with the coming of the Restoration," but Miyoshi took risks in the "dollar market" and "rice market" and made a fortune.[17] With the money he earned in such trade, he later became a president of a bank and has now become very successful.

Both Tomosada and Miyoshi had a level of success under the shogunate but then succeeded in businesses linked to nation-building projects specific to the post-Restoration era; export and banking intersect with the pressing need to establish Japan's position among the world powers. In effect, these characters acquired their current positions by capitalizing on the needs of the new world and adapting to the Meiji system "in accordance with the passage of time." Their lives, as they have them now, began with the Restoration itself, and their success is procured within the newly established socioeconomic structure.

In contrast to Tomosada and Miyoshi, who epitomize success, Komachida Kōji, the father of the protagonist Komachida Sanji, embodies failure. His is the story of a rise and fall, which begins with the Meiji Restoration. Kōji had fought with the imperial army during the Boshin Wars and thus "had connections with those in the government."[18] Recognized for "his contribution to the Restoration," he became a public servant at a ministry soon afterward; he attained "extravagant pay from the government and enjoyed an exceeding amount of glory, leading a luxurious life with his wife and mistress," at least temporarily.[19] Along the way, however, he also incurred many debts with money lenders, and during a major reform at the ministry for which he worked, Kōji was dismissed for being "an inappropriate human resource (*jinzai*) for the new world," clearly unable to positively engage with nation-building projects that meet the needs of the new world.[20] Like Tomosada's and Miyoshi's, the conditions of Kōji's rise and fall are specific to the post-Restoration era, albeit in an entirely opposite manner. Throughout the course of the story, he lives with his failure, striving to pay off his debts.

These representations of success and failure in *Tōsei shosei katagi* designate the Meiji Restoration as the beginning of "the present"—the Meiji Restoration is the time when the current lives of these characters begin. This designation of "the beginning," moreover, reconstructs "the past" and places a clear value judgment upon it. Not only are the two success stories a result of the characters' adherence to the Meiji system but they are also contingent upon a complete conversion—a conversion away from the political, economic, and social systems of the past. In order to succeed, both Tomosada and Miyoshi needed to relinquish the positions they had occupied in the past; or rather, jettisoning the past is the very condition for success. By representing success in this manner, *Tōsei shosei katagi* constructs the era prior to the Restoration—the *bakufu* system to which these characters once belonged—as "the bygone past." The current system within which they live exists as if independent from that of the *bakufu*; the two systems are completely discontinuous in *Tōsei shosei katagi*.

In effect, the present in *Tōsei shosei katagi* is a naturalized one. The political, economic, and social order of Meiji is fixed; it exists, and there is nothing that can be done to change it. In fact, no character in the text questions the basic paradigm that shapes the world within which he lives.[21] Even the "failed" characters in *Tōsei shosei katagi* are resigned to the idea that the Meiji order is here to stay. While the successful characters continue their path toward wealth, the failed characters struggle to make ends meet within their reality, their present.

I will later discuss in detail how the success and failure of the older generation are carried over to the members of the next generation, namely, Komachida Sanji, the protagonist of the story, and his best friend, Moriyama Tomoyoshi. These two characters, too, attempt to find their positions within the fixed parameters of the present. They do not seek to rearrange the present system, nor do they question the foundation upon which it is built. In this textual world, no one seeks a revolutionary change; no one dreams for an alternative order beyond the here and now. Such a construction of the present is a clear criticism of the Freedom and People's Rights activists who designated the Meiji Restoration as an "incomplete" revolution.

However, this does not mean that the text uncritically endorses the Meiji system and its patron, the Meiji government. Success in this work is brought to those who neither fought for nor contributed to the Restoration (Moriyama Tomosada), and failure befalls those who did (Komachida Kōji). *Tōsei shosei katagi* thus valorizes the conversion from the past, not the active contribution to the Restoration itself. Additionally, the absence of government-sponsored schools and those belonging to the realm of utmost success further constitutes a critical commentary on the Meiji order; if *Tōsei shosei katagi* had uncritically endorsed the new order of Meiji, the realm of utmost success would have been granted a central voice in the text. Instead, the text focuses on and gives voice to the private schools and the world of uncertainty; even the successful characters in this work, Moriyama and Miyoshi, do not enjoy the highest level of success. While affirming the Meiji system through the designation of such a beginning, *Tōsei shosei katagi* also maintains a critical stance against the Meiji order itself.

"Historical": The System of Self-Enrichment and Preservation

An inquiry into the socioeconomic sector to which the successful characters of *Tōsei shosei katagi* belong shows how they sustain their system of power: they compose a tightly knit group of "human resources" (*jinzai*)—those who have both the ability (*sai*) and the resources to contribute to the nation-building projects. The government is at the center of this community, which exists solely for its own enrichment and preservation. Not only are individuals assets to the nation but relationships among them are "cashed in" and mobilized for collective enhancement. Success in the present only exists within this system, while failure signifies exclusion from this system.

Consider the figure of Moriyama Tomosada, who achieved success at the export company. Having entered the international market in trade, Meiji Japan was in great need of foreign currency. To establish an economy comparable to those of the Western powers, the government invested in various businesses to enrich the country and encouraged the development of export businesses. As president of a bank, Miyoshi, too, can be located within the same system. Domestically, the Meiji government instituted numerous policies to gain capital; for example, the land tax revisions of 1873 and the abolition of the stipend system of 1876. Those who received favorable treatment (high-ranking *shizoku* and the aristocracy) increased their wealth by investing in businesses that were endorsed and thereby protected by the government—these businesses included banks, shipping companies, and coal mines. In the second decade of the Meiji period (1878–87), moreover, the government was desperately trying to control deflation. Matsukata Masayoshi (1835–1924), the minister of finance, took various measures to rejuvenate an economy that had floundered after the Seinan War. His most notable measures included privatization of government-owned factories and initiation of financial programs to support profitable businesses. Matsukata's policies safeguarded entrepreneurs and businesses whose agendas corresponded with those of the government, while forcing others to go out of business. In short, business and political leaders together defined what constituted the human resources of the time, sustaining the system of self-enrichment.

The continuation of this ruling system lies in its ability to produce and reproduce the next generation of supporters. The figure of Tomoyoshi shows how the ruling system produces the next generation of supporters and how privileges were handed down to sons. Although the narrative does not explicitly state this, the privileges Tomoyoshi enjoys are likely brought about by his father's personal/business affiliations. In the third chapter, Tomoyoshi states that he went to Yoshiwara, a well-known licensed prostitution quarter in Tokyo, with "his friends who work for Mitsubishi."[22] Tomoyoshi's father had become successful "seven or eight years ago" in his export business, that is, at the end of the first decade of Meiji, which is precisely when the Mitsubishi group began to monopolize sea transport and seized most of the government-supported trade.[23] The relationship that Tomoyoshi has with those at Mitsubishi most likely stems from his father's business dealings.

In order to preserve Mitsubishi's monopoly, financial support from privileged entrepreneurs was vital. In this light, it is no coincidence that the Moriyamas, the ones with the Mitsubishi connection, have a close tie with Miyoshi, president of a bank: Tomoyoshi lives with Miyoshi's nephew Ninna; Moriyama's friend Sonoda, a *shizoku* from Shizuoka (like the Moriyamas), works at Miyoshi's bank. Sonoda's relationship with Miyoshi is a close one, which is evident from the fact that Miyoshi "had lately given a house he owned to Sonoda."[24] Miyoshi himself had become the president of a bank through "the support of acquaintances who visited him to consult him about starting a bank."[25] Among these men, personal relationships are "cashed in"—they are assets that further produce and reproduce money. We see interactions of personal/business relationships that are continually transformed into money. Tomoyoshi successfully positions himself within this privileged community, which in turn brings him success of his own.[26]

Soon after Tomoyoshi becomes a lawyer, he visits Shizuoka with his father "to take care of things for the political party he had lately joined."[27] Tomoyoshi apparently shares his father's political views as well as his personal/business affiliates. Like any politician, it is crucial for Tomoyoshi to have the support of his hometown at election time. Clearly, he will inherit his father's power and support in Shizuoka.

Tomoyoshi, moreover, teaches at Tōkō Gakkan, "a law school" that is presumably a private school founded by a lawyer. Being the eldest son of the Moriyama household, he obviously has no financial reason to work. His teaching more likely stems from his political ambitions. Given that suffrage was granted only to men over twenty-five years of age who paid more than fifteen yen in taxes, the vote was limited to those with wealth.[28] A law school is a place where he can seek new connections with voters, the fathers of the students who attend the school, who can afford to send sons to a law school (as opposed to temple-hut schools, or *terakoya*).

Tomoyoshi thus inherits his father's business affiliates as well as his political supporters in his hometown. He builds on his father's ties by further befriending those who are part of the system of self-enrichment and expands his circle of supporters. Tomoyoshi's success is inextricably connected to, if not contingent upon, his status within the privileged community.

Tomoyoshi is portrayed as a diligent student who devotes his time to studying while frowning upon others who frequent the pleasure quarters. He is described as a person who succeeds in a world that is governed by the principle of the survival of the fittest, which suggests that the "ability" that Tomoyoshi possesses is the sole reason for his success.[29] However, he is clearly located within the human resources network of Meiji. In fact, the way in which he is represented in the text problematizes the very ideology of the survival of the fittest and in turn questions whether the Meiji socioeconomic structure is governed by such a principle at all. Ability alone cannot lead one to success; it needs to be endorsed and protected by the governing system. This will be further evident in a comparison between Tomoyoshi and Sanji.

The Komachida Family: "Outside" the System of Self-Enrichment

The way in which the system of self-enrichment operates is highlighted by those who embody failure, namely, Komachida Kōji and his son Sanji. In sharp contrast to Tomoyoshi, Sanji has a father who had been denied his place in the privileged community; no connection is passed down to him. After his dismissal from the ministry, Kōji regrets that he did not educate himself and "depended solely on personal connections" to succeed in the new world.[30] Determined to send his son to school so that Sanji would not follow in his footsteps, Kōji desperately tries to make money for his son's education. How Kōji procures Sanji's tuition is quite indicative of his position.

Sanji is fifteen when Kōji is laid off for not having the ability to contribute to the ruling system, and this is the year Sanji begins to attend a private school. The text says only that Kōji "managed to send [Sanji] to a private Western school despite his strained circumstances."[31] After being laid off, Kōji gets a new job as a bank clerk, which earns him a meager salary, but this job is hardly sufficient to finance his son's education given the old debts. Within the chain of events that follow his dismissal, he dismisses his mistress, Otsune, and his wife begins to work at home. In his situation, Kōji makes the most logical decision: reduce the number of dependents and have his wife work to increase their overall income. His separation from Otsune and his decision to have his wife work are the only recourses available to him.

Two years later, when Sanji is seventeen, his mother falls ill. As a result, Oyoshi—Sanji's adopted sister (later Tanoji, a geisha with whom Sanji falls in love)—begins to manage the household and cares for and takes over the work of her stepmother. Oyoshi's labor, in other words, allows Sanji to continue his studies during this time. In the following year, however, Sanji's mother dies, and Kōji, unable to pay off his "debt of forty or fifty yen," sends Oyoshi out to become a geisha.[32] Sanji, who "had taken a leave from his school after his mother's death," later goes back to school when Kōji's "debt is paid off."[33] Despite the fact that the cause and effect of these two events are not explicitly described, the implication is that Kōji needed to further reduce the number of dependents (and most likely get money from the geisha house) to keep Sanji in school. Thus, Sanji's return to school is contingent upon Oyoshi becoming a geisha.

This highlights the economy of elitism of Meiji. Unlike Moriyama Tomoyoshi, who secures his position through his father's wealth and connections, Komachida Sanji acquires and retains his status as a student through Otsune, his mother, and Oyoshi, his stepsister. The events that follow Kōji's dismissal show what a character removed from a network of success needs to do to procure money: he "sells off" the women in his household. Although Tomoyoshi and Sanji are both students at a private school, their positions within the new system of Meiji are asymmetrical, because one enjoys the privileges of the system of enrichment, whereas the other can get his position only from the sale of women given the exclusion from the system. Their juxtaposition brings to the fore the structure of the ruling community: we see the privileges Tomoyoshi enjoys precisely because Sanji is deprived of them. They are both portrayed as serious students who are quite gifted in their abilities. What distinguishes them is their position in the governing socioeconomic paradigm, which clearly undermines the "success and advancement" ideology.

That *Tōsei shosei katagi* does not endorse this system of enrichment is expressed in its choice of protagonist: the narrative situates Sanji as its protagonist, not Tomoyoshi. After Tomoyoshi appears in chapter 5 to listen to Sanji confess his love for Tanoji, he does not reappear until chapter 16, when the story begins to identify Tanoji's birth family, the Moriyamas. If Moriyama Tomoyoshi had been the protagonist, *Tōsei shosei katagi* would have either been one in which his party, Kaishintō, emerged victorious or a simple success story in which he would achieve prominent status within the Meiji society. Either way, it would have inevitably replicated the textual world of "a beautiful woman and a man of talent," where the political arena takes center stage.

Instead, Sanji is given the role of protagonist. His comments about politics, such as, "There is no merit in joining a political party; in fact, only harm is done by it," reject the dominant mode of success rather than reinforce them.[34] In fact, Sanji's claim against party politics marks a strong disapproval of Freedom and People's Rights politics. Reasons behind such criticism can be better understood by looking at the way party politics was being played out in the early to mid-1880s. As mentioned earlier, suffrage was given only to those with significant wealth. As the Freedom and People's Rights activists started to place more emphasis on winning parliamentary seats, the movement began to reveal itself as a movement exclusively for the upper *shizoku* class. Hence the political arena, like the socioeconomic sector portrayed in *Tōsei shosei katagi*, had become increasingly compartmentalized by excluding those without money and connections. It is not a coincidence that Freedom and People's Rights activists move in and out of the government, making various compromises in the face of the movement's decline. In 1887, for example, key leaders of the movement, such as Itagaki (former Jiyūtō president) and Ōkuma (former Kaishintō leader), were offered the chance to become barons, a rank in the new aristocracy required for those aspiring to be at the center of the government.[35] They quickly left the movement and grabbed the first opportunity to regain power. Sanji's criticism, therefore, is not groundless, especially for a character excluded from the privileged sector.

But *Tōsei shosei katagi*'s strongest rejection of this mode of success is expressed by not granting a dominant voice to such realm of "the historical." The system of success clearly shapes the world within which Sanji lives, and it is here to stay. The readers can access this system and are made aware of its basic mechanism. However, it remains forever in the periphery. Inscribed within the dichotomy of historical/social, therefore, is the urge to create a new space of *shōsetsu* that is putatively dissociated from the system of self-enrichment that exerts control over all political, legal, economic, social, and educational spheres. By focalizing on Sanji and his internal struggle, *Tōsei shosei katagi* effaces "figures making history"; debates on political issues, business dealings, the development of legal systems, and so on are not brought to the fore in this work. The story of *Tōsei shosei katagi* is configured in a textual world that peripherizes the political.

Such a setting is on a par with the depoliticizing tendencies of the autonomy of knowledge, which manifests a will to power in the formation of a new identity away from the political arena. *Tōsei shosei katagi* presents itself as a medium that grants an identity to a life "outside" the institutionalized system of self-enrichment and preservation. In effect, the social defined in *Shōsetsu shinzui* posits a new textual space for the *shōsetsu* in which a story would unfold *alongside of, but never within* the governing system. Yet this space of *shōsetsu* is far from being an egalitarian space that supports those in the lower economic strata. It features its own will to power, just as the proponents of the autonomy of knowledge had. Such will to power is inscribed in Sanji's position as the protagonist of the *shōsetsu*. I will elaborate on the full implication of such a position toward the end of this chapter.

The Socioeconomic Position of Yūjo: *Male-Male Domain and Male-Female Domain*

Tōsei shosei katagi selects a male-female romance as the main story of the *shōsetsu* and a *yūjo* as Sanji's female counterpart in love.[36] The world of *yūjo* underwent tremendous change with the unprecedented transformations brought about by the Meiji Restoration. Financial hardships caused by social upheaval forced women from the former upper classes to enter the pleasure quarters, bringing with them artistic skills and social demeanor previously found only among the upper crust. In early to mid-Meiji, it was very common for women of former samurai families to become *yūjo*. This phenomenon is portrayed through Tanoji, who was once Sanji's adopted sister and the daughter of a respectable public servant.

How the *yūjo* gain and lose their socioeconomic stability identifies the contingencies that shape Sanji and Tanoji's relationship. The market economy that shapes the world of *yūjo* operates very much like the network of self-enrichment that constitutes the sphere of success for men. In both worlds, personal relationships are assets that produce and reproduce money. Just as men capitalize on their personal connections, women "cash in" on their relationships.[37] Of course, the appearance and artistic skills of *yūjo*—perhaps the equivalent of men's "ability"—play an important role in their paths to success. However, they also need to be protected and supported by men of wealth, invariably those in the privileged sphere.

Consider Otsune, who at the beginning of the story appears as Komachida Kōji's mistress. She was once a geisha in Sukiyamachi, an area in downtown Tokyo. When Kōji succeeds and gains a job at a ministry, he takes Otsune in as his mistress, at which point she retires as a geisha and rises up the social ladder. Despite her status as a mistress, her relationship with a public servant gives her respectability and financial stability. As soon as Kōji is laid off, however, she is the first to be dismissed. Losing both her economic stability and social position, she is forced to revert to her old life as a geisha.

The ways in which male fortunes shape the status of women can also be seen in the stories of Tanoji and Kaodori, both of whom were separated from their birth parents during the Battle of Ueno. They were adopted by successful men—successful at least at the time of adoption. Tanoji, then named Oyoshi, became Kōji's daughter and "the child of a prosperous household."[38] Likewise, Kaodori became a daughter of "a wealthy farmer (*gōnō*) residing at Mikawa" named Mizuno Teishichi.[39] The narrative makes it clear that Tanoji and Kaodori were both legally adopted.[40] Gaining a place in the official registry (*koseki*) of successful men signifies stability for women who do not have parents to support them. Within their respective households, both Tanoji and Kaodori temporarily succeeded at gaining an institutionally recognized status.

The situation quickly changes with the tragedies that befall the women's stepfathers. In order to reduce the number of dependents after his dismissal, Kōji sends Tanoji out to become a geisha. Mizuno, who had become quite prosperous with his success in the rice market, loses all his savings and incurs a large debt by continuing to invest in the market. As a result, he can no longer support himself and Kaodori and is forced to sell her off to Yoshiwara, the largest licensed prostitution quarter in Tokyo.[41] As their male supporters lose their socioeconomic positions, Tanoji and Kaodori lose theirs.

Becoming a *yūjo*, however, does not simply signify a downfall for the women in *Tōsei shosei katagi*. In fact, it means severing old socioeconomic ties and securing new ones. Upward mobility is also possible through new connections and relationships. Otsune, for example, leaves Kōji and enters a new circle of acquaintances, as she "borrows some money from people she knew previously" and "publicizes her return through her own means."[42] The narrative does not specify who these people with money are. However, given her later connection with the Moriyamas and Sonoda, the people here may refer to Miyoshi and his personal/business connections. In fact, Otsune and Miyoshi had met prior to her relationship with Kōji, and Miyoshi had thought highly of her ever since.[43]

Otsune's entry into Miyoshi's circle of acquaintances allows her to raise her socioeconomic status once more. By the end of the story, she has become Sonoda's mistress; in fact, she is "about to officially become his legal wife (*honsai*)."[44] Sonoda, it will be recalled, works at Miyoshi's bank and is from Shizuoka, as are the Moriyamas. Otsune thus regains status and social stability by gaining access to this group of men. At least for the time being, her success seems irreversible.

However, the world Otsune enters is not that associated with the highest level of success. The Moriyamas, Sonoda, and Miyoshi have gained a modicum of status by organizing a tightly knit network of human resources, but none of them practice politics at the center, nor do they have the aristocratic titles necessary for entering the Upper House. Otsune will retain her standing as long as Sonoda and Miyoshi maintain their positions. In comparison to other female characters in *Tōsei shosei katagi*, such as Ohide and Kaodori, who cannot develop ties with men of wealth, Otsune is extremely successful in the women's world. Even so, her success is not absolutely stable.

It would actually have been more favorable for Otsune to have become affiliated with the Meiji elites after her separation from Kōji. In fact, her recognition of the advantages of serving their taste is inscribed in her appearance. When she returns to the geisha world, she wears her hair in the "Shinbashi style," a style associated with the Shinbashi pleasure district that was newly developed by the Meiji government officials.[45] This is significant because, being a Sukiyamachi geisha, her original style would have resembled that of the eminent Yanagibashi district, whose main patrons were the *bakufu* elites.[46] Although Yanagibashi maintained its prestige in the early years of Meiji, Shinbashi soon attracted wealthy patrons and became the central entertainment district for the Meiji ruling class. By the time of the Seinan War of 1877, which ended in a decisive victory for the Meiji government, Shinbashi had outstripped Yanagibashi in status, forcing Yanagibashi and its affiliates to convert their styles. By 1883, Sukiyamachi geisha were described as having "the mannerisms of Yanagibashi and the splendor of Shinbashi."[47] The world of *yūjo*, then, is extremely susceptible to shifts in power. To ensure survival, Sukiyamachi geisha like Otsune needed to adapt to the changing world, to convert their fashions to suit the needs of the new ruling class.

Tanoji, with whom Sanji falls in love, is also a Sukiyamachi geisha whose identity is contingent upon the sphere of success. However, Sanji does not have a place in that world; if Otsune's future is unpredictable, Tanoji's prospects with Sanji seem dismal. Numerous obstacles are inherent in their socioeconomic positions, and they must overcome them in order to consummate their relationship.

Male-Male versus Male-Female Domains and Seishitsu versus Socioeconomic Positions

Though this may be self-evident from my discussion so far, the privileged sphere is anchored on male-male relationships. Tomoyoshi's success is brought about by his father's support and connections; the close relationship between the

Moriyamas, Ninna, Miyoshi, and Sonoda clearly attest to this view. In sharp contrast, Sanji is supported by a female network that constitutes his mother, Otsune, and Oyoshi. Through their financial support, Sanji is able to stay in school and get the education he needs. The historical/social dichotomy, and hence *Shōsetsu shinzui*'s definition of the *shōsetsu*, gains a new, gendered dimension in which the historical constitutes the male-male domain and the social, the male-female domain.

To give a voice to the social, *Tōsei shosei katagi* attempts to sever these two textual domains—or at least efface the male-male domain and make the male-female domain dominate the textual order. However, the choice of a *yūjo* as Sanji's partner in love makes it almost impossible to entirely suppress the male-male realm. One specific incident clearly foregrounds how the textual struggle to efface the male-male realm plays out in the socioeconomic factors that govern Sanji and Tanoji's relationship.

In chapter 10 of *Tōsei shosei katagi*, Sanji encounters Yoshizumi, a frequent visitor to the pleasure quarters who is attracted to Tanoji and hence extremely jealous of Sanji. Upon seeing Sanji and Tanoji together, Yoshizumi begins to torment Sanji:

> How envious I am! Of course, I would like to say that you have both the flair and substance, but you have the flair but no substance. How else can we characterize your having a geisha as your mistress while being financially dependent on your father? Your reputation in the quarter seems well established, unlike your reputation at school. . . . I hear that you'll be expelled soon; no, excuse me, I mean graduate soon; you have a bright future ahead of you. . . . No wonder Tanoji is in love with you. Why don't you take her in and live in a two-tatami-mat room? I'll pay your rent.[48]

Unlike the drunken Yoshizumi, who is accompanied by two others, Sanji "had been sober and alone."[49] He thus desperately tries to control himself and tolerates Yoshizumi's slander. However, Sanji is "innately short-tempered" (*seirai kanshaku mochi*) and creates a scene as a result.[50] Tanoji, in order to save the "unsophisticated" (*yonarenu*) Sanji, sides with him and pulls him out of the room to put an end to their conflict.[51] Soon after this incident, Sanji is called into the principal's office and is suspended from school until further notice. Sanji himself later reflects on this event and says, "Given my [righteous] disposition, I am very angry about what happened."[52] Sanji is, however, reluctant to get even with Yoshizumi because that may result in further embarrassment.

The episode summarized here is mainly conveyed in the text by a student named Tsugihara. According to Tsugihara's narrative, the characters' dispositions or temperaments, such as Yoshizumi's jealousy or Sanji's short temper, are the primary reason for the conflict. By emphasizing the role of the characters' dispositions as the cause of their actions, his narrative adds depth to character development, which, as I will discuss shortly, occupies an important place in *Shōsetsu shinzui*.

Yet it is important to note that an examination of the power relations inscribed in the scene offers a very different explanation. At one point in the text, Yoshizumi is introduced as a lawyer. Although he is not at all respected for his skills in law, his family has substantial wealth (*sōtō na shindai*).[53] His membership in Miyoshi and Sonoda's powerful circle is also suggested in the opening scene, in which a "wealthy-looking group of seven men and women"—Yoshizumi, Miyoshi, and Sonoda among them—stroll around the Asukayama area together.[54] Yoshizumi, moreover, is a close friend of a teacher named Kashimori, who teaches at the private school Sanji attends. Yoshizumi's affiliation with Kashimori—as well as with Miyoshi and Sonoda—clearly places him among the privileged network of men.[55]

Sanji needs to tolerate Yoshizumi's behavior given Yoshizumi's connection with Kashimori, the private-school teacher, because any bad report could jeopardize his status at school. In fact, Sanji's frequent visits to Tanoji had become public knowledge soon after his initial meeting with Yoshizumi. Rumors that Sanji had become a "delinquent" (*hōtōka*) spread among his teachers and peers, endangering his position at school.[56] Such a reputation could impede Sanji's successful completion of his studies, which is extremely important, not only for him but for his father. Recall that Kōji did everything in his power—even selling Tanoji to be a geisha—to send Sanji to school. Sanji thus has the obligation to rebuild the Komachida household and recover Kōji's past status. Although Tsugihara claims that Sanji initially remained quiet because he was outnumbered by Yoshizumi and his friends, we see that this is not the only reason for Sanji's silence. Even if the situation had been reversed (Sanji being escorted by his friends and Yoshizumi alone), the power relations among the characters would have remained the same. The hierarchy established between them is based on the connections they have (or the lack thereof); it cannot be inverted by sheer number.

Sanji's anger toward Yoshizumi also cannot be fully explained solely through his disposition. The language Yoshizumi uses heightens the power relations between them: Yoshizumi's slanderous remarks about Sanji's financial situation clearly emphasize the differences in their current socioeconomic positions. By suggesting that he will pay rent for Sanji and Tanoji, Yoshizumi stresses his own financial power, all the while making fun of Sanji for being dependent on his father. Yoshizumi further hints at his connection with Kashimori when he slips and claims that Sanji is going to be "expelled soon." Yoshizumi's remarks emphasizing Sanji's subordinate status understandably make the latter angry; Sanji's "short-tempered" character cannot be the only reason for his outburst.

Later in the story, the narrator reflects on this incident and claims that the conflict began because Sanji was an "unsophisticated youth" (*yonarenu seinen*) and hence unequipped with the social skills necessary to maneuver his way through the situation.[57] The power dynamics of the scene, however, would not have changed in the least even if Sanji had been sophisticated. Social skills could not have overturned the hierarchy that governs Yoshizumi and Sanji's relationship.

If we examine Sanji's encounter with Yoshizumi in light of the characters' socioeconomic positions, we are able to create an entirely different narrative of the scene than that explicitly offered by Tsugihara or the narrator. However, such power dynamics are never foregrounded on the textual surface; the narrative consistently avoids mention of the power relations that exist among the characters. Sanji himself explains that his anger derives from his righteous disposition and refrains from examining the issue of positionality. The narrator, Tsugihara, and Sanji all attribute the cause of the conflict to everything *but* the power structure that governs the characters at the scene. It is as if the narrative as a whole conspires to conceal the socioeconomic factors that bind the characters.

What does the text accomplish by obscuring the socioeconomic positionality of the characters that produces the hierarchy evident in the scene? The key to answering this question lies in characterization, or the portrayal of a character's disposition, characteristic, or attribute (*seishitsu*).

A concern with characters' disposition occupies a significant part of *Shōsetsu shinzui*, as it espouses to produce "true-to-life" figures on the textual surface. In discussing the configuration of the protagonist, *Shōsetsu shinzui* again rejects the portrayal of attributes based on "eight Confucian virtues," which it designates as "idealist," and instead promotes a "realist" method (*genjitsuha*): "The writer creates his characters by using his own imagination to select and judiciously combine a collection of various characteristics found in living men. He relies for the most part on experience and observation to help him formulate those characteristics that will make up elements of people's personalities."[58]

Perhaps predictably, *Shōsetsu shinzui* is much more specific about how dispositions ought *not* to be portrayed (that is, by deploying the language of *zen'aku jasei*), but it is less clear about how to portray characteristics that rely on the writer's "experience and observation." Although portraying a set of characteristics may seem simple, there are a variety of conditions that need to be met on the textual surface. The struggle of producing such characters is a "side effect" of rejecting the literary cosmos of Confucian virtues and the *zen'aku jasei* language. Had *Tōsei shosei katagi* mobilized such language, it would have been using a prescribed formula of attributes alluding to innumerable literary precedents. But if the text was to create a new set of characteristics that do not rely on prior practices, which *Shōsetsu shinzui* promoted and *Tōsei shosei katagi* attempted, it had to treat a character as an empty sign whose identity, personality or otherwise, needs to be filled. Such configuration of characters' disposition can produce problems for other textual objectives, such as effacing the male-male domain. As we shall see later, the need to create true-to-life characters at times interferes with the need to restrict the textual realm to the social. The choices the narrative makes thus foreground the specific rhetorical strategies to delimit the social.

By definition, a given disposition is something that *appears* inherent in a given individual; it is something that seems to grow from the "inside" of a person and not something coerced or induced by some other stimulus. For a writer to endow a character with a disposition on the textual surface, the disposition must be accompanied by a certain act that is *attributable* to the disposition itself. For example, for Sanji to have a "short-tempered" character, he must act accordingly so that we, the readers, can recognize it as his defining characteristic. Moreover, the act must *appear* to have grown out of the character instead of being produced by an external force. If the reader can find other reasons for the action, such as the power relations inscribed in a given scene, the character's disposition cannot take substantive form because the action will not be attributed solely to the disposition. The power relations between characters must therefore be suppressed at a given moment for a disposition to be constructed in the text.

The descriptions of the characters' dispositions, whether they be of Sanji's unsophisticated and short-tempered nature or of Yoshizumi's jealous and wicked tendencies, overshadow their political, economic, and social positions, and hence the hierarchy between them. In *Tōsei shosei katagi*, there is a textual struggle between the depiction of personal attributes and the portrayal of the socioeconomic positions of the characters. The two narratives clash: while one is foregrounded, the other recedes into the background; one must be erased for the other to appear. The section of *Tōsei shosei katagi* that relates Sanji's encounter with Yoshizumi clearly leans toward characterization, forcing the socioeconomic factors to withdraw from the textual surface.

One other question arises from the way in which the scene comes to a close: Why is Sanji saved by Tanoji? Of course, there is nothing special about this in itself; it merely emphasizes Sanji's lack of social skills, which is one aspect of his character. However, if we consider the possibility of Tomoyoshi coming to rescue Sanji, we see significant implications in this scene. In fact, from the progression of the narrative, it would have been quite simple to have Tomoyoshi accompany Sanji. The scene we have been discussing occurs when Sanji leaves his house for the first time after a long period of seclusion because he is invited to celebrate Tomoyoshi's graduation. Tomoyoshi, however, is almost forcefully taken out of the scene: he is unable to attend his own celebration because of a storm.[59] The narrative set the expectation that Tomoyoshi and Sanji would be together, which raises the question of what would have happened had Tomoyoshi witnessed the conflict. Such a hypothetical examination will foreground another textual struggle that is played out in *Tōsei shosei katagi*, namely, the struggle between the narrative of characterization and that of the male-female domain.

The power dynamics of the scene would have changed completely if Tomoyoshi had been present to mediate between Yoshizumi and Sanji. Both Tomoyoshi and Yoshizumi belong to the same network of human resources and share certain connections, such as the ones with Miyoshi and Sonoda. With Tomoyoshi by his side, Sanji's identity would have been first and foremost that of being Tomoyoshi's friend, and thus potentially a member of Yoshizumi's network, rather than a powerless student who is trying to take his favorite geisha away from him.

Moreover, neither Tomoyoshi nor Yoshizumi could have uttered a single word without considering their political positions in their community. The story would have had to accommodate interactions that are governed by the power relations among their own affiliates. In this situation, what could Tomoyoshi have done to control the conflict between Yoshizumi and Sanji? He can hint at his connections, such as the one with Miyoshi, to put an end to the conflict altogether. Known for his upright character, Miyoshi would most likely side with Tomoyoshi and renounce Yoshizumi's behavior. It would definitely be unwise for Yoshizumi to offend someone like Miyoshi, who has the money and power to invest in and protect the group to which they all belong. By skillfully suggesting Miyoshi's name, Tomoyoshi could have saved

Sanji without insulting Yoshizumi too much, thereby establishing himself as a socially adept character.

In effect, this incident would have been highly appropriate for constructing the character of Tomoyoshi, who is repeatedly described as a man of intelligence and social skills (*josai nai*); his peers think highly of Tomoyoshi for being "very talented in social interactions."[60] However, as far as the readers are concerned, he has not been put to test. The importance of portraying a fully rounded character as discussed in *Shōsetsu shinzui* presumably applies to Tomoyoshi as well; he is, after all, one of the main characters of *Tōsei shosei katagi*. In this sense, Sanji's conflict with Yoshizumi would have given Tomoyoshi the perfect opportunity to exhibit his social skills and substantiate people's claims about his disposition.

However, a story evolving from such an exchange would feature the male-male relationships shaped by the hierarchy instituted within the world of success, easily overshadowing the story of Sanji, whose identity lies alongside of—never within—such a community. The need to develop a fully rounded character called Tomoyoshi can only be secondary to the need to retain the focus of the story on the male-female domain.

For the story of male-female relationships to dominate the textual surface, it must deliberately exclude exchanges or interactions between those belonging to the male-male sphere. Or perhaps more accurately, the existence of the male-female domain is contingent upon the textual effacement of the male-male realm. The deliberate and often forceful effacement makes the male-female domain *appear* as if it exists independently of the political, economic, and social systems that govern the male-male relationships. But those socioeconomic systems clearly shape the actions of the characters, even if they are never described.

Illusory or Self-Deluding Love and Komachida Sanji's Interiority

The previous sections focused on how *Tōsei shosei katagi* dissociates its protagonist from the sphere of success and effaces the political arena associated with it. We now turn to the subject position of the protagonist, Komachida Sanji, the embodiment of civilized emotion, a pillar by which the social realm comes into being. Sanji represents the figure of the "learned man" (*gakusha*) whose "neutrality" and its political implication are the loci of our inquiry.[61] His neutrality is textually produced, most evidently though his interior struggle with love. Through Sanji we see how the protagonist of the *shōsetsu* begins to turn inward and finds his identity in love. The story of love in *Tōsei shosei katagi* exists in a realm that deliberately and by design inhibits the exchanges and power dynamics that would otherwise exert considerable power within it. An examination of Sanji's internal struggle, the main theme of the *shōsetsu*, shows that it, too, reinforces the boundaries of such a realm.

Recall that *Shōsetsu shinzui* defines the internal struggle as the war between impure desires (*retsujō*) and reason (*dōri*):

> All human beings, even those who are wise and good, are creatures of carnal desires. Sages and fools alike harbor evil desires—what sets a man apart as good or wise is simply that he suppresses them and uses the exercise of his reason or the strength of his conscience to drive away the hounds of passion. . . . Surely, before [very intelligent, dignified men] attain that irreproachable behavior that others see, they must face many attacks of impure desires. The impure impulses and reason war within them; good conduct is only possible when reason wins.[62]

Komachida Sanji's interiority quite faithfully actualizes this theory. Sanji's reason tells him that he should sever his ties with Tanoji, but his base impulses drive him; consequently, he cannot completely separate himself from her. Sanji repeatedly claims that he is enslaved by "illusory" or "idealistic" love (*kakū no renjō*) or "self-deluding" or "idealistic" tendencies (*kakū no heki*), while his conscience tells him to do otherwise.[63] The following is his soliloquy: "People, when young, have self-deluding tendencies. How foolish it is to seek fantasy so desperately that one loses sight of oneself. Self-deluding tendencies of course are not restricted to love, but the most dangerous of them is fanciful love. . . . Oh Tanoji, you and I are both unfortunate victims of my foolish fantasy."[64]

Sanji thus agonizes over what he characterizes as self-deluding tendencies or idealism. In fact, given that he is too preoccupied with it, he does not consider the specific problems he would face if he were to try to overcome the obstacles. Sanji would, for example, need to find the means to pay off Tanoji's debts, as well as have enough money to finance their life together.[65] Unlike Tomoyoshi, who has already become a lawyer and a Freedom and People's Rights activist, Sanji has yet to decide on his career. In order to live with Tanoji, he must also persuade his father, who relies on Sanji to rebuild the Komachida household. From his father's perspective, the most desirable marriage for Sanji would be one with a woman from a wealthy family, a union that would allow him to join the elite. The stakes are even higher for Tanoji, who belongs to a world within which her survival depends on relationships with successful men. She cannot survive if her primary ties are with a man who does not have the resources to support her. Moreover, for a *yūjo* to maintain her value, she must be "available" to many men. If it becomes known that she has a specific lover, her value as a commodity will inevitably go down. Her status as a geisha can only be hurt by Sanji's existence.

Such issues are surprisingly not brought to the fore in *Tōsei shosei katagi*. Sanji focuses solely on restraining his self-deluding tendencies without acting upon the socioeconomic obstacles that lay between them. In fact, his decision to restrain his idealistic tendencies ultimately peripherizes the socioeconomic sector from the textual surface. Precisely because Sanji does nothing to consummate his relationship, the story of love and the story featuring the characters' political, economic, and social positions do not intersect in *Tōsei shosei katagi*. They are dissociated from one another, as if they are two separate stories evolving independently. These stories could have cohered to produce a variation to the overall narrative progression. If Sanji had tried to find a job in order to support himself and Tanoji, his political stance would have become apparent through the path he chose to pursue. His internal conflict would then have been constructed around his sacrifice of his own goal—to become a *gakusha* who does not get involved in politics—in order to be with Tanoji. Alternatively, if Sanji had sought a career in government-affiliated institutions, he would have become Tomoyoshi's opponent in the political arena, producing an internal struggle that would revolve around betraying his friend for his love. *Tōsei shosei katagi*, however, comes to an end without the two stories merging. The characters' socioeconomic positions remain forever in the background, completely removed from the central theme of love.

Sanji's interiority, his internal conflict with his "illusory love," thus appears to transcend his political, economic, and social position. It is not a coincidence that Sanji's internal struggle remains the same throughout the work: a simple conflict between his desires and his reason. His suffering, in other words, is fixed; there is nothing but his attempt to suppress his "base impulses." As long as his internal struggle revolves around separating himself from Tanoji, he does not have to act upon the obstacles that shape their relationship, and his socioeconomic positionality will not become an issue. This interiority, therefore, can be maintained only by evading action. The space of interiority, the new space of the *shōsetsu*, is a realm of internal struggle that sustains itself by evading action. This is the space of "neutrality," which, as we shall see shortly, finds its counterpart in the subject position of a *gakusha*.

The Politicality of Komachida Sanji's Position: The Gakusha

Tōsei shosei katagi created a protagonist who does not seek institutionalized paths to success. Yet Sanji, as the locus of the new space of the *shōsetsu*, needs to locate a positive identity: this is what he labels the *gakusha*. Talking about Tomoyoshi joining the Kaishintō, Sanji states, "There is no merit in joining a political party; in fact, only harm is done by it. One would look upon theories lightly, become an empty talker, and wouldn't be able to play up to the role required of a *gakusha*, which is to influence public opinion." For Sanji, *gakusha* is a subject position that maintains a critical distance from any political party; it is one that sways public opinion without becoming involved in politics.

Representative intellectuals of 1880s Japan *were* political activists, invariably implicated in the power struggle that shaped the educational arena between government supporters and Freedom and People's Rights activists. However, Sanji uses the term *gakusha* to posit a practically neutral role. In fact, his definition perfectly aligns itself with the *gakusha* posited by proponents of autonomy of knowledge, such as Fukuzawa and Ono. Such an intellectual does not recognize the hierarchy instituted between government affiliates and the advocates of the political movement; he treats the two opposing sides as one unitary group from which to disengage himself. As a result, he appears to maintain an equal critical distance from both, while retaining a neutral stance for himself.

This definition of *gakusha* seemingly transcends the contemporary system, as if to exist outside, or alongside, the governing modalities of power in Meiji. Through such a *gakusha*, *Tōsei shosei katagi* bestows Sanji a putative subject position that can coexist with the successful characters of the naturalized present but one that can still be critical of the Meiji order.

The position of *gakusha* that arises from Sanji's definition clearly aligns itself with the identity granted to him as the subject of love: they share one main characteristic, namely, neutrality. *Gakusha*, just like his interiority, is ostensibly neutral and appears to transcend the sociopolitical systems. The manner in which they are generated on the textual surface is also the same. Recall that Sanji's internal experience, which constitutes his identity in love, seems to be severed from his positionality because he continually evades action. Not coincidentally, Sanji remains a student until the end of the narrative. Although he posits a *gakusha* who does not get involved in politics, he has not become this *gakusha*. His neutrality, in other words, is produced precisely because he is *yet to be*. If, for example, Sanji had acted upon his ideal and ventured to become a *gakusha* in accordance with his own definition, the governing modalities of power would have mobilized and destroyed that neutrality. Given that there was no institution that would support such a neutral *gakusha*, Sanji would have had to maneuver his way through existing institutions in order to establish himself as a *gakusha*. If he became a *gakusha* at a private school, he would be a part of the scheme of the Freedom and People's Rights Movement to produce more supporters. If he had gone to state-sponsored schools, he would have sided with the Meiji government. Either way, he would not have been able to retain his neutral stance. Precisely because he avoids action, the systems that prohibit neutrality remain dormant. These systems invariably shape his positionality—this is clear from the rest of the narrative—but they are held in abeyance, allowing the neutrality of Sanji's subject position as a *gakusha* to sustain itself.

Neutrality of the *gakusha* is thus a product of forceful severance from the political, economic, and social systems. The identity of the *gakusha* is contingent upon his disengagement from the worldly sector; or perhaps more specifically, the dissociation is the very condition of such a representation. Success, which can occur only by inscribing himself in the worldly sector, is thus never within the reach of the *gakusha*. However, only through this neutrality can the *gakusha* putatively posit a space where he can coexist with those in the worldly sector. The neutrality, artificially created through multilayers of textual manipulation, is thus the condition for an affirmative identity in the new space of the *shōsetsu*. It is precisely in the creation and sustenance of this neutrality that we find a voice, and hence its will to power. To maintain this positioning, Sanji must continually evade action, alienate himself from the worldly sector, and find his identity in the very state of alienation. Through Komachida Sanji, we see the moment that a figure of an alienated intellectual, the textual embodiment of "the social," is produced.

Sanji is further embellished with a characteristic highly appropriate for such an identity: he is the "unsophisticated" type who lacks the social skills necessary in the worldly domain. Within the textual world of *Tōsei shosei katagi*, the intellectual *inherently* lacks the quality necessary to attain practical success. Not coincidentally, Sanji's polar opposite, Tomoyoshi, is described as being talented in socializing; he is able to climb up the social ladder with his highly developed skills. Such characters do not qualify as the subject of love in the *shōsetsu*; they cannot demarcate the new space of the *shōsetsu*, its raison d'être. Whereas Sanji's identity is constructed through his separation from worldly accomplishment, Tomoyoshi is a worldly character who can never become the protagonist of the *shōsetsu*.

Such an equation is carried over to representative works that follow *Tōsei shosei katagi*, beginning with Futabatei Shimei's *Ukigumo* (*Drifting Clouds*, 1887). In this work, Bunzō, an intellectual and failed public servant, loses his job for lacking social skills. Unlike his colleague Noboru, who is promoted because of his social adeptness, Bunzō shuts himself in his room and continues to ponder his next action *internally*. The *shōsetsu* ends without Bunzō taking any action whatsoever; he is left with nothing, except his identity as an intellectual. Bunzō clearly takes after Sanji, and Noboru after Tomoyoshi. Bunzō is the quintessential anti-hero who has everything that a protagonist of the *shōsetsu* must have. Noboru, however, is simply not qualified to be the hero of a *shōsetsu*. He is shrewd, calculating, and worldly; he is a character who can ingratiate himself with his boss in order to gain a promotion. Although unable to be a protagonist of the *shōsetsu*, Noboru, like Tomoyoshi, does not need any interiority; he has successfully inscribed himself in the institutionalized system of Meiji. Bunzō, however, needs to seek his identity elsewhere. And following the prescribed formula, the alienated intellectual named Bunzō finds his identity, his interiority, in love.

Another somewhat different example is Mori Ōgai's "Maihime" ("The Dancing Girl," 1890). A renowned masterpiece of Meiji fiction, "Maihime" features Ōta Toyotarō, a government-sponsored student in Germany, who falls in love with a dancer named Erisu. He begins to live with Erisu and, as a result, loses his status as a public servant. His friend Aizawa attempts to persuade Toyotarō against giving up his chances for a successful career and tells him to sever his ties with Erisu. Aizawa sounds very much like Tomoyoshi when he preaches the importance of social advancement. Toyotarō, torn between his love and Aizawa's advice to return to Japan, finds his identity in agonizing *internally*. The narrative thus focuses on Toyotarō struggling over the choice between Erisu and his successful future in Japan. What is noteworthy here is that Toyotarō turns inward precisely because he is severed from the worldly domain; he is granted an interiority because he has removed himself from the worldly sector. Aizawa, on the other hand, does not have (or need) an interiority because he has a successful career where his identity lies. In the end, Toyotarō relinquishes his identity as a subject of love and hence his interiority by choosing his career over Erisu.[66] It is not a coincidence that the story ends here. Given that the *shōsetsu* became a medium that focuses on the protagonists' internal struggle, the story must come to a close when the protagonist is deprived of interiority of love. Although the pattern of development differs in "Maihime," it is clear that Toyotarō takes after Sanji and Aizawa after Moriyama.

The depoliticizing tendencies of *Shōsetsu shinzui* are clearly replicated in *Tōsei shosei katagi*. Both contribute to the production of a new space for the *shōsetsu* as they demarcate the textual realm by peripherizing and effacing the political. As we have seen throughout the book, this new space is inextricably linked to the historical time that generated it. Shifting paradigms of knowledge, educational reforms, the Freedom and People's Rights Movement, and Japan's self-identity within the global context coalesce in the production of this medium, as well as its depoliticizing tendencies. How this *shōsetsu* was retrospectively (re)configured through subsequent literary histories, and how it came to embody the ideological core of modern Japanese literary studies, is the topic of the following chapter.

SIX

Unraveling the Mechanism of Concealment

Historicizing Shōsetsu shinzui

Retrospective Discoveries of Shōsetsu shinzui *as Origin*

As Peter Kornicki and others have noted, the actual impact of *Shōsetsu shinzui*, contemporaneous with its publication, was rather minimal. Kornicki, after all, found only a "few trifling mentions" of the work in the six years after its publication.[1] *Tōsei shosei katagi* was much better received and an object of much discussion. The discrepancy between the actual, minimal impact and the later claims of great impact highlights the retrospective and ideological nature of the designation of *Shōsetsu shinzui* as the origin of modern Japanese literature. Kornicki has also shown that the discussion of emotions, customs, and manners (*ninjō, fūzoku, setai*) was certainly not original to *Shōsetsu shinzui*. Yet *Shōsetsu shinzui* stood out for the later critics and literary historians as a text that could accommodate their theoretical and ideological claims and their varying needs for an origin, all of which contributed toward the concealment of "the concealment of politics." In our effort to unravel the mechanism of this double concealment, inextricably linked to the repeated discovery of *Shōsetsu shinzui* as the origin of modern Japanese literature, the actual impact contemporaneous with *Shōsetsu shinzui*'s production is not as important as the historical moments that solidified its originary position.

What does it mean to identify the point when *Shōsetsu shinzui* became the origin of modern Japanese literature? It is not enough to locate the first mention of *Shōsetsu shinzui* as a groundbreaking event, which, as I will discuss shortly, began as early as the mid-1890s. We must identify the historical contingencies that made *Shōsetsu shinzui* appear appropriate for the specific needs of the times, preparing the stage for the various (mis)readings of *Shōsetsu shinzui*. These include the establishment of the boundaries of literature integrating the *Shōsetsu shinzui* clichés; the practice of mimesis that ultimately engaged with the notion of "self" (in all its variation) in the *shōsetsu*; and the urge to produce a narrative of origin, one that links the past with the present, especially the moment when Meiji became a historical object to look back on as an era where the "modern" (*kindai*) began. These discursive conditions somehow coalesced around *Shōsetsu shinzui*, making it the origin of modern Japanese literature. Whether the text itself anticipated these conditions is not an issue; what is at stake is whether, at given historical moments, the textual space appeared amenable to the needs of its interpreters when projected onto it.

I focus on the manner through which the *Shōsetsu shinzui* clichés, which remained empty in *Shōsetsu shinzui* itself, acquired positive referents, and how such referents were continuously reinforced by historical forces, ultimately embodying a common thread of modern "apolitical" *shōsetsu*. This required about forty years to take form, despite various breaks and discontinuities; and, in many ways, we are still bound to the varying assumptions it embodies. A comprehensive survey of the forty years in question is a sheer impossibility. What I wish to do is highlight two historical moments that I deem crucial to understanding the status of *Shōsetsu shinzui* as the origin of modern Japanese literature: the turn of the century and the post–Great Kanto Earthquake era (1923). First, however, as a prelude to these two historical moments, I will briefly recount how literature, which later developed into what we know as "national literature" (*kokubungaku*), entered the Tokyo Imperial University curriculum, which is inextricably linked to the production of literary history. This supplements the discussion in the introductory chapter and shows how the realm of literature, through the compilation of literary history, was defined vis-à-vis the *Shōsetsu shinzui* clichés. I then proceed to the discussion on *shōsetsu* of the 1900s, when a new mode of reading surfaced, one that associates the literary creation with the personal lives of the writers. This marks the establishment of a mimetic order, in which the idea of self emerges to dominate the literary circle. The emergence of this mode of reading coincides with the establishment of reading *Shōsetsu shinzui* as a text that advocated realistic portrayal of interiority.

I subsequently move on to the 1920s and 1930s to examine the moment when the urge to reframe Meiji as a historical period and a beginning of "modern" civilization surfaced. At around the same time, we witness the rise of Meiji literary studies, along with the desire to document Meiji, which in part arose from the devastation of the Great Kanto Earthquake. The emergence of Meiji literature as an object of study in many ways solidifies *Shōsetsu shinzui*'s status as the origin of *modern* Japanese literature. Extending the discussion to the series of debates on politics and art, I then show that in the 1930s, the group of *shōsetsu* whose lineage was traced back to *Shōsetsu shinzui* was putatively defined as apolitical, which contributed, coincidentally or otherwise, to the establishment of *Shōsetsu shinzui*'s status as an apolitical manifesto that is at the core of the politics of concealment.

A Prelude: Early Bungakushi *and Literature in the Academy*

Works of literary history (*bungakushi*) began to be published in 1890, primarily by Tokyo University graduates of Koten Kōshūka (Program for Study in the Classics) and Kokubungakka (Department of National Letters), such as Hagino Yoshiyuki (1860–1924), Ochiai Naobumi (1861–1903), Mikami Sanji (1865–1939), Haga Yaichi (1867–1927), and Ueda Kazutoshi (1867–1939). There were, of course, narratives that we can now call literary history written prior to this time, including the opening passage of *Shōsetsu shinzui*, but works with the specific title of *bungakushi* began with these scholars.

The scholars were consistent neither in their selection of texts nor in the criteria they used to choose the works to be included. They also used different modes of categorization, and hence the end products were by no means uniform. Haga Yaichi and Tachibana Senzaburō's *Kokubungaku dokuhon* (*Guides to National Letters*, 1890) categorized the works by poets and writers, ranging from Kakinomoto no Hitomaro (685–705) and Ki no Tsurayuki (872?–945) to Chikamatsu Monzaemon (1653–1724) and Bakin. Ōwada Tateki (1857–1910), who taught at the Program for Study in the Classics, wrote *Wabungakushi* (*A History of Japanese Letters*, 1897) using different styles of writing, such as sinitic-Japanese style (*kanbun*) and classical Japanese style (*wabun*), as modes of categorization, as well as other genre markers, such as "puppet plays" (*jōruri*), and Japanese poetry (*waka*) in narrativizing the history of Japanese letters. Others, such as Utsumi Kōzō's *Nihon bungakushi* (*A History of Japanese Literature*, 1900) and Suzuki Hiroyasu's *Shinsen Nihon bungaku shiryaku* (*New Selections for an Abridged History of Japanese Letters*, 1892) framed the texts chronologically. What constituted Japanese literature was in flux and did not stabilize for a long time.

However, we can locate a common denominator in the manner in which they approached the texts. In contrast to traditional antiquarian study of letters, which was a study of "dead" texts as it were, the new scholars sought to read texts as a reflection of the time in which they were written. We thus see many references to terms such as "mirror of life" (*jinsei no kagami*), "reflection of the time" (*jisei no han'ei*), and "a reflective mirror of society" (*shakai no hansha kagami*) in situating works of literature.[2] Moreover, in describing texts as a reflection of time, literary historians constantly linked the texts to people's "internal lives" (*shinteki seikatsu*) and "emotions and thoughts" (*kanjō shisō*). Mikami and Takasu's *Nihon bungakushi* claims, for example, that "literature is a reflection of people's heart/mind (*jinshin*)."[3] Haga Yaichi, in his *Kokubungaku jikkō* (*Ten Lectures on National Letters*, 1899), says that literary history traces "the thoughts and feelings of our ancestors, expressed through our national language."[4] In compiling literary history, Takeshima Hagoromo sought to discover "vicissitudes of our people's spirit" (*kokumin ga seishin no hensen*) and identify their "internal movements" (*naimenteki katsudō*).[5] The references to "internal lives," mind, and emotions and thoughts are thus everywhere apparent. Despite the tendency in Japanese scholarship to attribute such terms to *Shōsetsu shinzui*, the internal focus of literary history was a trend that emerged independently of *Shōsetsu shinzui*.

Although literary historians designated feelings and emotions as a significant component of literature, they did not share *Shōsetsu shinzui*'s agenda to posit "emotions" as the primary theme of the *shōsetsu* or literature. With their internal focus, literary historians sought Japanese "national character" in literature, which had to be one of civilized beings, given the social Darwinian doctrines that governed this historical time; they accordingly valued thoughts, reason, and rationality over emotion.[6] In spite of this, however, the references to internal lives in literary histories clearly gave form to literature as a discipline, however amorphous it may have been, setting the stage for retrospective discovery of *Shōsetsu shinzui* as the origin of literary practices.

The literary histories that emerged within the academy focused primarily on the classics; most of them went as far as the Edo period, and the few that extended the discussion to the present apologetically added several pages in conclusion.[7] This shows that Meiji writings were not generally considered as an object of study. This trend continued throughout the Meiji period, and as I will discuss later in this chapter, Meiji literature was not established as an object of study in and of itself until the 1920s.

However, the urge to compile a Meiji literary history appeared as early as 1894, when Ōwada Tateki published the first complete volume entitled *Meiji bungakushi* (*History of Meiji Letters*).[8] In the introduction, Ōwada claims that there are three stages in Meiji literature: the era of Western import that dates from the Restoration (1868), the post–Seinan War period (1877) marked by reactionary movements against Western import, and the post-1890s era marked by the development of constitutional politics. He focuses on the *shōsetsu* as the primary genre that developed during these three phases. In relation to the second phase, Ōwada discusses Shōyō and his contributions to the world of the *shōsetsu*, along with Fujita Mokichi (1852–92), Yano Ryūkei (1850–1931), Aeba Kōson (1855–1922), and Sudō Nansui (1857–1920), all of whom were quite active in the literary scene in early to mid-Meiji. Along with direct quotations from *Tōsei shosei katagi* and another work by Shōyō entitled *Imotose kagami* (*Mirror of Marriage*, 1886), Ōwada says the following about Shōyō:

> Shōyō not only popularized the name *shōsetsu* but worked toward reforming and expanding it. He claimed that the many *shōsetsu* existing in our country were dissociated from actual society (*genjitsu shakai*) and that they merely thematize what the writers themselves imagine are real. He fervently criticized the old form of the *shōsetsu* and then published works that adhered to the Western ways. Cutting off the hackneyed "happy ending" structure of old, Shōyō with his pen paved the way for tragic *shōsetsu* that do not allow easy resolution.[9]

The treatment of *Shōsetsu shinzui* becomes more dramatic with Haga Yaichi in his *Kokubungakushi jikkō* published in 1899. He says that Tsubouchi Shōyō was "the first pure 'man of letters' (*bungakusha*) to appear from Tokyo University": "His *Shōsetsu shinzui* evaluated the different types of *shōsetsu* and rejected Bakin's didacticism (*kanzen chōaku*); he also published his own fiction such as *Tōsei shosei katagi* and *Imotose kagami*. I think that this can appropriately mark the beginning (*isshin kigen*) of Meiji literature."[10] Similarly, Shioi Ukō (1869–1913) and Takahashi Tatsuo (1868–1946) in *Shintai Nihon bungakushi* (*A New History of Japanese Literature*, 1902) situate Shōyō as a man who "rejected trivial *shōsetsu* of Edo and opened a new path. . . . As a result, although the writers of Edo were lowly, the writers [of Meiji] are more lofty and elegant."[11]

In the 1890s, therefore, two forces are important to our inquiry. As literary histories begin to situate literature as an expression of internal lives, we begin to see entries that describe *Shōsetsu shinzui* and *Tōsei shosei katagi* as texts that embody a break from the past. Despite the fact that Meiji texts were yet to be considered "knowledge," the boundaries of literature and *Shōsetsu shinzui*'s break from the "trivial" and "didactic" writings of the past emerge simultaneously.

Note, however, that even when many of these literary histories dramatize the emergence of *Shōsetsu shinzui* and *Tōsei shosei katagi*, they merely treat the event as a mere moment in the history of Meiji literature whose influence does not continue in the present. *Shōsetsu shinzui* simply represents a moment in literary history, albeit a dramatic one. In effect, many of these narratives emphasize *Shōsetsu shinzui*'s break from the past but do not extend the text's influence forward, which is a necessary condition of the narrative of "origin." Such a continuity between the break and the present begins to appear in literary histories at the turn of the century, especially after the Russo-Japanese War (1904–5).[12]

Literary Histories at the Turn of the Century: Mimesis and "Self-Representation"

The turn of the century, especially after the Russo-Japanese War, is important in this inquiry because at this time mimesis emerges as the dominant mode of representation. The appearance of this mimetic condition gives positive referents and meaning to the terms "emotions, customs, and manners" and *ari no mama* (literally, "as it is"), crucial terms that were presented only negatively in *Shōsetsu shinzui* through its rejection of Bakin.

In the literary histories of the post–Russo-Japanese War period, we see the term *shajitsu*—which now signifies "realism" or "mimesis"—appearing as the dominant criterion by which to define *shōsetsu*. In fact, *shajitsu* appears as early as 1897 as the common denominator of Meiji *shōsetsu*, which were invariably traced back to *Shōsetsu shinzui*. The literary critic and thinker Takayama Chogyū (1871–1902) espouses Shōyō's position in his famous "Meiji no shōsetsu" (The *Shōsetsu* of Meiji, 1897): "When Shōyō entered the scene, publishing *Shōsetsu shinzui* and *Tōsei shosei katagi*, he exposed the fallacy of didacticism (*kanzen chōaku*) and opened the path toward *shajitsu shōsetsu*; everyone then began to pursue it, completely altering the literary attitude."[13]

It is noteworthy that Chogyū gives much agency to *Shōsetsu shinzui*, especially as it discusses *shajitsu shōsetsu*, which can be read as a narrative of origin. However, interestingly, and perhaps a little surprisingly from our perspective, he characterizes works written by the members of the Ken'yūsha school between the late 1880s and mid-1890s as *shajitsu shōsetsu* that followed the path opened up by *Shōsetsu shinzui*. This shows that *shajitsu* initially did not signify the establishment of mimetic order. To be precise, until the advent of naturalism, *shajitsu* meant being free from the didactic structure that promised a prescribed resolution—encourage virtue, castigate vice. It is not a coincidence that tragic *shōsetsu* were considered representatives of *shajitsu shōsetsu* until the emergence of naturalism. In examining the many references to *shajitsu* in the

1890s and 1900s, it is therefore important to keep in mind that *shajitsu* had yet to take on the meaning of "mimesis." Even in the post–Russo-Japanese War period, the equation "*shajitsu* = realism" remained rather unstable. To avoid the anachronism, I will retain the term *shajitsu* without translating it until my discussion moves into the 1920s and 1930s.

The use of *shajitsu* as a common denominator of Meiji fiction thus began in the late 1890s, but it increased dramatically in the 1900s: Iwaki Juntarō's *Zōho Meiji bungakushi* (*An Expanded History of Meiji Literature*, 1909), for example, highlights the call for *shajitsu* in his discussion of *Shōsetsu shinzui* and *Ukigumo* as the primary reason for their break with the past.[14] In 1909, the magazine *Taiyō* published a special issue entitled "Bungeishi" (A History of Literary Art), in which *Shōsetsu shinzui* is designated the "primary cause of the popularity of *shajitsu*."[15] Predictably, perhaps, the increase in such references coincides with *shajitsu* taking on the meaning of mimesis. Yet the prior notion of *shajitsu* remained, as evident in Shimamura Hōgetsu, who, in 1915, refers to *shajitsu* as the driving force that produced subsequent genres such as "*kannen shōsetsu* [sentimental *shōsetsu*], *shinkoku shōsetsu* [serious *shōsetsu*], and *shakai shōsetsu* [social *shōsetsu*]," referring to Ken'yūsha-affiliated writers such as Hirotsu Ryūrō (1861–1928) and Izumi Kyōka (1873–1939).[16]

As references to *shajitsu* as the defining feature of contemporary *shōsetsu* increased, the language that describes *Shōsetsu shinzui*'s emergence became even more dramatic. The literary critic Ikuta Chōkō claims the following in his *Meiji jidai bunpan* (*A Guide to Meiji Letters*, 1907):

> *Shōsetsu shinzui* is truly a revolutionary (*kakumeiji*) of the world of the *shōsetsu*. The loud cry of this revolution—the loud cry that attempted to introduce a brand-new trend to our nation's literary world—woke up even the lifeless, old-fashioned writers of the time. The imprudent didacticism was defeated in the eyes of the public, and *shajitsu* was valued. Portraying the psychology (*shinri*) with emotions (*ninjō*) as the main aim of the *shōsetsu* became the general trend; the world of the *shōsetsu* was, for the first time, given the opportunity to interact with the world literature of the nineteenth century, and the light of literature shined radiantly. . . . This requires special mention in the history of literature of our nation, and Shōyō's contribution as the writer of *Shōsetsu shinzui* will never be erased.[17]

Such a dramatic characterization of the shift further coincides with the emergence of a narrative that links *Shōsetsu shinzui*, Futabatei's *Ukigumo*, and the naturalist school based on *shajitsu*, while devaluing the works in between, such as those by the Ken'yūsha school, as superficial. As Chogyū's "Meiji no shōsetsu" has shown, when *shajitsu* was initially discovered as a common trait of Meiji fiction, it was a characteristic shared by many works produced subsequent to *Shōsetsu shinzui*, especially by the Ken'yūsha school. With naturalism, however, these works began to be characterized as "having the facade of *shajitsu*" (*shajitsuteki sakufū*) but not quite actualizing it.[18] As far as the supporters of naturalism were concerned, works of the Ken'yūsha school still adhered to a prefigured landscape and hence portrayed superficial reality that was not based on "deep observation" (*fukai kansatsu*).

The meaning of *shajitsu* clearly began to shift as naturalist works were discovered to embody the successful *shajitsu*. "Deep observation" and "objective portrayal" (*kyakkan byōsha*) became key terms in denoting realism in naturalist works. In comparison, Ken'yūsha works were based on limited "subjective" perspective (*shōshukan*) rather than objective portrayal. Categorizing the main members of the Ken'yūsha school, such as Yamada Bimyō (1868–1910) and Ozaki Kōyō (1867–1903), under the section "first-generation *shajitsu* school" (*daiichiji shajitsu shugi*), *Bungei hyakka zensho* (*Encyclopedia of Literary Arts*, 1909) says the following:

> As to the works of the Ken'yūsha school led by [Bimyō and Kōyō], even if they appeared to have followed the *shajitsu* espoused by Shōyō, in actuality they featured pseudorealism. I feel that I am bending the words by describing them under the rubric "first-generation *shajitsu* school"; it is not an exaggeration to say that their works are a figment of their imagination (*kūsō no bungaku*). The writers who deeply observe (*fukaku kansatsu suru*) and research life (*jinsei*) with a faithful perspective appeared after Kitamura Tōkoku, Takayama Chogyū, and Tsunashima Ryōsen.[19]

Taiyō's "Bungeishi," in the chapter entitled "Hisō shajitsuha no zensei" (The Popularity of Superficial *Shajitsu* Writers), similarly criticizes the works of the Ken'yūsha writers Kōyō, Bimyō, and Hirotsu Ryūrō, among others:

> They are, strictly speaking, not adherents of *shajitsu* because they lean toward superficial portrayal (*hisō no mosha*) or they merely borrow the *shajitsu* form in order to present their own taste. In other words, they seem to capture the social emotions by their own narrow subjective perspective; accordingly, it is not possible to see life or deep observation (*fukai kansatsu*) in their works.[20]

Notice the criticism against subjective perspective in these entries, which precludes deep observation. According to the advocates of deep observation (and hence objective portrayal), it follows that Ken'yūsha writers could only super-ficially follow *Shōsetsu shinzui* because they based their portrayal on a subjec-tive perspective. This criticism of subjective perspective clearly replicates the wording that *Shōsetsu shinzui* used in rejecting the "writer's design" (*sakusha no ishō*) and Bakin, evident in the use of phrases such as "figments" of the writer's thoughts and "superficial portrayal." In this criticism of Ken'yūsha writers, *Shōsetsu shinzui* already exists as a text that argued for objective portrayal as it rejected the writer's design. The turn-of-the-century literary histories thus reformulated *Shōsetsu shinzui* rejection of the writer's design, which was linked to the writers' political thoughts specific to 1880s Japan.

Here is another example of such (re)interpretation of *Shōsetsu shinzui*. "Meiji bundan ni okeru ikuta no kōkei" (Many Scenes of the Meiji Literary Circle, 1912) says, "Shōyō was the first in our country to say that life (*jinsei*) is not to be preached but portrayed."[21] *Shōsetsu shinzui*'s claim that *shōsetsu* teaches not directly but indirectly—an argument that was devised to sever *shōsetsu* from other major disciplines such as history and politics—is reappropriated here to argue how artistic portrayal of life through deep observation educates its reader. The writer of this unsigned article further quotes the now most famous passage from *Shōsetsu shinzui* to make his point:

> The main characteristics of the *shōsetsu* are emotions. Customs and manners follow next. . . . A writer is like a psychologist. He must create his characters based on the principles of psychology. If he creates, by his own design, charac-ters who deviate from human emotions (*ninjō*) or, worse, from the principles of psychology, those characters would merely be figments of the writer's imagina-tion rather than those belonging to the human world.

The writer comments on this passage, saying, "Adding the writer's opinion, con-trolling life and using it for didactic means only deviates from essential purpose of literature."[22] Notice the tautology inherent in this narrative, which is at the core of the mechanism of concealment: "The essential purpose of literature" is posited through *Shōsetsu shinzui*'s definition of literature. The objective portrayal that is allegedly upheld by the quoted *Shōsetsu shinzui* passage is posited against "controlling life," which is a reinterpretation of its criticism of didacticism. The mimetic order is treated as a given, and accordingly, the criticism of didacticism is dissociated from the political context of 1880s Japan. The idea that *Shōsetsu shinzui* advocated objective portrayal thus originates around this time.

Accompanying the narrative of objective portrayal and *shajitsu* is the ap-pearance of "human life" as an object of serious art. The focus on human life brought artistic *shōsetsu* and reality closer, which is evident in Shimamura Hōgetsu's *Meiji bungaku hensenshi kōwa* (*Vicissitudes of Meiji Literature: A Lecture*, 1915). In it he claims that with the advent of the naturalists, "The fissure that lay between art and life, apparent in works of the Meiji 30s [1897–1906], was finally filled. Art now truly adheres to our daily existence (*seikatsu*) and has taken a step toward a literary art (*bungei*) that is deeply meaningful."[23]

The question we must ask is, How did such a condition of reading become possible? The historical time in which such *shajitsu* appears in literary histories shares its moment with the emergence of what the contemporary literary critic Hibi Yoshitaka calls "literature of self-representation" (*jiko hyōshō no bungaku*). In his *Jiko hyōshō no bungakushi* (*A Literary History of Self-Representation*, 2002), Hibi brilliantly documents the moment that literature of self-representation began to appear, which he carefully differentiates from the I-novel (*shishōsetsu*), a genre that has long been claimed as the "unique" literary form specific to Japan.[24] He does so by highlighting the historical discrepancy between the emergence of such fiction (which he locates around 1906–7) and the actual appearance of the word *shishōsetsu* in the 1920s. He makes a compelling case for the emergence of a new mode of reading predicated on an intersection between fiction and real life.

This certainly does not mean that literary critics before 1907 did not debate fiction's impact on life and society. In fact, terms such as "human life" (*jinsei*), "the human world" (*ningen sekai*), "instinct" (*hon'nō*), and "society" (*shakai*) were common in the media in the 1890s. Debates on deterioration of literature (*bungaku kyokusui ronsō*), for instance, argued over the place of emotions (*ninjō*) in literature. Many of the discussions in the 1890s revolved around the moral impact of literary works as writers debated their philosophical outlook vis-à-vis fiction. In 1893, for example, Yamaji Aizan (1864–1917) and Kitamura Tōkoku (1868–94) engaged in a debate on the intersection between life and literature (*jinsei sōshō ronsō*). Arguing over the autonomy of literature and literature's utility, they both tried to define the role of *shōsetsu* by foregrounding their philosophical outlook on human life, morality, and beauty. The emergence of Takayama Chogyū on the literary scene also saw efforts to define the relationship between literature and life. Chogyū, in the famous "Biteki seikatsu o ronzu" (On Aesthetic Life, 1901), claims, "Since aesthetic life exists to satisfy the demands of essence of life (*jinsei hon'nen*), this life has absolute value in and of itself."[25] What constitutes aesthetic life and its relation to "instinct" spurred much debate. Such categories were mobilized to discuss not only Japanese literature and *shōsetsu* but also "foreign" literature, such as Russian and British. In effect, they defined the realm of "literature."

Despite the many references to life, society, and the human world, however, they remained abstract, mobilized primarily as philosophical categories.[26] In the place of such abstract discourse, a new mode of discourse that links the real and the fictional worlds began to appear in the 1900s, in part as a result of media expansion with the Sino-Japanese War (1894–95) and the Russo-Japanese War (1904–5). In such media, the writers' real life began to take center stage.[27]

Drawing on many studies that precede him, Hibi states that the link between reality and fiction is exemplified by the many articles—which began to appear around 1906—that introduce new literary works by discussing the real-life models used for characters in the text. Hibi analyzes the growing media coverage not only of the writers but the actual models of the fictional characters, which set the stage for a new interpretive mode that links the real world and fiction.

For example, *Bunshō sekai* (*The World of Literature*) and *Kokumin shinbun* (*Nation's Newspaper*) created sections where writers could talk about the models they had in mind when producing a given work of fiction. *Bunshō sekai*, very much tied to the naturalist school, had a special issue entitled "Jijitsu to sakuhin" (On Truth and Fiction) in September 1907 in which Kunikida Doppo (1871–1908), Tokuda Shūsei (1871–1943), Oguri Fūyō (1875–1926), and others wrote on the models of their characters. Doppo begins his discussion of "Gen'oji" (Old Gen, 1897) by saying "Old Gen and the pauper are both based on real people."[28] He continues discussing *Haru no tori* (*The Spring Bird*, 1904) in the following manner: "The protagonist of the story, the retarded boy, is a person with whom I was intimately acquainted when I resided in the town of Saigi in Bungo prefecture. The background story of this boy is all true. However, his tragic death in Shiroyama is my fiction."[29] In the same installment, Tokuda Shūsei says:

> To take an example, there was a model for Osaki in my "Kumo no yukue" [The Fate of the Clouds, 1900]—the stubborn and emotional, peculiar sort of girl. Though, of course, she is a little different from the character in my work. [The model] was a girl of a temple. She had good penmanship (and was quite well read); she sang well too. She was very high spirited like a man, and she'd throw rocks at Christians when they gave a speech. The two are similar in that they are both emotional and peculiar, but the [real girl] was a little older, wasn't very pretty, and was not as innocent.[30]

Even if such information was not used to interpret a given work, the information had become readily available to the reading public.

There were also many readers' columns established.[31] *Kokumin shinbun*, for example, put "Bungeikai shōsoku" (News of the Literary World) on the front page around 1908, listing the many witness accounts and/or rumors about writers. We find entries such as these:

> Miyake Setsurei, who is writing "Genseikai to fukuseikai" [The Primary World and Secondary World] in the journal *Nihon oyobi nihonjin* [*Japan and the Japanese*], will end his serialization around October this year. He will publish it in one complete volume soon after that with the title *Uchū* (*Universe*). I heard that the British Consulate is translating every installment.[32]

> It seems that Oguri Fūyō again severed his ties with Mayama Seika. This is about the sixth or seventh time they have done this with each other, but it seems that it may last a long time [before they make amends again].[33]

The growing desire for information about writers is further apparent in *Bunshō sekai*'s "Gendai bungakusha shōden" (A Short Biography of Contemporary Writers), which was included in the April 1, 1907, edition of *Bunshō sekai*; the biographies were presented with an interesting layout: they occupy the top one-third of a page for approximately twenty or so pages, almost in headnote form, as the rest of the page serialized *shōsetsu*, poetry, and essays. They provide birthplace, birth date, educational background, representative works, and even current addresses.

Literary journals and newspapers such as *Shinchō*, *Bunshō sekai*, and *Kokumin shinbun* thus thrived on discussions that fostered a mode of reading that links the fictional world and reality. This was the condition in which Shimazaki Tōson's *Namiki* (*Pathway*, 1907), which spurred the infamous "model scandal," and Tayama Katai's *Futon* (*The Quilt*, 1906) were received, stimulating the media into identifying the models and prompting debates on the ethical nature of using models.[34] Such a discursive condition also set the stage for debates on the uniformity of art and life that appeared around this time, which revolved around whether a writer ought to live life in accordance with the philosophy espoused by his fiction or whether art and life ought to be separate. Dovetailing this debate was an increasing concern for moral degeneracy in the media; naturalist works were criticized for promoting immoral behavior, and many writers were forced to defend their works against the moralists who devalued naturalist works' artistic worth.[35] None of these discussions would have been possible without the close proximity between fiction and real life.

Whether the media told the truth about the models or writers or whether naturalist works affected the actual lives of the readers is not the issue. What matters is that the boundary between fiction and reality was blurred, fostering a mode of reading that identifies the real *behind* the fictional work. The discursive condition further induced this mode of reading by providing information to produce this "real" behind the fictional work. This is a crucial discursive condition of mimesis that *Shōsetsu shinzui*'s advocacy of *ari no mama* portrayal has come to represent. Note, as I have argued throughout the book, *Shōsetsu shinzui* itself does not argue for mimetic description. It was through retrospective designation, after such a condition was set in place, that *Shōsetsu shinzui* was discovered as a text that promoted mimesis. Yet once *Shōsetsu shinzui*'s call for *ari no mama*, which was empty upon the text's production, was equated with mimesis, and hence positive identification was made and essentialized, the specific manner in which it was posited—against the political habitus—was concealed. Because the process through which *ari no mama* was posited was concealed, its depoliticizing tendencies were effaced.

Perhaps more than apparent from the discussion above, the establishment of the mimetic order coincides with the appearance of "the self" (*jiko*)—and all its variations, such as "selfhood" (*jiga*), "self-awareness" (*jiishiki*), and "psychology" (*shinri*)—as a key literary theme.[36] Predictably, this contributes to the discovery of *Shōsetsu shinzui* as the origin, given the designation of "emotion" (*ninjō*) as the main theme of the *shōsetsu*. Deep observation of life, a condition of "true art," was one that went hand in hand with the search for and improvement of the self. This was the self represented in the works as well as the subject of expression, that is, the writers. Katagami Tengen (1884–1928), in his "Mikaiketsu no jinsei to shizenshugi" (Unresolved Life and Naturalism, 1908), says, "For a person struggling with real life (*genjitsu seikatsu*), expression is that of a struggle. . . . There is no meaning to expression of real life without writing about the heart that attempts to express its own struggle."[37] Tengen, in his "Jiko no tame no bungaku" (The Literature for the Self, 1908), also says:

> By "literature for the self" I refer to works that express what one sees with one's eyes and what one truly feels in one's own heart. The contemporary writers can now clearly see the importance of not deceiving oneself and being faithful to thought, emotion, and observation; in other words, we can see the importance of not concealing one's own truth (*jiko no shinjitsu*).[38]

Such a link between self, life, and literary expression based on deep observation is at the core of the narrative that links *Shōsetsu shinzui* and naturalism. The literary histories written around this time emphasize the intersection between such self-expression and real life as the most complete literary form, invariably embodied by the works of naturalists. Ikuta Chōkō, in his *Meiji jidai bunpan*, praises Tōson's *Hakai* (*The Broken Commandment*, 1906) as a portrayal of "meaningful life" that features "actual depiction of life that intersects with its interiority (*naimen*)."[39] *Zōho Meiji bungakushi* situates the "new literature" as one that promotes "the most natural imagination of the self (*jiko*)" instead of flowery rhetoric that induces tears.[40] *Bungei hyakka zensho* describes naturalist works as those written by "the modern men (*kindaijin*) who have attained 'self-awareness' (*jiishiki*); the spirit and emotion that run through them were nothing that the previous *shōsetsu*, written at whim, could attain."[41] *Bungei hyakka zensho* appropriately traces such self-awareness to the appearance of *Shōsetsu shinzui* by saying that "the psychological dissection (*shinri no kaibō*) and objective portrayal (*kyakkanteki byōsha*) not only adhere to the *shajitsu* movement but are two defining pillars of naturalism. [Shōyō] had already foreseen the path."[42] *Shōsetsu shinzui* clearly took on a life of its own in the first decade of the twentieth century.

The Production of "Modern" Shōsetsu *and Meiji Literary Studies: Discovery of "Meiji" in the 1920s–1930s*

In his *Nihon no "bungaku" gainen* (*The Concept of "Literature" in Japan*, 1998), a monumental work that explores the historical development of the term *bungaku*, Suzuki Sadami states that the first reference to Meiji as "modern" (*kindai*) in literature-related works occurred as early as 1921, with Takasu Baikei's *Kindai bungeiron* (*On Modern Literary Art*, 1921). Yet according to Suzuki, the use of "modern" as a reference to Meiji literature does not become the norm until the late 1920s and early 1930s. In substantiating this claim, he lists many works of literary histories that have the rendering "modern" in the title; we will examine some of them later.[43]

The reference to modern is, of course, not limited to the title of works. For our purposes, it is important to decipher when the term "modern" was endowed on works that are traced back to *Shōsetsu shinzui*. In the early to mid-1920s, aside from several exceptions like Tayama Katai's *Kindai no shōsetsu* (*Shōsetsu of the Modern Era*, 1923), the majority of the literary histories and other critical works used the designation "Meiji" literature or "Meiji" *shōsetsu*. Others also used "new" literature (*shin bungaku*), emphasizing the division between pre– and post–*Shōsetsu shinzui*.[44] Toward the end of the decade, we begin to see the designation "modern thought" (*kindai shisō*) referring to individualism (*kojin shugi*) that is embodied by the works of naturalism, which allegedly perfected the ideals espoused by *Shōsetsu shinzui*. In the 1930s, we find many more usages of "modern." The literary critic Hijikata Teiichi (1904–80) says, "The naturalist movement was an unprecedented literary revolution, and Meiji literature rightfully gained its status as 'modern literature' (*kindai bungaku*) with it."[45] Kanzaki Kiyoshi (1904–79), a social critic, characterizes Futabatei's work as one that offers a "detailed portrayal of reality," which he glosses parenthetically as "modern literature" (*kindai bungaku*).[46] Shinoda Tarō, albeit negatively, says that "the mainstream literature, ever since *Shōsetsu shinzui*, has consisted of works that thematized the individual's psychology (*shinri*), taste, and daily existence (*seikatsu*), works that only showed the weakness of 'modern literature' (*kindai bungaku*)," which, he goes on to argue, simply reflect the lives and feelings of the bourgeoisie and the intelligentsia.[47] Despite these writers' varying agendas in evaluating the *shōsetsu* that feature psychological realism, the designations "modern *shōsetsu*" and "modern literature" stabilize by the mid-1930s.

As Suzuki Sadami and others have noted, this aligns itself with the new perception of the Meiji that began to emerge around the mid-1920s to 1930s.[48] This urge to resituate the Meiji period shaped not only the view of the past but also the study of Meiji history and literature and contributed to forces that strengthened *Shōsetsu shinzui*'s originary status. References to Meiji appeared in various forms around this time. The first and perhaps most notable is the establishment of the Meiji Bunka Kenkyūkai (Meiji Cultural Studies Group) in 1924. It was founded with the aim of "studying the various social phenomena since the early Meiji period and presenting them as materials for national history (*kokuminshi*)."[49] Led by Yoshino Sakuzō (1878–1933), the group initially consisted of eight primary members who met weekly to study Meiji history, political thought, and so on.[50] Many critics who became central players in Meiji literary studies were also associated with the Meiji Cultural Studies Group, most notably Kimura Ki (1894–1979) and Yanagida Izumi (1894–1969). The research group founded a journal entitled *Shinkyū jidai* (*Times Old and New*) in February 1925 (renamed *Meiji bunka kenkyū* [*A Study of Meiji Culture*] in 1926 and *Meiji bunka* [*Meiji Culture*] in 1929) to publicize their studies. Their study was in part shaped by the experience of the Great Kanto Earthquake of 1923; the devastation and subsequent reconstruction brought forth a new sense of the present and its relationship to the past. The earthquake also produced the urge to document Meiji given that the earthquake destroyed invaluable documents. In fact, the members of the Meiji Cultural Studies Group have often been criticized for being mere collectors of documents. However, as Yoshino's "Meiji bunka no kenkyū ni kokorozashiseshi dōki" (My Motives for Meiji Cultural Studies) shows, there is much more:

> The democracy of old was one espoused by men who blindly valorized the West without having a full understanding of the concept. The historical condition (*jisei*) had not developed enough to accommodate it. Any attempt to implement it would have failed accordingly. In contrast, the democracy of the present is one that emerged from the need of the historical condition. The autocratic/despotic bureaucratic politics that was necessary before no longer works. The people's intelligence has developed to the extent that the masses now have the true taste of freedom and independence. However, those of the old do not see this change and treat the claims for democracy as an abstract concept. Their decisions [against democracy] are based on their own past experiences. They—without malice—suppress the youths' demand. And they truly believe it is the best for society. But society cannot go on like this. We must debunk their illusion. What should be done to this end? The easiest way is to teach them the transformation of historical condition, to tell them the difference between the old and new that shapes the changes in political thought.[51]

This is how Yoshino decided to embark on Meiji cultural studies. The basic premise of his endeavor was the difference between the Meiji period and the present: he sought to recount the past to show how different the present had become. As the contemporary Japanese historian Narita Ryūichi argues, Yoshino produced a "foreign culture" out of Meiji, which is marked in the title that the Meiji Cultural Studies Group gave its journal: *Shinkyū jidai* (*Times Old and New*).[52] Meiji cultural studies feature an attempt to institute a clear division between the old and new and narrate the present by differentiating it from the past. This understanding guided their study and compilation of materials. In 1926, they established Meiji Shinbun Zasshi Bunko (A Collection of Meiji Newspapers and Journals) in the Law Department of Tokyo Imperial University, a collection to which many Meiji specialists are still indebted. Out of this collection, the group compiled and published twenty-four volumes of *Meiji bunka zenshū* (*An Anthology of Meiji Cultural Writings*) between 1927 and 1930.

Yoshino Sakuzō and his followers were certainly not the only group of people who sought to sever the present from the past. One other clear example was the Marxist-influenced intellectuals who sought to situate the time frame since the Meiji Restoration as the rise of bourgeois capitalism and a fulfillment of a bourgeois revolution, which set the stage for the proletarian revolution. Shinoda Tarō, for example, in his "Meiji bungaku kenkyū ni kansuru ichi kōsatsu" (A Perspective on Meiji Literary Studies, 1932), discusses the historical groups by which to categorize literary works:

> All literature produced between the Meiji period and today ought to be con-solidated. . . . How would I categorize the literature of the Meiji, Taishō, and Shōwa periods? Anyone who would agree to consolidate the literature of the three eras would not object to calling them "bourgeois literature" or literature of the age of capitalism. Of course, we could call them "literature of individual-ism," but since individualism is the main concept of the bourgeoisie, it is easier to call them bourgeois literature.[53]

Kanzaki Kiyoshi also describes the Meiji period as a "revolutionary culture of the youthful bourgeoisie," one that he seeks to reassess in examining the devel-opment of linguistic reforms that reflect the incomplete nature of the bourgeois revolution.[54] The critic Karaki Junzō (1904–80) likewise situates Meiji as an era of the development of the bourgeoisie, whose literature was "a preparatory stage for our critical ability and philosophy to reach the international level."[55] In more ways than one, these Marxist-influenced intellectuals all sought to re-evaluate the present by consolidating the past, though clearly with a different agenda from that of their counterparts in the Meiji Cultural Studies Group.

Such varying desires to break away from the past were quickly institution-alized through the media and educational arenas. Meiji literary studies, for example, emerged around this time: Honma Hisao's (1886–1981) involvement with the journal *Waseda bungaku* (*Waseda Literature*) shows one such exam-ple. Honma, though not directly affiliated with the Meiji Cultural Studies Group, quickly praised the endeavor and sought to expand such reassessment of Meiji in the realm of literature. In his "Kibō futatsu mittsu—Meiji bunka kenkyūkai e" (Two or Three Wishes: An Address to the Meiji Cultural Stud-ies Group, 1924), he says that although the "fifty years of Meiji" are banal and boring compared to the modern civilization of the West, "as long as it is a culture that our ancestors built, the study of Meiji from a new position must be a top priority; this is necessary to understand our current selves and further understand ourselves as Japanese."[56] Honma put such need into practice with the publication of special issues of *Waseda bungaku* entitled *Meiji bungakugō* (*Issues on Meiji Literature*) from March 1925 to June 1927. The issues marked an attempt to resituate the Meiji past from writers' current positions; they featured many "records of reminiscence" (*kaikoroku*) by writers active in the early de-cades of the Meiji period, such as Tsubouchi Shōyō, Kōda Rohan, Baba Kochō (1869–1940), and Ichishima Shunjō. The issues recount the early chaotic years of Meiji to naturalism, many of which are described through writers' accounts of their personal experiences among the literati. The narratives of reminiscences were supplemented by studies of Meiji works and writers written by younger critics like Yanagida Izumi, Miyajima Shinzaburō (1892–1934), and Takasu Yoshijirō (1880–1948).

Concurrently with this project, Honma and other critics, who were either affiliated with the Meiji Cultural Studies Group or were deeply sympathetic to the cause, compiled and published *Meiji bungaku meicho zenshū* (*An Anthology of Masterpieces of Meiji Literature*, 1926), giving readers access to many literary works of the Meiji period. Among them, Shōyō's *Tōsei shosei katagi* was included in the first volume and *Shōsetsu shinzui* in the third volume. Furthermore, in the same year, *Nihon bungaku kōza* (*Essays on Japanese Literature*, 1926–27), edited by Fujimura Tsukuru, professor in the Department of National Literature at the Tokyo Imperial University, was published. It featured nineteen volumes, including famous essays on Meiji literature such as Ikuta Chōkō's "Meiji bungaku gaisetsu" (An Outline of Meiji Literature) and Yanagida Izumi's "Meiji no hon'yaku bungaku kenkyū" (A Study of Meiji Translation Literature). In many ways, these works mark the beginning of Meiji literary studies.[57]

The study of Meiji literature quickly spread to academia. The scholars and students of Tokyo Imperial University established Meiji Bungakkai (Meiji Literary Circle) in February 1932. The national literature scholars in the academy contributed to the proliferation of the records of reminiscence. The August 1934 installment of the Tokyo Imperial University journal *Kokugo to kokubungaku* (*National Language and Literature*) features a special issue entitled "Meiji Taishō bungaku o kataru" (Speaking on Meiji and Taishō Literature), in which the famous scholars of national literature and national language studies offered their recollections. Ueda Kazutoshi, for example, reflected on "Kokugogaku no sōsōki" (The Formative Years of National Language Studies); Mikami Sanji and Inoue Tetsujirō were given the theme "Kokugo kokuji mondai no kaiko" (Recounting the Problems of National Language and Orthography); and Sasaki Nobutsuna recollected his experience at Koten Kōshūka (Program for Study in the Classics). These were then recorded by the young scholars of the Meiji Literary Circle. Such collaborative effort certainly did not mean that there was no friction between the national literature scholars in the academy and others participating in Meiji literary studies.[58] Although I am unable to go into detail here, Sekii Mitsuo discusses how the Meiji Cultural Studies Group and its affiliates, such as Kimura Ki and Yanagida Izumi, implicitly criticized the philological tendency of national literature instituted since Haga Yaichi's dominance. For the Meiji Cultural Studies Group, reading literature meant reading the society in which it was produced; as far as the members were concerned, national literature sought the beauty of Japanese uniqueness in literature that has been alienated from society.[59]

Renarrativizing Meiji thus expressed the urge to consolidate the past as a reference point to narrativize the present in the late 1920s and 1930s. This was not limited to literary studies. According to Narita Ryūichi, in the discipline of history, too, the study of the Meiji Restoration took off in the early 1930s, particularly with the publication of the series entitled *Nihon shihon shugi hattatsushi kōza* (*On the Development of Japanese Capitalism*, published in seven volumes).[60] Moreover, as Kobayashi Takiji states in "Uyokuteki henkō no shomondai" (Problems of Rightist Tendencies, 1933), we find many historical *shōsetsu* being published around the same time, whose narratives are set in the late Edo and early Meiji era, an era of turmoil.[61] Whether it be through records of reminiscences, fictional rendering of the past, or a study of Meiji literature, intellectuals both inside and outside academia with varying philosophical and political agenda chose the Meiji period as a vehicle to narrativize the present.[62] Within this milieu the many narratives of literary history, produced along with the establishment of Meiji literary studies in the late 1920s and early 1930s, designate *Shōsetsu shinzui* as the origin of "modern" *shōsetsu*.

Literary History of the 1920s and 1930s

An attempt to produce a narrative of Meiji necessarily posits "Meiji" as a single entity, which calls for a single set of criteria by which to define it. The common denominator of the *shōsetsu* produced at the turn of the century, namely, realism and self-portrayal, invariably traced to *Shōsetsu shinzui*, was mobilized again for this purpose. *Meiji Taishōshi* (*History of the Meiji and Taishō Periods*, 1931), in the section entitled "*Shōsetsu shinzui* no shutsugen" (The Emergence of *Shōsetsu shinzui*), claims that the publication of *Shōsetsu shinzui* "is the direct cause that prompted the production of a new literary art of the new time" because it argued for the portrayal of the "truth of life" (*jinsei no shin*) "as it is" (*ari no mama*).[63] The internal focus of *Shōsetsu shinzui* was also emphasized: after quoting the famous passage of *Shōsetsu shinzui* where it defines the primary aims of *shōsetsu*, the literary critic Senuma Shigeki says, "With such a beginning . . . psychological portrayal became the core of modern *shōsetsu* and brought about unprecedented success to *shōsetsu*."[64] Many also followed the literary histories written at the turn of the century in link-ing *Shōsetsu shinzui* and the naturalists while devaluing others in between. Miyajima Shinzaburō's *Meiji bungaku jūnikō* (*Twelve Lectures on Meiji Literature*, 1925) defines the intent of *Shōsetsu shinzui* as "making art intersect with life or existence (*jisseikatsu*)." He continues, "But Professor Tsubouchi's call was only heard correctly by Futabatei; his call was answered only at the third stage [of Meiji, that is, post–Sino Japanese War], in fact only truly answered at the fourth stage [the advent of naturalism]."[65] Takasu Yoshijirō, in his *Meiji bungakushiron* (*On Meiji Literary History*, 1934) says that the naturalists successfully went against the Ken'yūsha school, which did not "sufficiently understand the meaning of realism":

> Going back in time, it was Tsubouchi Shōyō's *Shōsetsu shinzui* published in 1885 that indirectly intersected with naturalist depiction. [*Shōsetsu shinzui*] preached psychological and objective portrayal and defined criticism of life (*jinsei hihan*) as the primary objective of the *shōsetsu*. The literati of the time more or less understood Shōyō's call for "objective portrayal," but they didn't seem to understand psychological depiction. It was only Futabatei who understood this and produced a new form of expression. Accordingly, no one could possibly understand the meaning of "criticism of life," and even if someone did, no writer had the ability to actualize it in writing.[66]

Despite the variation in these writers' focus, the narrative that links *Shōsetsu shinzui* and the naturalists we saw after the Russo-Japanese War—which can now be called the lineage of the "modern *shōsetsu*"—appears to be replicated here.[67]

This narrative, however, was situated quite differently. Whereas the earlier narratives valorized naturalism for actualizing the realism that *Shōsetsu shinzui* allegedly promoted, the 1920s and 1930s narratives posited the realism of the naturalists as a negative reference point by which to advocate a new literary movement. The criticism against realism was first led by the proponents of Shinkankakuha (New Sensationist School), composed of writers such as Yokomitsu Riichi (1898–1947) and Kawabata Yasunari (1899–1972). A strong advocate of new sensationism, Kataoka Teppei (1894–1944) situates the new sensationist movement as "a rebellion against realism," which derives from the dissatisfaction with the works of the realists, such as Shiga Naoya (1883–1971), as "commonsensical prose" of those who "have not traveled far beyond the naturalists."[68] As the proponents of new sensationism argued against the realists in such a manner, they mobilized and hence reified the modern *shōsetsu* formula, which was invariably traced to *Shōsetsu shinzui*. The validity of the modern *shōsetsu* formula was never scrutinized in such criticism; whether or not naturalism in fact actualized *Shōsetsu shinzui*'s theories was never questioned. It was treated as a given and reinforced as it continued to be reproduced.

Furthermore, while the earlier narratives of literary history endorsed the self embodied by the naturalists and designated it as a fulfillment of what *Shōsetsu shinzui* purportedly preached by its focus on "emotions," the writings of the 1920s and 1930s were quite critical of this "self" and its description. We find many references to "trivial descriptions of personal surroundings" (*shinpen zakki*): Hijikata Teiichi, for example, is extremely critical of the naturalists' focus on "the desire of the flesh and trivial records of personal surroundings," which reflect their "lack of social concerns and empirical spirit."[69] Such a view was on a par with that of Aono Suekichi (1890–1961), who, in his "'Shirabeta' geijutsu" (Researched Art, 1925), criticized the contemporary *shōsetsu*, a lineage of which he traced to the work of naturalists, as works of "personal impressionism" that derive from mistaken and superficial understanding of "reality," "life," and "self."[70] Similarly, critics often attacked the naturalists' portrayal of the self as one that is isolated from society: Kataoka Yoshikazu (1897–1957) says that naturalists had an "incomplete" notion of human awareness and hence "eliminated the social aspect of human existence."[71] Karaki Junzō, too, claims that the problem with the naturalists was their severance with the social, arguing that Marxist literature reintroduced "social solidarity" into "human existence."[72]

Perhaps predictably, Marxist critics and/or those influenced by Marxism were the main proponents for such a narrative. The modern *shōsetsu* formula that connected *Shōsetsu shinzui*, *Ukigumo*, and the naturalists also worked well with their agenda in recapturing the Meiji past as the development of bourgeois literature, a base upon which they would develop their proletarian literary revolution. The typical narrative accordingly features a struggle between the development of bourgeois realism and feudalistic elements, the former represented by *Shōsetsu shinzui*, *Ukigumo*, and naturalist lineage, and the latter by the writers of Ken'yūsha.[73] The development of bourgeois realism coincides with that of individualism in these narratives, which is used as a negative reference point by which to promote a proletarian position: Kurahara Korehito's (1902–91) "Puroretariya rearizumu e no michi" (Toward Proletarian Realism, 1928), for example, calls for a proletarian subjectivity by which to portray reality, as opposed to the individualistic perspective of modern bourgeoisie that dominated the works of the naturalists.[74] Criticism of individualism (*kojin shugi*), whether it be identified in the form of trivial descriptions of personal surroundings (*shinpen zakki*) or the self's severance from society, was therefore a way for these critics to promote a new proletarian literature that would over-come and annul bourgeois individualism and realism.

Just as the new sensationist movement reified the modern *shōsetsu* lineage by its criticism of its realism, the proletarian literary movement essentialized a collective Meiji literature that began with *Shōsetsu shinzui*—one with the non-social, individualistic perspective of the bourgeois realism. The literary histories' emphasis on "personal impression" and alienation from the social realm, which allegedly governs Meiji literature, contributes to the image of the *shōsetsu* that is apolitical, an image that, as we shall see shortly, is reified through the many debates over politics versus art.[75] Through the debates, we find the binary "poli-tics versus art" being posited; the modern *shōsetsu* is then discovered as "art" that is associated with a certain apoliticality, whose defining characteristic was psychological realism of the socially isolated self.

The many debates in the 1920s and 1930s between the Marxist critics and the so-called *geijutsuha* (proponents of art for art's sake, consisting of "real-ists" and the new sensationist writers—despite their criticism of the realists) play a crucial role in reinforcing the mechanism of concealment within which *Shōsetsu shinzui* is implicated.[76] At the risk of simplification, I wish to map out the discussions that were prevalent at the time. For Marxist/socialist critics, art and politics were one and the same; or perhaps the better way to put it is that they tried to adhere to that belief. The following statement by Kurahara Korehito, the theoretical leader of the proletarian literature movement, is rep-resentative of their view: "All art . . . is necessarily an agitation, and proletarian art is consciously an art of agitation. Hence the proletarian artistic movement is continuously a 'political' movement in the broadest sense of the term; in this sense, an 'artistic program' is always a 'political program.'"[77] Writers and critics of proletarian literature accordingly criticized works that did not adhere to such standards; their main target was the works of bourgeois individualism, which were invariably traced to *Shōsetsu shinzui*.

This is not to say, however, that there were no conflicts in their understand-ing of politics and art. In fact, one of the most famous essays that prompted a debate over the political value of literature among the Marxist critics was written by the renowned Marxist critic Hirabayashi Hatsunosuke (1892–1931); in it, he posited the dualism of art and politics, which garnered a tremendous amount of criticism from his peers. Hayashi Fusao (1903–75), who started his literary career as a proletarian writer, also rejected political subjugation of literature. In response, Miyamoto Kenji (1908–2007) was relentless in his at-tack, and one of the criticisms characterized Hayashi as showing an "apolitical, pure-literature-oriented trend."[78] The logic was this: to leave the proletarian literature movement, as Hayashi did, was to become complicit with the apolitical trend of "pure literature." By pure literature, Miyamoto clearly had in mind the lineage of the modern *shōsetsu* traced to *Shōsetsu shinzui*.

The proponents of art for art's sake certainly did not remain silent in the face of Marxist critics' rejection of their works as bourgeois literature. Nakamura Murao's famous "Dareda? hanazono o arasu mono wa!" (Who Dares to Assail Our Flower Garden? 1928) argues against the often oppressive definition of literature presented by Marxist critics who reject all forms of fiction that do not adhere to their political philosophy. Similarly, many argued against overt politicization of literature: Minegawa Hiroshi claims that "as long as art is the product of the intellectual class, it is our mission to protect literature from politics."[79] Ozaki Shirō, too, argues that "as long as art is art, it is natural that it deviates from political concepts."[80]

Such a schematic description obviously does not do justice to the complexity of the issue at hand; in many ways, what constitutes politics and art shifted depending on the context in which each proponent argued and who the opponents were. Yet what is important for us to note is how the numerous debates and essays increasingly placed the political and artistic realms in opposition to one another. In fact, as a binary opposition, they sustain each other. As Funahashi Seiichi very tellingly said, the emergence of "art-for-art's-sake" proponents was a product of the rise of the proletarian literature, suggesting that the advocates of art for art's sake emerged to resist such a force; accordingly, they continued to become what the other was not.[81]

We witness a compelling rereading of *Shōsetsu shinzui* that appears around this time, which can be seen in Shinoda Tarō's characterization of *Shōsetsu shinzui* in 1934: *Shōsetsu shinzui* was an attempt to sever literature from sociopolitical issues as well as an attempt to posit the "artistic independence" in and of itself.[82] *Shōsetsu shinzui*'s effort to posit *shōsetsu* in the realm of art, which was shaped by the contingencies of its historical time, was renarrativized in this manner, resituated as a text that depoliticized literature in ways that are entirely dissociated from the time of its production. Characterization of *Shōsetsu shinzui* such as that of Shinoda clearly essentializes *shōsetsu*'s apoliticality and further sanitizes the realm of *shōsetsu* by concealing its position within the sociopolitical system from which it emerged.

This discussion points us to the mechanism of concealment. At a time when the urge to consolidate Meiji as a past is becoming prominent, and as the linear narrative that links *Shōsetsu shinzui* to naturalism based on "realism" and "self" in all their variations is being reproduced and essentialized, the "artistic" was defined as that which is not political. These conditions are coincidental. Despite various descriptions of art that were exchanged in the debate, the realm of the modern *shōsetsu*, especially the bourgeois art of the naturalist vein that thematizes psychological realism, was being defined as nonsocial and nonpolitical. The "political" of politics versus art cannot be equated with the "political" habitus that *Shōsetsu shinzui* rejected in its criticism of Bakin nor with the political realm that was peripherized in *Tōsei shosei katagi*. Yet the modern *shōsetsu* whose lineage was traced to *Shōsetsu shinzui* was reconfigured in the 1920s and 1930s as the politically sanitized realm.

The increase in government suppression, which was symbolically expressed in the death by torture of Kobayashi Takiji in 1933, brought about a decisive decline in the proletarian movement.[83] By this time, the binary between politics and literature was essentialized: the proletarian literature writers who disavowed Marxism and hence performed "acts of conversion" (*tenkō*) were characterized as those who "returned to literature."[84] Despite the clear political positionality of the writers, in such a paradigm, the acts of conversion signified relinquishing politics, which further signified a return to literature. The decline of the proletarian literary movement appropriately brought about a period known as the "revival of literature" (*bungei fukkō*). By then, pure literature was already in a politically sanitized form.

As I have repeatedly argued, the depoliticization of the *shōsetsu* at the time *Shōsetsu shinzui* was written had overt political implications specific to the time of its production. It constituted a will to power within the existing sociopolitical system precisely because it marked an attempt to produce a new space, a space where the *shōsetsu* found its raison d'être. The dissociation from the political sector was the condition upon which this space of the *shōsetsu* was found.

This brings me to one of the primary differences that marks the time of *Shōsetsu shinzui*'s production and the 1930s: the status of "literature" itself. Literature as a category had already acquired recognition in the 1930s. In fact, the debates between politics and art are predicated on the existence of literature as an ontologically independent category. Whichever side one took, the debates revolved around what "literature" ought to be. For example, literature is an essential existence in Hayashi Fusao's self-reflective essay "Sakka to shite" (As a Writer, 1933); he claims that he had long wavered between "two poles of 'politics' and 'literature'" and that in his mind he had at times "subjugated literature to politics" while "separating literature from politics" in others. Now, he claims, he decided to "devote [his] entire life to literature" and relinquish "politics."[85] Notice the same ontological status that "literature" and "politics" occupy in his argument. In response to Hayashi, Kobayashi Takiji argues that "literature can achieve its full potential only when incorporated in political struggle" and "the effort to perfect literature by isolating it from politics only weakens literature in the future."[86] Quite evident from the discussions of these writers, whether one claims that literature is politics or that literature is separate from politics, literature's ontological status is clearly assumed. Proletarian literature was, after all, already accepted as a *literary* genre. The debates that occur with such an assumption are entirely asymmetrical with the dichotomy of politics and literature of the late nineteenth century.

Historical contingencies have coincidentally and continuously reinforced the positive referents of "emotions, customs, and manners" and *ari no mama*, and further reinforced the linear narrative that was produced based on these referents, which were in many ways independent of *Shōsetsu shinzui* and its historical contingencies. The production of the mimetic condition, coupled with the discovery of the self that was established after the Russo-Japanese War, engaged with the urge that arose in the 1920s and 1930s to resituate the Meiji period; these conditions were coincidentally accompanied by the debates on the dichotomy of politics/art that putatively "sanitized" the realm of art. All these forces coalesced in producing and sustaining the ideological narrative of the modern *shōsetsu*, (re)producing the originary status of *Shōsetsu shinzui*.

Afterword

I described two levels of concealment in this book: first, the concealment of politics in 1880s Japan, a process through which literature as category was produced; and second, the concealment of "the concealment of politics" by the twentieth-century literary histories, which suppressed the specific condition through which "literature" emerged as they repeatedly designated *Shōsetsu shinzui* as the origin of modern Japanese literature. In this afterword, I wish to discuss further implications of such a double concealment.

As I argued throughout the book, literature as a category was produced through the rejection and concealment of the politics of its time. The political habitus featured the discursive affinities claimed by both sides in the central conflict involving the Freedom and People's Rights Movement and the Meiji elites. First, radical political activism, linked to the violent uprisings (*gekka jiken*), was represented through the language of good/bad and right/wrong (*zen'aku jasei*) shared among the activists in a form of communal recitation. The language of communal recitation was embodied in the works of Kyokutei Bakin and the lineage of the *hakuwa* tradition traced back to the Chinese classics *The Water Margin* and *The Epoch of the Three Kingdoms*. Second, the political arena of the Meiji elites, which included both the Freedom and People's Rights activists and government supporters, was represented through works that drew on *Karyū shunwa* (*Romantic Stories of Blossoms*), narratives of "a beautiful woman and a talented man" (*kajin saishi*) that thematized the protagonists' political success and consummation of love. As the chapter on *Tōsei shosei katagi* made clear, this was the domain in which the Meiji elites, through their own exclusive network of resources, established a system of self-enrichment. In other words, the *shōsetsu*, as it found its raison d'être in "emotions, customs, and manners" (*ninjō, fūzoku, setai*), rejected the Freedom and People's Rights activism as well as the Meiji elites, as it defined itself in opposition to these forces.

Through the rejection of such politics, the *shōsetsu* demarcated a space of its own, a space of putative neutrality that exists alongside but never within the existing modalities of power. The new space was defined as "the social" (*sewa*)—in which the nonpolitical protagonist finds his identity in his internal struggle in love. This space nullifies the dominant opposition in the political landscape between the Meiji government and the Freedom and People's Rights Movement and treats the political arena as a single arena of the elites from which to distance the space of *shōsetsu*.

This new space was defined in response to numerous historically contingent anxieties. Although I have claimed a concrete link between the concealment of politics and some of these anxieties, I presented others as discursive movements parallel to the concealment of politics. Regardless of the degree of connection, the category of literature emerged as an embodiment of these anxieties. Recall that the advocates of the maxim "the autonomy of knowledge" facilitated the production of the *shōsetsu* when they saw that they were being defeated in the political struggle. The *shōsetsu* synchronized with the forces that sought to conceal Japan's vulnerable status in East Asia by seeking rhetorical fulfillment of its status as the "civilized" leader in East Asia. Its production was endorsed by redefinition of knowledge haunted by Japan's desire to become the West, a desire that could never be fulfilled. It further engaged with anxieties over political representation that brought about radical activism. The domestic struggle over what constituted modern knowledge and the need for internal reform, which embodied a political struggle between advocates of Confucian principles and Western learning, endorsed the production of the *shōsetsu*. In other words, the production of literature in 1880s Japan was about what makes Japan Japan, its relation to the world, and domestic turmoil over political representation, as well as its place in the shifting paradigms of knowledge that constantly negotiated with its imperial longing.

Yet the literary histories that designated *Shōsetsu shinzui* as the origin of modern Japanese literature constantly dissociated that literature from the moment of its production and concealed the anxieties that literature embodied. In spite of their varying agendas specific to each historical moment, they continued to conceal the anxieties as they took for granted the existence of "literature." As long as the existence itself is not questioned, the anxieties that fostered its production are never brought to the fore.

Part of what fosters this concealment is the link between *Shōsetsu shinzui* clichés and *Shōsetsu shinzui* itself. Recall that the association between the medium of *shōsetsu* and emotion, customs, and manners appeared in the 1880s independently of *Shōsetsu shinzui*. *Shōsetsu shinzui* was merely one of the many texts that expressed the connection. By putatively separating emotion, customs, and manners and *Shōsetsu shinzui* and recasting them onto the discursive landscape of 1880s Japan, I identified the epistemological shift in literature. Yet once *Shōsetsu shinzui* was discovered as the origin, these terms became associated with it, giving *Shōsetsu shinzui* the sole agency in bringing about the birth of modern Japanese literature. This birth, however, should not be equated with the epistemological shift; in fact, this narrative is precisely what conceals the emergence of literature as a category by presupposing the existence of literature that had yet to come into being. In effect, the uncritical association between emotion, customs, and manners and "as things are" (*ari no mama*) with *Shōsetsu shinzui* dissociates *shōsetsu* from the moment of its production and makes us lose sight of the multiple layers of discourse that the production of the *shōsetsu* engages.

When the boundaries of literature demarcated in *Shōsetsu shinzui* are taken for granted, the discussion of literature is confined to the definition of literature offered in *Shōsetsu shinzui*. This is most evident with the representation of "frivolous or trivial writings" (*gesaku*). *Gesaku* was designated as the negative precursor to *shōsetsu*. *Shōsetsu shinzui* created fallacious continuity between Edo and Meiji *gesaku*, whose main characteristic was didacticism that needed "reform." Such a characterization of Edo and Meiji *gesaku* grossly simplified the changes brought forth by new printing technology, government-sponsored reforms, and shifting paradigms of knowledge. Perhaps more important, within the confines of literature, *gesaku* appears only as a repressed "literary" genre. Such a treatment of *gesaku* erases the choice *gesaku* signified: a deliberate selection over the *hakuwa* line that had depoliticizing and de-Asianizing impulses inscribed within it.

The treatment of Bakin within such a paradigm only replicates the process of depoliticization. Bakin in many ways signified what the term *shōsetsu* meant before its coupling with "novel." Within the confines of literature, however, "encourage virtue, castigate vice" (*kanzen chōaku*) and the language of *zen'aku jasei* represent "uncivilized" and "superficial" characteristics. How Bakin was implicated in the Freedom and People's Rights Movement, how his language consolidated the political energy, and how works that share such language were directly linked to the violent uprisings and hence to the discourse of the imaginary revolution against the Meiji government are all concealed in the "literary" Bakin. Without freeing Bakin from the confines of literature and recasting his works onto the moment in which they were discovered as "barbaric," the link between the *zen'aku jasei* discourse of the domestic political turmoil and the de-Asianizing impulses of the time cannot be foregrounded. The alignment between depoliticization and de-Asianization—between the language with which Bakin's cosmos was reduced and the language that constructed "Asia" of de-Asianization, the barbaric other by which to define Japan's superiority—expresses Japan's anxiety specific to 1880s Japan. It foregrounds the will to power that facilitates the production of the *shōsetsu*. In effect, literary studies of Bakin sanitize Bakin's place in the political discourse and hence contribute to the further concealment of the political.

Such treatment of Bakin was reinforced by the turn-of-the-century literary histories that equated psychological realism with emotions (*ninjō*) and *ari no mama*, which were invariably linked to *Shōsetsu shinzui*. *Ari no mama* was specifically posited against *kanzen chōaku*, which was based on the language of *zen'aku jasei*. The literary histories, by giving positive referents to terms that were quite empty at the time of *Shōsetsu shinzui*'s production, erased the role of Bakin as a negative embodiment of the *shōsetsu*. As a result, they concealed the *shōsetsu*'s urge to seek out a new space called "the social" where emotion, customs, and manners would be depicted. The literary histories of the 1920s and 1930s further reinforced the equation between psychological realism and *ari no mama* and emotions as they (re)configured the modern *shōsetsu* formula as a medium that portrays the nonpolitical, socially alienated self. Despite the fact that nonpolitical in the 1920s and 1930s signified "nonproletarian," literary histories rewrote the *shōsetsu*'s apparent apoliticality in their terms.

Given the erasure of the specific contingencies in which literature was generated, such (re)configuring of emotions and *ari no mama* sanitizes literature of all the anxiety that it embodies. This literature is thus a site of double concealment. The study of literature within the confines of *Shōsetsu shinzui*'s literature can only conceal the concealment of the political and hence the anxieties inscribed in it.

These anxieties became apparent as I explored the parallel discursive movements that facilitated the epistemological shift in the understanding of literature.

The discursive space of "knowledge" is one of them. Knowledge engaged with the production of the *shōsetsu* at various levels. With the maxim "autonomy of knowledge," knowledge sought the space of neutrality and hence synchronized with the *shōsetsu*. Knowledge was also used as Japan posited its relationship vis-à-vis East Asia, defining Japanese knowledge as a means to "naturally" educate the "less civilized," unlike Confucianism/China that "directly interferes," thereby replicating the *shōsetsu* as a medium that naturally elevates the reader's mind. With the subsequent establishment of "national literature" (*kokubungaku*) in the academy, this anxiety-ridden literature became implicated in the nationalization process through the compilation of literary histories that sought to discover an expression of national character. The internal focus of literary histories further facilitated the establishment of the *shōsetsu*.

The new geographical awareness that shaped the world order in the nineteenth century is another. This new world order and the cofigurative model of desire shaped the many claims for Japan's superiority in East Asia as it sought to "become" the West by discovering a more barbaric other. As Japan's claim to be the leader in East Asia was constantly questioned in the mid-1880s, Japanese intellectuals reverted to rhetorical fulfillment of Japan's superiority and concealed the vulnerability of Japan's geopolitical reality. Such forces for rhetorical fulfillment synchronized with the production of the *shōsetsu* that sought to disengage itself from the political arena and produce a new space of neutrality. The realm of *shōsetsu*, by limiting its narrative to a space in which Japan's geopolitical reality does not enter the picture, thus acted out the concealment, temporarily giving relief to the anxiety.

However, anxiety that arose from the cofigurative model of desire could never be erased, and the desire to become the West constantly reproduced imperial longing. In this regard, the two historical moments we saw in the last chapter that dissociated *Shōsetsu shinzui* from the moment of its production and concealed the anxieties embodied in the production of literature warrant further thought. I highlighted the turn of the century as the time when the mimetic order was established along with a new mode of reading that blurred the boundaries of reality and fiction. I then selected the 1920s and 1930s as the time when the Meiji period was discovered as the past, an origin of the modern, which coincided with the definition of the artistic *shōsetsu* as a "nonsocial, nonpolitical" realm. In these moments, literary histories effectively rewrote the *Shōsetsu shinzui*'s clichés and facilitated the concealment of the anxieties that produced literature.

Interestingly, these two moments coincide with Japan's establishment in the new world order. The turn of the century marked Japan's victory in the Russo-Japanese War, allowing the Japanese to claim "equality" with the West. In the 1920s and 1930s, we see the emergence of the Japanese Empire and territorial expansion in East Asia. In short, there are two apparently contradictory forces at work here. Take the latter period as an example: Instabilities of Meiji undeniably became the past in the 1920s and 1930s as the Japanese Empire began to take firm hold of East Asia. Yet the apoliticality of the modern *shōsetsu* produced through the debates on politics and art in the 1920s and 1930s rewrote the depoliticization of *shōsetsu* specific to the nineteenth century and further concealed the anxiety inscribed in literature. I do not mean to claim any causal or logical link between these two forces. I just want to suggest that, in spite of Japan's rise among the world powers, the anxiety inscribed in literature never became the "past."

The period when *Shōsetsu shinzui* was appropriated as origin is just one period ripe for reflection. Although I cannot deal with it here, a similar project can be carried out for the post–World War II period. The dichotomy of politics and art was again revisited soon after the war. The debates over political superiority and self-sufficiency of literature—and ultimately how the "modernized self" (*kindai jiga*) is resituated vis-à-vis literary history—shape the modern *shōsetsu* formula. The manner in which such debates engage with Japan's defeat and the writers' and critics' self-reflection on their complicity in war is a complex yet fascinating problem to which I cannot do justice at the present time. It certainly marks another moment when the modern *shōsetsu* was (re)configured, further concealing the politicality of *Shōsetsu shinzui*'s ideological status. The anxiety specific to the production of literature in the nineteenth century thus haunts the Japanese literary studies of the post–World War II era to which we are, in many ways, still bound.

Notes

CHAPTER I

1. Now a standard translation of "novel," *shōsetsu* was, as I argue later, a contested term in the early Meiji period. I will provide the definition of *shōsetsu* later in this chapter. Given the importance of the term, I will retain *shōsetsu* throughout the book without resorting to the term "novel."

2. Kamei, *"Shōsetsu"ron*, 3.

3. Tsubouchi Shōyō, *Shōsetsu shinzui*, in *Tsubouchi Shōyōshū*, vol. 3 of *Nihon kindai bungaku taikei*, 70–71 (hereafter cited as *Shōsetsu shinzui*). All the page numbers are from this edition. I owe a great deal to Nanette Twine's translation of *Shōsetsu shinzui*; I most often quote her directly and will thus list the page numbers for her translation as well. Nanette Twine, *Essence of the Novel*, 24–25. I have also consulted *Shōsetsu shinzui*, compiled in *Tsubouchi Shōyōshū*, vol. 16 of *Meiji bungaku zenshū*; *Shōsetsu shinzui* (Tokyo: Nihon kindai bungakkan, 1976); and *Shōsetsu shinzui* (Tokyo: Iwanami bunko, 1936). An extensive analysis of this passage is provided in Chapter 3.

4. In the final chapter, I examine when and how such narrative was produced, hence historicizing the dominant narrative that situates *Shōsetsu shinzui* at the beginning of modern Japanese literature.

5. As I will discuss in more detail in Chapter 6, the term *shajitsu* was quite unstable and did not necessarily signify "realism" at the turn of the century. The interpretation of *shajitsu* as "realism" is one of the reasons for the retrospective designation of *Shōsetsu shinzui* as the origin of modern Japanese literature.

6. Takayama Chogyū, "Meiji no shōsetsu," compiled in *Saitō Ryokuu, Ishibashi Ningetsu, Takayama Chogyū, Uchida Roanshū*, vol. 8 of *Nihon gendai*

bungaku zenshū (Tokyo: Kōdansha, 1967), 261 (hereafter cited as "Meiji no shōsetsu").

7. Ikuta Chōkō, *Meiji jidai bunpan* (Tokyo: Hakubunkan, 1907), 68–69 (hereafter cited as *Meiji jidai bunpan*).

8. To be precise, such narrative of literary history continued well into the 1980s and in some cases into the 1990s. For example, Ino Kenji identifies *Shōsetsu shinzui* as "the first critical work to define the fundamental features of the modern novel." Ino, *Meiji bungakushi*, 228–29. Ishida Tadahiko says, "I cannot deny that the modernity in the *shōsetsu* began with *Shōsetsu shinzui*." Ishida, *Tsubouchi Shōyō kenkyū*, 165. Yamada Yūsaku too claims, "In order to turn toward the 'West' in terms of theoretical concepts, Japan needed a pioneer. Shōyō was that pioneer and Japanese literature gained a direction toward the 'modern' with his *Shōsetsu shinzui*." Yamada, "Jobun," iii.

9. Among many works produced by these critics, I wish to specifically mention Maeda, *Kindai dokusha no seiritsu* and *Kindai Nihon no bungaku kūkan*; Kamei, *Kansei no henkaku* and *Shintai, kono fushigi naru mono no bungaku*.

10. Asukai, *Nihon no kindai bungaku*, 53.

11. See also Komori, *Kōzō to shite no katari* and *Buntai to shite no monogatari*.

12. Kōda Rohan, "Meiji nijūnen zengo no nibunsei," compiled in *Meiji bungaku kaisōshū*, ed. Togawa Shinsuke (Tokyo: Iwanami bunko, 1998), 1:272–73 (hereafter cited as "Meiji nijūnen zengo no nibunsei").

13. Kornicki, *Reform of Fiction*, 35–37.

14. Nakayama, "'Bungakushi' to nashonaritī," 83–119. Nakayama states that *Shōsetsu shinzui* clichés are used in over 60 percent of the literary histories he examined from the Meiji period. The main gist of his article is not on *Shōsetsu shinzui* but the varying types of clichés used in the constructions of literary histories and how they are usurped and reappropriated in subsequent literary histories.

15. *Mosha suru* means "to copy" in contemporary Japanese, which is often taken to mean *shajitsu*, denoting mimetic description. As Maeda Ai suggests, however, *mosha* in Shōyō's day had a different signified: *mosha* was like a signature marker used by Edo painters, which denoted "so-and-so painted this." Maeda, "Kindai bungaku to katsujiteki sekai," 329. For a more extensive discussion on *mosha*, see Chapter 3.

16. For both of these references, see Kornicki, *Reform of Fiction*, 33–34. As Kornicki points out, Shōyō was by no means unique in his references to "emotions, customs, and manners" in describing the *shōsetsu*.

17. We cannot rule out the possibility that Sakazaki is referring to Shōyō's preface to his translation of Bulwer-Lytton's *Rienzi* (entitled *Gaisei shiden*, published in 1884), which is considered to be the precursor to *Shōsetsu shinzui*. However, given that neither the preface nor *Shōsetsu shinzui* was immediately rec-

ognized by the reading public as a seminal work of *shōsetsu* theory, it is also possible that Sakazaki landed on such terms through other means. "Shōsetsu haishi no honbun o ronzu" is signed by Mui Masato, identified as Sakazaki Shiran. This article appeared in *Jiyū no tomoshibi* in March 1885 and is included in Yoshida and Asai, *Kindai bungaku hyōron taikei 1*, 23.

18. "Bungaku sekai no kinkyō" first appeared in *Chōya shinbun*, February 27, 1890, unsigned. Modern literary critic Ochi Haruo, however, speculates that it was written by Ozaki Gakudō (1858–1954). This, too, is compiled in Yoshida and Asai, *Kindai bungaku hyōron taikei 1*, 98–99.

19. Uchida Roan, "Jogaku zasshi no shōsetsuron," initially published *in Tokyo yoron shinshi* on September 11, 1889, has been more recently published in *Uchida Roanshū*, vol. 24 of *Meiji bungaku zenshū* (Tokyo: Chikuma shobō, 1978), 143 (hereafter cited as "Jogaku zasshi no shōsetsuron").

20. For a discussion of this concept of the habitus, see Bourdieu, *Outline of a Theory of Practice* and *Logic of Practice*.

21. *Seiji shōsetsu* did not become identifiable as a literary genre probably until around the time Tokutomi Sohō published his famous criticism, "Kinrai ryūkō no seiji shōsetsu o hyōsu" (On the Recently Popular *Seiji shōsetsu*, 1887), in which he identified the defining characteristics of *seiji shōsetsu* as he negatively evaluated such works. Tokutomi Sohō, "Kinrai ryūkō no seiji shōsetsu o hyōsu," *Kokumin no tomo*, vol. 6 (July 1887); it is reprinted in *Kokumin no tomo,* vol. 1 (Tokyo: Meiji bunken, 1966) (hereafter cited as "Kinrai ryūkō no seiji shōsetsu o hyōsu"). "*Seiji shōsetsu*" as titles to works (e.g., *Seiji shōsetsu: Setchūbai* [Political *shōsetsu*: Plums in the Snow]) began to appear around 1886–87.

22. In conceptualizing this view of discourse, I consulted not only the prominent theories of discourse such as Foucault, *Archaeology of Knowledge* and *Order of Things*, but also the theory of autopoesis, which finds its origin in biological theory. It was soon applied to social contexts, most notably by Niklas Luhmann. See Luhmann, *Social Systems* and *Observations of Modernity*. See also Kawamoto, *Ōtopoiēshisu.*

23. *Kangaku* is typically translated as "Chinese learning," but I wish to refrain from invoking a regionally specific designation for *kangaku* and retain the term without translating it. Classical writings of *kangaku* may have originated in China, but the practice of *kangaku* has a long history in Japan, and it is quite misleading to suggest that *kangaku* and its Confucian foundation are "Chinese" and *not* "Japanese." When linguistic traditions are discussed, the division between Japan and China is not only hard to draw but is ideologically charged, especially as the impulses of de-Asianization (often equated to "de-China") became strong in 1880s Japan. This is especially important because, as we shall see in Chapter 4, proponents of "de-Asianization and Westernization" began to isolate "Chinese" by

designating Confucian principles as "Asian" and hence "non-Japanese," all the while seeking affinity with the West. For a brilliant discussion on the ambivalent status of Sino-Japanese tradition in the Meiji period, see Saitō, *Kanbunmyaku no kindai*.

24. The translation of this passage from Suzuki Akira's (1764–1837) *Hanareya gakkun* (*Teachings in the Hanareya*, 1814) is provided in Naoki Sakai's *Translation and Subjectivity*. Sakai continues to define *bungaku* in the following manner: "[*Bun*] meant the texture of a certain social reality that is 'lived' by people and whereby the people are ruled. . . . Primarily, it was neither a set of abstract doctrines nor imperative statements that were determined in conceptual terms. Its distinctive feature lay in its concreteness and its immediacy to those who abided by it. Conceptualized thus, *bun* was in fact akin to what we today understand by ideology. People were supposed to internalize the *bun* of behavior patterns, and it was by 'living' this texture that they were successfully ruled. . . . Nevertheless, *bungaku* was not merely a given, a gift, since the compound contained another character, *gaku*, which meant work, labor, the laborious process of learning. *Bun* was something that had to be learned through repetitive practice" (23–24).

25. Nishi, *Hyakugaku renkan*, 12.

26. *Chunqiu* is a historical account of events that occurred between the years 772 BC and 381 BC and is said to have been compiled by Confucius. *Guoyu* consists of historical chronicles from Western Zhou to 453 BC. *Shi ji*, written by Sima Qian (145–86 BC), is one of the primary *kangaku* classics that records history from the beginning of China to about 86 BC. *Hanshu* is a classic that covers the history of Western Han from 206 BC to AD 8.

27. See Tomi Suzuki's *Narrating the Self* for a discussion of *shōsetsu* and *haishi*'s "critical framework" (18) that the translated and political works of fiction inherited.

28. For an extensive discussion of the category of *shōsetsu*, see Fujii, *Nihon "shōsetsu" genshi* and Noguchi, *Shōsetsu*.

29. 「小説家流、蓋出於稗官、街談巷語、道聴塗説者所造也」.

30. Takizawa (Kyokutei) Bakin, for example, often referred to his work as a *shōsetsu* in humbling himself and his creation.

31. Despite the fact that *hakuwa shōsetsu* is often referred to as "Chinese vernacular fiction," I wish to note here that the *hakuwa* lineage is not necessarily Chinese, especially after the increase in works of adaptations in Edo Japan. Just like *kangaku*, therefore, I will henceforth refrain from using the regionally specific designation "Chinese" in referring to the *hakuwa* tradition, except when referring to specific works, such as *The Water Margin* or *The Epoch of the Three Kingdoms*. As we will see in the next chapter, there are attempts in *Shōsetsu shinzui* to isolate "Chinese" writings as those that are not "Japanese," which are on a par with the de-Asianizing impulses of the time.

32. Both of these works are said to be written between the end of the Yuan dynasty (1279–1367) and the early Ming dynasty (1368–1661).

33. Nishi, *Hyakugaku renkan*, 76. He lists *The Epoch of the Three Kingdoms* and *The Water Margin* as Japanese/Chinese equivalents of romance.

34. "Rhetoric and Belles-Lettres" is a section of Chambers and Chambers, *Chambers' Information for the People*.

35. Matsumura Shun'suke, *Kaimei shōsetsu: Harusame bunko*, in *Meiji kaikaki bungakushū 1*, vol. 1 of *Meiji bungaku zenshū* (Tokyo: Chikuma shobō, 1966), 309.

36. Takabatake Ransen, *Kōsetsu kono tegashiwa*, in *Meiji kaikaki bungakushū 2*, vol. 2 of *Meiji bungaku zenshū* (Tokyo: Chikuma shobō, 1967), 145.

37. Sakurada Momoe, *Nishi no umi chishio no saarashi*, in *Meiji seiji shōsetsushū 1*, vol. 5 of *Meiji bungaku zenshū* (Tokyo: Chikuma shobō, 1966), 11 (hereafter cited as *Nishi no umi chishio no saarashi*).

38. Tōkai Sanshi, *Kajin no kigū*, compiled in *Meiji seiji shōsetsushū 2*, vol. 6 of *Meiji bungaku zenshū* (Tokyo: Chikuma shobō, 1967), 3.

39. There have been many debates about when Shōyō actually wrote *Shōsetsu shinzui*. Most critics now follow Yanagida Izumi, who claims that the first draft was complete by the time Shōyō graduated from Kaisei gakkō (later Tokyo Imperial University) in 1883. See Chapters 2 and 3 for more extensive discussions on why *hakuwa*-type narratives grew in number in the 1880s.

40. *Shōsetsu shinzui*, 42; Twine, *Essence of the Novel*, 3.

41. It is often said that translators took liberty with the original, freely taking out and/or inserting passages, as if the Meiji translators were wrong in doing so. For example, Fujikawa Yoshiyuki says that "not only were the works not faithful to the original but [translators] inserted passages self-indulgently and altered sentences at whim." Fujikawa, "Hon'yaku bungaku no tenbō," 318. However, it is more appropriate to say that the idea that a translation had to be accurate or faithful to the original did not exist. The ideology of translation in which the original is valorized as "god's word" was produced subsequently to the proliferation of the works in question. John Mertz, in discussing the translated works, says the following: "The works are . . . neither 'Japanese' nor 'foreign,' neither 'original works' nor 'true translations.' They defy the basic categories of both national and authorial attribution." Mertz, *Novel Japan*, 252.

42. Many other Kaishintō affiliates translated British novels, especially works of Edward Bulwer-Lytton (1803–73), who was by far the most popular British writer in early-Meiji Japan; unlike the Jiyūtō affiliates, however, they did not frame their translations with language and themes reminiscent of *hakuwa shōsetsu*. Reserving my discussion on the works translated by Kaishintō members until later, I wish to focus here on the works that adhere to the *hakuwa* tradition, given that they enjoyed tremendous popularity among the literati of the time.

43. Narushima Ryūhoku, "Ōshū kiji: Karyū shunwa daigen," in Oda Jun'ichirō, trans., *Ōshū kiji: Karyū shunwa*, compiled in *Meiji hon'yaku bungakushū*, vol. 7 of *Meiji bungaku zenshū* (Tokyo: Chikuma shobō, 1972), 3.

44. For what constitutes "practical knowledge" (*jitsugaku*), see Chapter 2. Moreover, this is not to say that there were no literary works published before *Karyū shunwa*. Other notable works include Daniel Defoe's *Robinson Crusoe* (translated from Dutch) in 1872 and William Shakespeare's *Hamlet* in 1875. See "Meiji hon'yaku bungaku nenpyō."

45. There were, of course, further conflicts between scholars of *kangaku* and "native learning."

46. On Meiji "national literature" and its close affiliation with the emergence of the modern university system, see Brownstein, "From *Kokugaku* to *Kokubungaku*"; Suzuki, "Gender and Genre"; Shirane, "Curriculum and Competing Canons" and "'Kokubungaku' no keisei"; Shinada, *Man'yōshū no hatsumei*; Yoda, *Gender and National Literature*.

47. I must add, however, that a direct connection is also a possibility; in one of his records of reminiscence (*kaikoroku*), which he published in August 1934, Ueda Kazutoshi, one of the main leaders of academic *kokubungaku*, recalls being an avid reader of *Shōsetsu shinzui* around the time it was published. Ueda, "Kokugogaku no sōseiki," 1132.

48. The compilers have noted the influence of Hippolyte Taine's *History of English Literature* and Hutcheson Macaulay Posnett's *Comparative Literature* in deriving at such a definition of literature. See also Nakayama's "'Bungakushi' to nashonaritī" for a brilliant analysis of the rhetoric mobilized in literary histories.

49. Mikami and Takatsu, *Nihon bungakushi* (Tokyo: Kinkōdō, 1890). Reprinted as *Nihon bungakushi* (Tokyo: Nihon tosho sentā, 1982), 5.

50. See, for example, Liu, *Translingual Practice*; Yamamuro, *Shisō kadai to shite no Ajia*; Komori, *Posutokoroniaru*.

51. Yamamuro, *Shisō kadai to shite no Ajia*, 199.

52. Ibid., 199–210.

53. "Cofiguration" and "tropes of equivalence" are terms that grew out of theories of translation, exemplified by works of Naoki Sakai and Lydia Liu, which have shed new light on the problematics of modernity in East Asia. Sakai, *Translation and Subjectivity*, 15–16; Liu, *Translingual Practice*.

54. This idea was advocated by Hashimoto Sanai, who sought to bring about Asian consolidation by Russo-Japanese coalition. Yamamuro, *Shisō kadai to shite no Ajia*, 582.

55. This was the primary idea behind Hayashi Shihei's *Sangoku tsūran zusetsu*. Yamamuro, *Shisō kadai to shite no Ajia*, 581.

56. Yamamuro, *Shisō kadai to shite no Ajia*, 584.

57. As Joshua Fogel makes clear, the increase in actual travel and distribution of reports written by the travelers also contributed to such change. Fogel, *Literature of Travel.*

58. Sakai argues, "It is important to note that, through the representation of translation, the two unities are represented as two equivalents resembling one another. Precisely because they are represented in equivalence and resemblance, however, it is possible to determine them as conceptually different. . . . Just as in the cofiguration of 'the West and the Rest' in which the West represents itself, thereby constituting itself cofiguratively by representing the exemplary figure of the Rest, conceptual difference allows for the evaluative determination of the one term as superior over the other." Sakai, *Translation and Subjectivity*, 16.

59. As I will make clear in Chapter 4, this discussion of the cofigurative model of desire draws not only on Sakai's paradigm of cofiguration but also on Homi Bhabha's concept of colonial mimicry and ambivalence. Bhabha, *Location of Culture.*

60. These terms have multiple meanings. Chapter 2 provides a detailed description of each.

61. I borrow Kevin M. Doak's translation of Muryū's title. His paper features a brilliant analysis of varying representations of France used in early Meiji political discourse. Doak, "Civil Society," 16.

62. See, for example, Yamada, "Jobun," iii.

63. Hachimonjiya Jishō (?–1745) and Ejima Kiseki (1667–1736) were popular writers of *ukiyo zōshi* (literally, "stories of the floating world") in the Genroku period (ca. 1670–1710). Kasei culture (ca. 1800–50) refers to the time period in which Bakin wrote his works.

64. Shōyō, "Kaioku mandan," 348–49.

65. See, for example, Maeda, "Gesaku bungaku to *Tōsei shosei katagi*"; Takemori, "'Henka' 'hensen' to iu koto." In recent years, however, some works have reevaluated *Tōsei shosei katagi*, especially in its production of the new narrative voice. See Yamada, "*Tōsei shosei katagi*—katarite o megutte"; Komori, *Kōzō to shite no katari*; Kamei, "Seishi jitsuroku to shōsetsu haishi"; Yamada, "Bōkan suru katarite no haikei"; and "*Tōsei shosei katagi* ni okeru sakusha no ichi."

66. Quoted in Ino, *Meiji bungakushi*, 192.

67. It must be noted, however, that in *Ernest Maltravers*, Maltravers is not poor and Alice is not a wealthy woman. In fact, the situation is reversed. Maltravers is an aristocratic heir, and Alice is the daughter of a thief who tries to deceive Maltravers at the beginning of the story. Yet Maltravers's psychological development, which brings about the consummation of his love affair with Alice, appeared to embody the ideal for the Meiji students. This is apparent from the use of the trope of *kajin saishi* (a beautiful woman and a talented man)

in referring to Maltravers and Alice, the same trope used to refer to the characters in the stories produced in Japan with a similar plot structure.

68. Ino Kenji states that Sohō most probably had Suehiro Tetchō's *Setchūbai*
in mind when he wrote this criticism. Ino, *Meiji bungakushi*, 222.

69. Hibi, *Jiko hyōshō no bungakushi.*

CHAPTER 2

1. I will discuss the category of *gesaku* more extensively later in the chapter,
but as the translation "playful writings" shows, *gesaku* refers to a body of writing
considered secondary to serious, or scholarly, texts.

2. *Genji monogatari* (*The Tale of Genji*) by Murasaki Shikibu (978–1019?), written in the first decade of the eleventh century, is undoubtedly the most famous
and most celebrated text of the *monogatari* tradition. *Sagoromo monogatari* (*The
Tale of Sagoromo*) by Baishi naishin'nō senji (?) was written in the second half of
the eleventh century. *Hamamatsu chūnagon monogatari* (*The Tale of Hamamatsu*)
by the daughter of Sugawara Takasue (1008–?) was written about 1045–67.
Sumiyoshi monogatari (*The Tale of Sumiyoshi*), whose author is unknown, was
written in the early Kamakura period (1192–1333). Ichijō Zenkō (1402–81) is
the famous *kangaku* scholar and poet Ichijō Kanera, known for his scholarship
in poetic composition. By Ichijō's *gesaku*, *Shōsetsu shinzui* is possibly referring
to *Shōjin gyorui monogatari* (*The Tale of Devoted Seafarers*, 1452). Ono no Otsū
(1559–1616) was a writer and musician in the service of Yodogimi (1569–1615).

3. Ihara Saikaku (1642–93) was a writer of *ukiyo zōshi* (literally, "stories of the
floating world") and was famous for his *kōshoku mono*, which thematized love and
lust. Hachimonjiya Kishō (?–1750) was known for his adaptations of *jōruri* and
kabuki, two representative genres of drama. Fūrai Sanjin (1726–79), better known
as Hiraga Gen'nai, was an Edo scientist who also wrote *gesaku*. Santō Kyōden
(1761–1816) was a popular writer who published in a variety of *gesaku* subgenres,
such as "yellow-cover" books (*kibyōshi*), "humorous stories" (*kokkeibon*), "books of
wit and fashion" (*sharebon*), "books of sentiment" (*ninjōbon*), and "books for reading" (*yomihon*). These subgenres will be explained later in the chapter.

4. Jippensha Ikku (1765–1831) is most famous for *Tōkai dōchū hizakurige* (*By
Shank's Mare through the West*, 1802–9). Shikitei Sanba (1776–1822) is known for
Ukiyoburo (*Baths of the Floating World*, 1809). Tamenaga Shunsui (1790–1843) is
especially known for *Shunshoku umegoyomi* (*Colors of Spring: The Plum Calendar*,
1832–33), which features the playboy Tanjirō and his love encounters with geisha
and prostitutes.

5. Ryūtei Tanehiko (1783–1843) is celebrated for *Nise Murasaki inaka Genji*
(*The Rustic Genji*, 1829–42), a parody of *The Tale of Genji*. Kyokutei Bakin
(1767–1848) is arguably the most popular writer of "books for reading" of the late

Edo period. *Nansō Satomi hakkenden* (*The Account of Eight Dogs*, 1814–41) is his representative work.

6. *Shōsetsu shinzui*, 40; Twine, *Essence of the Novel*, 1–2.

7. The term *noberu* (or "novel") is provided alongside the word *shōsetsu* in the form of a *rubi*. *Rubi* are glosses that show how the sinified characters should be read. In the first edition, *noberu* is provided parenthetically.

8. *Shōsetsu shinzui*, 42; Twine, *Essence of the Novel*, 3.

9. For the use of the word *monogatari*, see Fujii, "Kodai bungaku shiron," 38–42.

10. See Okada, *Figures of Resistance*. I would like to thank Steven Carter for pointing out to me this oral component of *monogatari*. Orality associated with *monogatari* may well have been the reason that *Shōsetsu shinzui* did not choose the term *monogatari* to take on the main genre it sought to promote. See Chapter 3 for further discussion.

11. The term *haishi* was already being used in *Hanshu* (*History of the Han Dynasty*).

12. However, as Patrick Caddeau shows in his recent book *Appraising Genji*, late Edo scholar Hagiwara Hiromichi sought to read *Genji monogatari* as a *shōsetsu*, or popular fiction, applying the critical terms associated with the interpretation of *hakuwa* fiction in his reading.

13. As Nakamura Yukihiko notes, however, earlier usages can be found in Osaka and Kyoto writers such as Ueda Akinari (1734–1809) and Tsuga Teishō (1718–94?). Nakamura, "Gesakuron," 22.

14. Kanagaki Robun and Sansantei Arindo "Chosakudō kakiage," *Shinbun zasshi*, July 1872. Reprinted in *Nihon shoki shinbun zenshū*, vol. 40 (Tokyo: Perikansha, 1993).

15. Anderson, *Imagined Communities*.

16. *Shōsetsu shinzui*, 132; Twine, *Essence of the Novel*, 76.

17. For example, Fujita Meikaku's criticism of Yano Ryūkei's *Keikoku bidan* was governed by the "seven rules of *shōsetsu*." See Kamei, "*Shōsetsu*"ron, 109.

18. Nakamura, "Gesakuron," 19.

19. Other representative writers of this era are Ueda Akinari and Takebe no Ayatari (1719–74), who wrote *Ugetsu monogatari* (*The Tale of Ugetsu*, 1776) and *Nishiyama monogatari* (*The Tale of Nishiyama*, 1768), respectively. One point of interest is Akinari's introduction to *Ugetsu monogatari*, which specifically refers to both Luo Guanzhong's *The Water Margin* and Murasaki Shikibu's *Genji monogatari*, as if to identify the genealogy of his tale.

20. Suzuki, *Nihon no "bungaku" gainen*, 96–97.

21. Of course, different schools of scholars viewed Heian tales differently. A scholar of *kangaku* would have held the tales in disdain, more so than a scholar of *kokugaku*. Moreover, there were other forms of tales written (or compiled) by

men, such as *Hōgen monogatari* (*The Tale of Hōgen*), *Heiji monogatari* (*The Tale of Heiji*), and *Heike monogatari* (*The Tale of Heike*), which are often categorized as "war narratives" (*gunki mono*). The multilayered usage of the term *monogatari* and its implications are beyond the scope of this book. Here, I wish to highlight that the *gesaku* genealogy interestingly omits a large number of texts with *monogatari* included in the title, all the while creating the link with women's tales written between the late Heian and early Kamakura periods.

22. In the preface Shunsui wrote for *Shunshoku yuki no ume*, he glosses the character for *shōsetsu* with *monogatari*. For more examples, see Fujii, *Nihon "shōsetsu" genshi*, 241–42.

23. *Rubi* are glosses provided alongside *kanji* characters that, in contemporary Japanese, typically show how the characters should be read. A common practice in *yomihon* is *rubi* being used to provide a phonetic script equivalent or an equivalent vernacular term or phrase to the characters. The glosses may not provide a standard reading for *kanji* but may instead describe the *kanji* compounds to readers who are unfamiliar with them.

24. For a more specific discussion on how *gesaku* subcategories developed in Edo, see Kamei, Komori, and Takada's round-table discussion, "Teidan."

25. See ibid.

26. Nakamura Yukihiko identifies these three dimensions in his "Gesakuron."

27. See, for example, Ino's *Meiji bungakushi*.

28. *Shōsetsu shinzui*, 86–87; Twine, *Essence of the Novel*, 39.

29. Fukuzawa, *Gakumon no susume*, 12–13. This translation is from Kiyooka, *Fukuzawa Yukichi on Education*, with some modifications to clarify my argument (67).

30. I must also add here that, as Asukai Masamichi points out, Fukuzawa considered *shōsetsu* as an educational medium. He did not consider literary writings to be a form of knowledge, but he also saw that they serve an educational purpose. Asukai, "Seiji shōsetsu to 'kindai' bungaku," 87–88.

31. As Carol Gluck notes, the contents of national education did not include any "reference to moral influence, either Confucian or nativist." Gluck, *Japan's Modern Myths*, 104.

32. See Maeda, "Ondoku kara mokudoku e."

33. Nakamura, *Saigoku risshihen*, 429.

34. Smiles, *Self-Help*, 316.

35. Nakamura Masanao was a *kangaku* intellectual who sought to introduce Western thought via *kangaku*-based language, thereby showing much interest in Western knowledge as well. However, as we shall see later in this chapter, there were many other *kangaku* intellectuals who opposed the Western-based "practical knowledge."

36. *Shōsetsu shinzui*, 40–41; Twine, *Essence of the Novel*, 1–2.

37. For a detailed discussion on Meiji *gesaku*, see Okitsu, *Meiji kaikaki bungaku no kenkyū* and *Meiji shinbun kotohajime*.

38. By saying this, I certainly do not mean to underestimate the existence of rental bookstores already in place prior to the Meiji period, which played a significant role in distributing and circulating books.

39. On newspapers and magazines of the early Meiji period, see Yamamoto, *Kindai Nihon no shinbun dokushasō* and *Shinbun to minshū*; see also Kōno, *Shomotsu no kindai*.

40. Such division did not always remain the same. Especially by the second decade, we begin to find translated and political works of fiction being serialized in large newspapers such as *Jiyū shinbun*. Travel accounts such as Morita Shiken's (1861–97) *Senjō nikki* (*A Diary at Sea*, 1886) was serialized in *Yūbin hōchi shinbun*, one of the large newspapers of the time. Small newspapers were easier to read, with *rubi* on all of the characters, making the works accessible to the readers who were less literate than the members of the intelligentsia. For extensive discussions on small newspapers, especially on *Kanayomi shinbun*, founded by Kanagaki Robun in 1875, see Marran, "Allure of the Poison-Woman."

41. This translation of *Sanjō no kyōken* is given in Keene, *Dawn to the West*, 21.

42. Hardacre, "Creating State Shintō," 45.

43. Robun is clearly exaggerating when, in his response, he claims that there are only three *gesaku* writers, including himself. As I touch upon later, moreover, there were also *gesaku* writers who resisted such a role.

44. Kamei Hideo, in his *Meiji bungakushi*, claims that one of the differences between Edo and Meiji *gesaku* is the temporal setting of the works (31). In Edo, when writers thematized contemporaneous events, they tended to transpose the temporal setting to earlier periods, such as Muromachi. In Meiji, one of the main characteristics of documentary fiction (*jitsuroku*) was that the actual time and place were used in relaying the stories.

45. *Kanbun* refers to sinified Japanese prose.

46. Part 1 of *Ryūkyō shinshi* was written in 1859. Ryūhoku continued parts 2 and 3 after the Meiji Restoration and completed the book in 1875. *Ryūkyō shinshi* is compiled in *Narushima Ryūhoku, Hattori Bushō, Kurimoto Ryōunshū*. Kamei Hideo, in his *Kansei no henkaku*, discusses the role that *kanbun fūzokushi* played in producing the "modern narrative voice."

47. Maeda Ai suggests that beginning around 1877 the small newspapers had to rely on monthly subscribers to remain competitive in the market. Serialized fiction was found to be an effective way to attract them. Maeda, "Meiji shoki gesaku shuppan no dōkō," 48.

48. On Motoda's influential role in tutoring the emperor, see Asukai, *Meiji taitei.*

49. Motoda, "Kyōgaku seishi," 78–79. See also Gluck, *Japan's Modern Myths,* 102–28. A detailed account of educational history can be found in *Nihon kindai kyōiku hyakunenshi.* On Motoda's "Kyōgaku seishi," see 1:114–19.

50. Yamazumi, "Kaisetsu," 490.

51. See Gluck, *Japan's Modern Myths,* 108.

52. "Shōgakkō kyōin kokoroe," 126.

53. Changes in history education occurred simultaneously with the increasing emphasis on moral education. Article 15 of *Shōgakkō kyōsoku kōryō,* published in 1881, specified that Japanese history ought to be taught instead of world history to "develop patriotism and respect for the emperor." See Yamazumi, "Kaisetsu,"490.

54. *Nihon kindai kyōiku hyakunenshi,* 1:110. This movement to exert control over the educational system as well as the textbooks is inextricably linked to the government's effort to oust Freedom and People's Rights activists and their political principles from the educational arena. See Chapter 3 for further discussion.

55. Marran, "Allure of the Poison-Woman," 42.

56. For a list of reprints published between 1882 and 1885, see Maeda, "Meiji shoki gesaku shuppan no dōkō," 62–64.

57. Yanagida, *Shōsetsu shinzui no kenkyū,* 124.

58. Tsubouchi Shōyō, "Kyokutei Bakin," in Shōyō kyōkai, ed., *Shōyō senshū* (Tokyo: Daiichi shobō, 1977), 12:297 (hereafter cited as "Kyokutei Bakin").

59. Ichishima Shunjō, "Meiji bungaku shoki no tsuioku," compiled as an afterword to Tsubouchi Shōyō, *Shōsetsu shinzui* (Tokyo: Tokyōdō, 1926), 175 (hereafter cited as "Meiji bungaku shoki no tsuioku").

60. Maeda, "Meiji rekishi bungaku no genzō," 467.

61. In the first decade, there were also efforts to promote "internal reform" and moral instruction, but intellectuals leaned toward Western models for moral education in the first decade.

62. Motoda, "Kyōgaku seishi," 78.

63. Ono, "Shuku kaikō," 462.

64. "The Benefits of the *Shōsetsu*" discusses the four benefits of *shōsetsu*: "Ennoblement of Character," "Moral Instruction," "Supplementing Official History," and "Providing a Model for *Bungaku.*"

65. *Shōsetsu shinzui,* 84–86; Twine, *Essence of the Novel,* 37–38.

66. *Shōsetsu shinzui,* 76; Twine, *Essence of the Novel,* 29.

67. Fenollosa was an American philosopher who taught at Tokyo University. *Bijutsu shinsetsu,* published only in Japanese, was based on a lecture given at the university and had a tremendous impact upon the world of art in Japan. He criticized the Japanese valorization of Western art, which had supposedly led the

Japanese to neglect their own artistic tradition.

68. *Shōsetsu shinzui*, 43–44; Twine, *Essence of the Novel*, 4–5.

69. *Shōsetsu shinzui*, 44–45; Twine, *Essence of the Novel*, 5.

70. "Wagakuni ni jiyū no shushi o hanshoku suru ichi shudan," 15–16.

71. "Seiji ni kansuru haishi shōsetsu no hitsuyō," 22.

72. See Chapter 3 for a more extensive discussion on the government regulations to crack down on the Freedom and People's Rights Movement.

73. Nishi does not provide any specific examples for these categories but instead defines them, parts of which I provide here. Biography is "a type of writing that describes a person's life." Chronology is "a type of writing that lists the dates from the ancient times." Synchronology is a text that "compiles two or more lists of chronology" of different countries, such as those of China and Japan. Nishi, *Hyakugaku renkan*, 76–77.

74. This characterization of *Shōsetsu shinzui* is one that can be traced back as far as the end of the Meiji period, when the naturalist-oriented writers discovered *Shōsetsu shinzui* as a text that argued for artistic independence.

75. *Shōsetsu shinzui*, 52–54; Twine, *Essence of the Novel*, 11–13.

76. *Shōsetsu shinzui*, 72; Twine, *Essence of the Novel*, 26.

77. *Shōsetsu shinzui*, 55; Twine, *Essence of the Novel*, 13–14.

78. *Shōsetsu shinzui*, 60–61; Twine, *Essence of the Novel*, 17–18.

79. *Shōsetsu shinzui*, 91–92; Twine, *Essence of the Novel*, 43–44.

80. *Shōsetsu shinzui*, 150; Twine, *Essence of the Novel*, 90.

CHAPTER 3

1. Maeda, "Kindai bungaku to katsujiteki sekai," 329. This is also the basic premise with which Kamei Hideo wrote *"Shōsetsu"ron*, his book on *Shōsetsu shinzui*.

2. As I argue in Chapter 6, mimetic realism was not established until the turn of the century.

3. *Shōsetsu shinzui*, 70–71; Twine, *Essence of the Novel*, 24–25.

4. The eight cardinal virtues are benevolence, justice, courtesy, wisdom, sincerity, loyalty, filial piety, and obedience.

5. *Shōsetsu shinzui*, 70–71; Twine, *Essence of the Novel*, 25.

6. *Shōsetsu shinzui*, 157–58; Twine, *Essence of the Novel*, 96.

7. *Shōsetsu shinzui*, 70; Twine, *Essence of the Novel*, 25.

8. *Shōsetsu shinzui*, 69; Twine, *Essence of the Novel*, 25.

9. Throughout "The Vicissitudes of the *Shōsetsu*," a section prior to the "The Main Themes of the *Shōsetsu*," the term "superficial" (*hisō*) is used to characterize literary representations such as myth, fables, and allegory; furthermore, such superficial representations are considered to be a reflection of the "uncivilized

emotional state" of the times. See also Tsubouchi Shōyō, "Shōsetsu o ronjite shosei katagi no shui ni oyobu," in Yoshida Seiichi and Asai Kiyoshi, eds., *Kindai bungaku hyōron taikei 1: Meijiki I* (Tokyo: Kadokawa shoten, 1971), 28.

10. For a brilliant and extensive discussion of the multilayered construction of Bakin's *Hakkenden*, see Takada, *Hakkenden no sekai*. On Bakin's use of allegory, see Kamei, "Gūi to bungakushi." *Shōsetsu shinzui*'s criticism of Bakin has had grave consequences for Bakin scholarship precisely because the definition by which a given work was considered "modern," and hence "artistic," was predicated upon the rejection of Bakin.

11. *Shōsetsu shinzui*, 70; Twine, *Essence of the Novel*, 24–25.

12. *Shōsetsu shinzui*, 142; Twine, *Essence of the Novel*, 84–85.

13. It is worth noting here that the positive evaluation of *Genji monogatari* (eleventh century) and the negative evaluation of Bakin's works (eighteenth century) go against the Darwinian formula that is deployed throughout *Shōsetsu shinzui*.

14. Although the narrator of *Genji monogatari* explicitly states that she is narrating events from the past, the regime within which the narrator and the writer are situated is clearly the Heian imperial court, hence making the temporal setting the present.

15. Maeda, "Bakin to Tōkoku," 348.

16. Ibid.

17. Maeda, "Meiji rekishi bungaku no genzō," 467.

18. "Meiji bungaku shoki no tsuioku," 175.

19. "Kyokutei Bakin," 297.

20. Masamune Hakuchō, "Mukashi no nikki," *Kindai bungaku* 1, no.1 (January 1946): 14.

21. Even though education in *kangaku* classics was considered old-fashioned, many intellectuals continued to teach *kangaku* classics to their sons at home or at specialized schools. According to Maeda Ai, children of the *shizoku* class (the former samurai) and those of the wealthy houses began *sodoku* anytime between five and ten years of age. See Maeda, "Ondoku kara mokudoku e," 130.

22. Ibid., 132.

23. See ibid., 122–23.

24. *Nishi no umi chishio no saarashi* is a translation of Dumas's work *The Memoirs of a Physician*, by Sakurada Momoe. *Jiyū no gaika* is also a translation of Dumas's work, entitled *Ange Pitou*, by Miyazaki Muryū. In Muryū's text, the characters for *gaika* are glossed with *kachidoki*, so I have consistently referred to the text as *Jiyū no kachidoki*. In Roka's text, however, the characters for *gaika* are glossed with *gaika* in phonetic *kana* scripts, suggesting perhaps that the youth of the time referred to the sinified reading (*on'yomi*) of the characters regardless of the glosses given, which is indicative of the *sodoku* reading.

25. The year 1890 marks the founding of the Parliament, the date of which was set in 1881. As we shall see later, Asai's language here overlaps with words in *Jiyū no kachidoki*.

26. Tokutomi (Roka) Kenjirō, *Omoide no ki* (Tokyo: Minyūsha shuppan, 1901), 115 (hereafter cited as *Omoide no ki*). In translating *Omoide no ki*, I followed Kenneth Strong's translation of the work, published as *Footprints in the Snow*, with some modifications to highlight my arguments (119–20).

27. Though in a different context, Dipesh Chakrabarty says the following: "Ideas acquire materiality through the history of bodily practices. They work not simply because they persuade through their logic; they are also capable, through a long and heterogeneous history of the cultural training of the senses, of making connections with our glands and muscles and neuronal networks. This is the work of memory, if we do not reduce the meaning of that word to the simple and conscious mental act of remembering." Chakrabarty, Afterword to *Mirror of Modernity*, 295. Chakrabarty's statement sheds important light on the role of *sodoku*, as well as of communal memorization and recitation, in disseminating the works' content and ultimately producing a shared sentiment and solidarity among the Meiji intellectuals.

28. Aside from the *Jiyū shinbun*, the other main Jiyūtō-affiliated newspaper is *Nihon rikken seitō shinbun* founded by the Osaka Jiyūtō affiliates, in press from 1882 to 1885. *Chōya shinbun* also had Jiyūtō members writing for it. Jiyūtō had a small newspaper founded in 1882 (published until 1893), *Eiri jiyū shinbun*, and *Jiyū no tomoshibi*, founded in 1884. There were many local newspapers as well. Furthermore, along with the images of the French Revolution, images of Russian nihilism were prevalent. For example, *Rokoku kakumeitō* (*The Revolutionary Party in Russia*), which began serialization in the fourth issue of the *Jiyū shinbun*, overlaps in serialization with Sakurada's work. Russian nihilist–related articles increased dramatically with Vera Zassulic's attack of Trepoff, as well as the assassination of Emperor Alexander II in 1881, both of which are thematized in Muryū's *Mujitsu no shimoto* (*Cruel Treatment of the Innocent*, 1882), serialized initially in the *Eiri jiyū shinbun* and two months later published in book form. Many writings discuss the inevitable rise of the nihilists: for example, *Rokoku kyomutō no yurai* (*The Origins of Russian Nihilism*), published in September 1882, claims that, given the "condition of oppression and cruelty" (7–8), it is natural for the nihilists to come into being. As with works that thematize the French Revolution, writings that feature the Russian nihilist movement show strong identification with the oppressed. *Rokoku kakumeitō*, which was compiled in book form only two months later under the title *Rokoku kyomutō jijō* (*Conditions of the Russian Nihilists*), states that "the evil oppressive politics" and "the cruel conditions in Russia [were responsible for producing] the Russian Revolutionary

Party" (17–18). Baba Tatsui (1850–88), in his speech entitled "Nairan no gai wa kakumeika no ayamachi ni arazu" (Revolutionaries Are Not to Be Blamed for the Domestic Turmoil), claims that oppressive government produces domestic chaos and revolution: "Isn't it true that the oppression of the French government interfered with social reform and improvement?" *Jiyū shinbun*, July 21–22, 1882. He ends his speech with a warning that the existence of an oppressive government can produce nihilists, clearly suggesting that continued oppression in Japan will bring about a similar outcome.

29. I must hasten to add here that the use of such language was certainly not limited to the fictional works nor to People's Rights activists. Those in the government also mobilized this language, albeit in a completely opposite manner. In his letter to the minister of internal affairs, Mishima Michitsune, for example, refers to the participants of the Fukushima Incident as "evil people" (*kanmin*).

30. Quoted in Matsuoka, *Jiyū shinbun o yomu*, 81.

31. Itagaki, *Jiyūtōshi*, 2:3–14.

32. Yanagida, *Seiji shōsetsu kenkyū I*, 119–22. See also Asukai, "Miyazaki Muryū no gensō," 281–82.

33. *Nishi no umi chishio no saarashi*, 13.

34. In his "Miyazaki Muryū no gensō," Asukai speculates that the blood oath in question, signed either at the end of July or early August 1882, was scripted within a month of the installment that included the oath.

35. See ibid., 282.

36. By December 1882, the first sixteen sections had been compiled in book form, but the book was prohibited from sale in January 1883. Yanagida, *Seiji shōsetsu kenkyū I*, 117.

37. Asukai, "Miyazaki Muryū no gensō," 282.

38. Yanagida Izumi notes that Katō Heishirō, Itō Jintarō, and Mitamura Genryū, all of whom were engaged with the political movement in the 1880s, also attest to the popularity of these works, especially among the "fighters" of the Jiyūtō. See Yanagida, *Seji shōsetsu kenkyū I*, 121.

39. The first forty-two sections were published individually in two volumes even as Muryū was serializing; the first volume was published in October 1882, and the second followed two months later. Muryū apparently continued to translate a few more chapters and serialized them in the *Shinonome shinbun*, all of which were republished in individual volumes in 1889. The first fifty-five sections of the original serialization, out of a total ninety-six sections, are compiled in *Meiji seiji shōsetsushū I, Meiji bungaku zenshū*, vol. 5 (Tokyo: Chikuma shobō, 1966) (hereafter cited as *Jiyū no kachidoki*). My references to *Jiyū no kachidoki*, at least until section 55, will be to the *Meiji bungaku zenshū* edition.

40. Yanagida, too, speculates that Muryū translated from the English version.

Sakurada, however, was able read both German and English, so whether he translated from the English or the German version cannot be confirmed.

41. Dumas, *Taking of the Bastille*, 82.

42. *Jiyū no kachidoki*, 49.

43. Ibid., 58.

44. Dumas, *Taking of the Bastille*, 56.

45. *Jiyōu no kachidoki*, 37.

46. Kevin Doak discusses how Muryū uses the term *minzoku* (as opposed to *kazoku*, and not as an invocation of the usual connection with the Germanic concepts of the Volk) in naming the "national people," a production of which he skillfully analyzes. Doak, "Civil Society."

47. *Jiyū no kachidoki*, 32.

48. Ibid., 62.

49. The court proceedings were published daily in the *Jiyū shinbun* beginning July 20, 1883.

50. These are the members of the Jiyūtō who signed the blood oath.

51. *Omoide no ki*, 116; Strong, *Footprints in the Snow*, 120.

52. Maeda, "Meiji rekishi bungaku no genzō," 471.

53. I do not wish to argue that the use of force against the government is necessarily Muryū's position. In January 1883, while the participants of the Fukushima Incident are being questioned and tried, *Jiyū no kachidoki* focuses on a scene where Billot preaches to the crowd that violence is cruel: "Billot stood in front of Berthier and said loudly, 'We had always passionately hoped to overthrow the despotic government and regain true liberty. Because of that we took the Bastille and killed de Launay and de Losme. We killed de Launay only because he was presumptuous and would not let us take the prison. It was certainly not that we find killing pleasurable. Our intention is to fulfill the revolution peacefully.'" *Jiyū shinbun*, January 18, 1883. The text continues three days later: "I had always respected freedom and held it highly. . . . I left my wife and children to join the revolutionary party and took the Bastille. . . . But there is neither compassion nor reason in what the revolutionary party does nowadays; brutality and cruelty have taken over." *Jiyū shinbun*, January 21, 1883.

54. For an extensive discussion on *hifun kōgai* and the political subject "stalwart youth" (*sōshi*), which "performs" such language, see Kimura Naoe's *Seinen no tanjō*. Tokutomi Sohō's *Kokumin no tomo*, from its founding in 1887, played a significant role in making associations between the language of *hifun kōgai* and the radical activists of the Freedom and People's Rights Movement. However, it must be noted that the language of *hifun kōgai* was not isolatable as such until around 1887, which is about the time *seiji shōsetsu* becomes identifiable as a literary genre.

55. As Maeda Ai suggests in his "Ondoku kara mokudoku e," the rejection of

this communal site of recitation coincides with the shift in the practice of reading, namely, from oral recitation to silent reading. This shift is also reflected in studies of rhetoric that focused first on oratory skills, which was later supplanted by the "supremacy of the written medium." See Tomasi, *Rhetoric in Modern Japan*.

56. On Meiji practices of political oration, see Yanagida, "Seiji kōdan kotohajime."

57. "Meiji 13 nen shūkai jōrei" (Public Ordinance Act of 1880) and its subsequent revisions are reproduced in Matsumoto and Yamamuro, *Genron to media*, 440–44.

58. Sakazaki Shiran, for example, created a "political oration" group that included Miyazaki Muryū.

59. *Chōya shinbun*, February 4, 1883.

60. *Jiyū shinbun*, February 22, 1883.

61. Yanagida, *Zuihitsu Meiji bungaku*, 56.

62. Ibid., 61.

63. Komuro Shinsuke, *Tōyō minken hyakkaden* (Tokyo: Iwanami shoten, 1957), 19 (hereafter cited as *TMHD*). Following a trend in Japanese scholarship, I will refer to him as Shinsuke, which is an exception to the general rule that uses the surname when referring to the writer's real name. This is in part to differentiate Shinsuke from his father-in-law, Komuro Nobuo, also a political activist. Angaidō is Shinsuke's pen name, which scholars use when referring to his fictional works. When he is referred to as a political activist and compiler of *Tōyō minken hyakkaden*, however, the use of Shinsuke is the norm. Shinsuke began to conceptualize the work in 1880 and collected stories of righteous men buried in rural areas as he traveled around the country to give speeches at public gatherings in 1881–82. He began writing/compiling the first volume in January 1883, which was published in August of the same year. The second volume was published in January 1884, but Shinsuke had already sought publication authorization for this volume in September 1883, only a month after the publication of the first volume. The permission was not given until January 1884 because of the inclusion of the term *minken* (people's rights) in the title of the work; when he changed *minken* to *gijin*, the authorization was granted almost immediately. The second and third volumes, therefore, appeared under the revised title *Tōyō gijin hyakkaden*. The third volume was published in June 1884, but he had finished the third volume when the second volume was given authorization, hence six months before the actual publication. The biographies were extremely popular: by the time the third installment came out in June 1884, both the first and second installments were already being reprinted. Upon the publication of the first volume, moreover, some newspapers featured articles that specifically discussed the text. Shinsuke had apparently gathered enough material for a fourth volume, but in 1884 his

interest was elsewhere. As we shall see in the following chapter, he turns to a project that engages with Japan's position vis-à-vis Asia, a project that he had hoped to address since his visit to Korea in the aftermath of the Imo Mutiny in 1882. For *Tōyō minken hyakkaden's* publication history, see Gotō, "Gimin kenshō o meguru jiyūshugi to fashizumu; Hayashi, "Kaisetsu."

64. *Chōya shinbun*, September 6, 1883.

65. Ochi, *Kindai bungaku seiritsuki no kenkyū*, 175–76. Shinsuke was certainly not the only person to refer to "Monju Kusukeden" in the early Meiji years. Another, for example, was Udagawa, *Tenmei sōdō*.

66. Yanagida, *Zuihitsu Meiji bungaku*, 61–62.

67. *Undōkai* in contemporary Japanese means "athletic meet." In early Meiji years, however, it constituted a political gathering, especially by "stalwart youth" (*sōshi*, a name usually given to the fighters of the Freedom and People's Rights Movement). For an extensive discussion of *undōkai*, see Kimura's *Seinen no tanjō*.

68. This report on the public gathering, entitled "Takeyari tazusaete undōkai," is included in Yasumaru and Fukaya, *Minshū undō*, 223–24.

69. Biographies of Nakakamiyamura Buzaemon and four others feature peasants discussing how to free leaders who were wrongly incarcerated.

70. It is also worth mentioning that the readers/listeners of the *Jiyū shinbun* in which Muryū's *Jiyū no kachidoki* was serialized do not necessarily constitute the same group as the listeners of political oration. Political oration was, after all, also employed as a part of the effort to expand the movement to include the less literate, though as mentioned before, it replaced political speeches after government restrictions intensified in June 1882. Moreover, it is probably safe to assume that the readers of *Tōyō minken hyakkaden* overlap with those of *Jiyū no kachidoki*; in fact, one episode, "Sado Yoshihei no denki" (Biography of Sado Yoshihei), which was initially advertised to be included in the third volume, was serialized in the *Jiyū shinbun* from January 11 to January 20, 1884 (with several lapses in between).

71. *TMHD*, 18.

72. Ibid., 19.

73. Ibid., 20.

74. Walthall, "Introduction," *Peasant Uprisings in Japan*, 1–34.

75. *TMHD*, 34–35.

76. Ibid., 157.

77. Ono, "Shuku kaikō," 465.

78. For a discussion of what constitutes "Japanese knowledge" in this context and how it intersects with the mechanism of mimicry, see Chapter 4. Fukuzawa, *Gakumon no dokuritsu*, compiled in *Fukuzawa Yukichi zenshū*, 5:370.

79. Ibid., 377.

80. As we shall see in more detail in the following chapter, Ono also argued

for the use of Japanese in Tokyo Senmon Gakkō as a unique feature of its curriculum; this was a clear criticism of Tokyo University, whose classes were primarily taught by hired foreigners (*oyatoi gaijin*) in their language.

81. Takeuchi, *Gakureki kizoku no eikō to zasetsu*, 67.

CHAPTER 4

1. Bhabha, *Location of Culture*, 86. I must hasten to add here that this concept of mimicry is a contentious one. It is useful in deciphering the dynamic of colonial ambivalence and the complex, interdependent relationship between the colonizer and the colonized. However, it is problematic because Bhabha identifies subversive power in mimicry: "What [instances of colonial imitation] all share is a discursive process by which the excess or slippage produced by the *ambivalence* of mimicry (almost the same, *but not quite*) does not merely 'rupture' the discourse, but becomes transformed into an uncertainty which fixes the colonial subject as a 'partial' presence. By 'partial' I mean both 'incomplete' and 'virtual.' It is as if the very emergence of the 'colonial' is dependent for its representation upon some strategic limitation or prohibition within the authoritative discourse itself. The success of colonial appropriation depends on a proliferation of inappropriate objects that ensure its strategic failure, so that mimicry is at once resemblance and menace" (86). In effect, what he suggests is an optimistic view that colonial authority ultimately cannot sustain itself because of the ambivalence inherent in mimicry.

2. I owe a great deal to Komori, *Posutokoroniaru*, in deriving this model. However, by invoking Bhabha's concepts here, I do not mean to suggest that Japan's policies and attitudes in the 1880s manifest *colonial* desire relative to Korea and China as Komori does in his work. Bhabha's notions of colonial mimicry and ambivalence are helpful in formulating my thoughts on Japan's position in East Asia, but it is slightly anachronistic to read the policies in 1880s Japan as "colonial desire," which manifest much more clearly in 1890s and beyond. What we find in the 1880s is a kind of "imperial longing" that may eventually link up to "colonial desire," but it has yet to manifest itself as such. I would like to thank my colleague David Howell for pointing this out to me.

3. "Fukuzawa Yukichi no Chūgoku bunmeiron" is compiled in Hashikawa, *Kindai Nihon to Chūgoku*.

4. Main political affiliations of the major large newspapers in the years between 1882 and 1885 were the following: *Jiyū shinbun* (Jiyūtō), *Chōya shinbun* (Jiyūtō and Kaishintō), *Nihon rikken seitō shinbun* (Jiyūtō), *Yūbin hōchi shinbun* (Kaishintō), *Tokyo Yokohama mainichi shinbun* (Kaishintō), *Naigai seitō jijō* (Kaishintō), *Tokyo nichi nichi shinbun* (Teiseitō, government supporters), *Jiji shinpō* (*fuhen futō* ["no prejudice, no party"], led by Fukuzawa Yukichi and his followers), and *Asahi shinbun* ("neutral").

5. Shibahara, "Taigaikan to nashonarizumu," 504.

6. Fukuzawa, "Chōsen no kōsai o ronzu," *Jiji shinpō*, March 11, 1882. It is compiled in *Fukuzawa Yukichi zenshū*, 8:30. Yasukawa Jun'nosuke, in his "Nisshin sensō to Ajia besshi shisō," states that Fukuzawa's aggressive stance was criticized as "an act of plunder" even by his contemporaries (171–72).

7. "Tōyō renkōron," November 19, 1879.

8. Ono, "Gaikō o ronzu," 24.

9. "Kuni kore o sadamuru no gi," February 22–23, 1881.

10. "Kōa no mondai oyobi tōyō no gensei," June 6, 1884. See also "Tōyō shokoku no keisei," *Yokohama mainichi shinbun* (renamed *Tokyo Yokohama mainichi shinbun* in November 1879), June 27–28, 1879, which argues that, unlike India and China, whose national pride was degraded, Japan has maintained its national rights through strategic diplomacy with Euro-American countries and thus is becoming a top-quality country that has undergone various reforms.

11. Fukuzawa, "Gyūba Takuzō-kun Chōsen ni iku," *Jiji shinpō*, January 12–13, 1883. Compiled in *Fukuzawa Yukichi zenshū*, 8:505.

12. "Chōsen o shosuru no seiryaku," May 15, 1881. Korea was by no means the only other through which this position of teacher was sought: in 1879, *Yūbin hōchi shinbun* argued for a "dispatch of students" to India in order to produce a "spirit of independence" among the Indians. "Tōyō renkōron," November 19, 1879. Moreover, there were many arguments to prioritize domestic issues, and not all Japanese intellectuals argued for such a position.

13. Gaimushō, *Nihon gaikō bunsho*, 308.

14. Yamamuro, *Shisō kadai to shite no Ajia*, 314. Koreans did not respond to Japan's entreaty until 1881 primarily because they were concerned about Qing China's reaction. In fact, in 1881, Korea also sent an embassy to Qing China. For a detailed discussion, see Kwon, "Ryōsen shikō ni kansuru ichi kōsatsu."

15. Fukuzawa, "Gyūba Takuzō-kun Chōsen ni iku," 502.

16. Ibid., 504.

17. The Japanese term for what I render in English as "possessed" here is *koyū*, which in present-day usage means "specific to X."

18. Ono, "Shuku kaikō," 462.

19. *Waseda daigaku hyakunenshi*, 437–39.

20. In discussing this shift from Western knowledge (*yōgaku*) to Japanese knowledge (*Nihon no gakumon*), I wish to underscore the fact that I am by no means suggesting that Japan merely imported and imitated the preestablished Western knowledge. It is not possible for me to delve into the details of this shift, which is clearly mediated by different paradigms of "translation"; suffice it to say that words such as *import* and *imitate*, which appear to invoke modernization theory, can claim validity only when "translation" is deemed transparent.

The process of mimicry discussed previously cannot be narrativized in such terms but must be examined in reference to the varying and unstable representations of the "West," "Japan," and "Asia." On different paradigms of "translation," see Sakai, "Jobun," and Sakai, *Translation and Subjectivity*. See Komori, *Nihongo no kindai* for how Japanese language was mediated by and produced through a variety of "translations" from early to mid-Meiji. See also Lee, *"Kokugo" to iu shisō*; Yasuda, *Teikoku Nihon no gengo hensei*; Osa, *Kindai Nihon to kokugo nashonarizumu*.

21. "Kōa no mondai oyobi tōyō no gensei," June 6, 1884.

22. Fukuzawa, "Gyūba Takuzō-kun Chōsen ni iku," 502.

23. Even if the *shōsetsu* becomes free of the "writer's design" associated with didacticism, it by no means becomes free of design per se. It requires a new design, perhaps one that conceals itself.

24. "Chōsen no henpō," August 1–2, 1882.

25. "Chōsen ni shissu no gi," October 25–29, 1882.

26. "Chōsen no hanto utarazu bekarazu," August 7, 1882.

27. "Chōsen hatashite museifu naru ka," August 8, 1882.

28. See "Chōsen seiryaku," August 8–13, 16–19, 1882.

29. Kuroki, "Kōakai/Ajia kyōkai no katsudō to shisō," 12.

30. See "Annan no senpō," June 13, 1883.

31. "Wagakuni ga Shinfutsu ni taisuru no seiryaku," June 19–24, 1883.

32. See, for example, "Shinkoku heisei," October 16–17, 19–20, 23–25, 1883, and "Nisshin no kankei," November 3, 1883. Interestingly, the justification to side with France was given in a form of the rhetoric of the Freedom and People's Rights Movement, as it claimed that "France is a republic" unlike the "barbaric" (*yaban*) autocratic system of China. "Rō narukana sensei seifu no ken," June 26, 1883.

33. "Annan no senpō."

34. "Eitei ga Shinfutsu ni chūsai suruto wa hatashite makoto kana," August 1, 1883.

35. "Shinfutsu no wa," May 17, 1884. Matsuoka Kiichi, in *Jiyū shinbun o yomu*, states that *Jiyū shinbun* had yet to describe Qing China's incompetence as strongly as it did on this occasion (202).

36. Ozaki Gakudō, "Kokusaihō wa Shina to Chōsen to o ninshiki sezu," *Yūbin hōchi shinbun*, December 18, 1884.

37. "Waga hō no Shina ni taisuru seiryaku ikan," December 21, 23, 1884.

38. "Tōyō no kiun," April 13, 1884.

39. "Ippō o higo subekarazu," September 16–18, 1884.

40. "Tōyō shokoku wa bankoku kōhō no rieki o bunshu sezu," October 10, 1884.

41. "Shina no haiboku wa Nihon no sachi nari," August 29–30, 1884.

42. "*Ōshū* no taisei o ronjite Futsushin jiken no kyokusei o danzu," September 18, 20, 1884.

43. Ozaki Gakudō, "Shina to tatakau no rigai o ronzu," *Ozaki Gakudō zenshū* (Tokyo: Kōronsha, 1956), 2:161.

44. "Yamu o ezunba Futsukoku to dōmei subeshi," January 14, 1885.

45. In an article entitled "Sensō to nareba hisshō no san ari" in *Jiji shinpō*, Fukuzawa is certain that Japan will emerge victorious, to the extent that he wants to commit his wealth to support the war. *Jiyū no tomoshibi*, the textual embodiment of Jiyūtō radicals, was more than inclined to argue for military confrontation with Qing China. See, for example, "Kakugo wa yoika," December 29, 1884; "Satekosona," January 15, 1885; "Imada rakutan suru ni oyobazu," January 17, 1885.

46. "Nihonhei no buryoku o unai ni shimesu beshi," December 27, 1884.

47. I must here add that some newspapers argued against military confrontation, most notably *Chōya shinbun* and *Tokyo Yokohama mainichi shinbun*. As I have repeatedly suggested, however, these papers were not consistent in their positions, and they also published reports advocating military attack on China. As Kuroki Morifumi argued, Suehiro Tetchō, who was the primary writer for the *Chōya shinbun*, continued to write against military confrontation with China given its potential disadvantages to the national economy. Kuroki, "Kōshin jiken to *Chōya shinbun*."

48. Tokutomi Sohō, "Nisshikan jiken ni kansuru no iken," compiled in *Taigaikan, Nihon kindai shisō taikei*, ed. Shibahara Takuji, Ikai Takaaki, and Ikeda Masahiro (Tokyo: Iwanami shoten, 1988), 12:413.

49. *Kōa kōhō*, reprinted in Kuroki and Masuzawa, *Kōakai hōkoku/Ajia kyōkai hōkoku*.

50. For all practical purposes, Asianism signified Sino-Japanese coalition for the Kōakai members.

51. See Kuroki, "Kōakai/Ajia kyōkai no katsudō to shisō," 19.

52. Komuro Shinsuke, *Kōa kidan: Murenren, Jiyū shinbun*, April 13, 1884 (hereafter cited as *Murenren*).

53. Ibid., May 14, 1884.

54. Ibid.

55. Ibid., June 18, 1884.

56. As I briefly mentioned before, such a position was shared by members of Kōakai. Even Suehiro Tetchō, a member of Kōakai who was one of the very few that argued against immediate military confrontation after the Kapsin Incident, never went against the idea that Japan would be the leader of Asia.

57. Rather conveniently, moreover, Raishun never meets Lin Zexu, which was the initial objective of his trip to Beijing. If such a meeting had actualized, it

would have inevitably led to a debate of Raishun's goals and methodology. The narrative again prevents the story from developing in that direction.

58. See Fukuzawa, "Gyūba Takuzō-kun Chōsen ni iku." In more ways than one, this shows that his argument against direct interference, which was linked to Confucianism, did not target interference per se. Rather, it was more an antigovernment gesture with a will to power inscribed within it.

59. See, for example, Yasukawa, "Nisshin sensō to Ajia besshi shisō—Nihon kindaishizō no minaoshi," and Shō, "Datsu-a nyū-ō o mezasu kindai Nihon no Ajia ninshiki," both of which are compiled in Matsuura and Watanabe, *Sabetsu to sensō*. See also Yasukawa, *Fukuzawa Yukichi no Ajia ninshiki*.

60. Fukuzawa, "Datsu-a ron," compiled in *Fukuzawa Yukichi zenshū*, 10: 239–40.

61. Ibid., 240.

62. Fukuzawa, "Chōsen dokuritsutō no shokei," compiled in *Fukuzawa Yukichi zenshū*, 10:226.

63. Ibid.

64. Ibid., 222–23.

65. Fukuzawa, "Datsu-aron," 240.

66. *Murenren* is one of the first works of *kokken shōsetsu*. See Yanagida, *Seiji shōsetsu kenkyū I*, 353.

67. Tōkai Sanshi's *Kajin no kigū*, Yano Ryūkei's *Ukishiro monogatari*, and Suehiro Tetchō's *Nan'yō daiharan* are some such examples.

68. Shō Rō makes clear that "de-Asianization" meant "de-Confucianism." Shō, "Datsu-a nyū-ō o mezasu kindai Nihon no Ajia ninshiki," 224–25.

69. Fukuzawa, "Datsu-aron," 239.

70. Tokutomi Sohō, "Osaka no goku," *Kokumin no tomo*, vol. 5 (June 1887): 16–17. Reprinted in *Kokumin no tomo* (Tokyo: Meiji bunken, 1966), 1:59. On *Kokumin no tomo*'s view on uprisings led by the People's Rights activists, see Kimura, *Seinen no tanjō*.

71. See Hattori, "Saisetsu Bakin no bunshō ishiki."

72. See Caddeau, *Appraising Genji*.

73. The nativist movement to identify "Japan" vis-à-vis "China" and *kangaku* was clearly present in the Edo period. However, the urge to separate "Japan" from "China" in 1880s Japan is governed by the existence of the West, which makes the power dynamic entirely asymmetrical to the Edo period.

74. Kimura, *Seinen no tanjō*, 240.

CHAPTER 5

1. *Shōsetsu Shinzui*, 80; Twine, *Essence of the Novel*, 33.

2. *Shōsetsu shinzui*, 154; Twine, *Essence of the Novel*, 93. The selection of male-

female romance plays a crucial role in the development of literary modernity in Japan. Jim Reichert states that *Shōsetsu shinzui* and *Tōsei shosei katagi* "participated in the development of modern Japanese literature by helping to establish new boundaries for the representation of love and sexual desire that were thought to be more in keeping with the conditions of an evolved society," referring to the manner in which the two texts marginalized male-male sexuality. Marginalization of male-male sexuality that Reichert notes is especially thought provoking in light of the *shōsetsu*'s focalization on the male-female domain discussed later in this chapter. Reichert, *In the Company of Men*, 70.

3. These are the works that Tokutomi Sohō had in mind when he wrote "Kinrai ryūkō no seiji shōsetsu o ronzu" (On the Recently Popular Political *Shōsetsu*). See Komori, *Kōzō to shite no katari*; Kamei, "Seishi jitsuroku to shōsetsu haishi."

4. Such a brief plot summary does not do justice to the numerous narrative and stylistic experiments the text offers. As many critics have argued, *Tōsei shosei katagi* features a search for a new narrative voice.

5. Tsubouchi Shōyō, *Tōsei shosei katagi*, in *Tsubouchi Shōyōshū, Nihon kindai bungaku taikei* (Tokyo: Kadokawa shoten, 1974), 3:223 (hereafter cited as *TSK*).

6. Although the passage does not mention students explicitly, there is no question that the rhetoric of "success and advancement" applies to students in the early years of Meiji.

7. Kamei Hideo claims that this number is most likely part of the playful rhetoric that connects "four directions," "60,000," and "seven years." When Tokyo University became Tokyo Imperial University in 1886, enrollment was only 437; thus, 60,000 is an unrealistic number. Kamei, "Seishi jitsuroku to shōsetsu haishi," 124.

8. *TSK*, 223–24.

9. In his "Seishi jitsuroku to shōsetsu haishi," Kamei analyzes the opening passage extensively and discusses how it portrays a pessimistic picture of the new but unstable world.

10. *TSK*, 222.

11. The term I translated here as "public gathering" is *undōkai*. See Chapter 3, note 66 for its meaning in the Meiji period.

12. The Boshin War refers to the numerous battles carried out between the imperial army and the Tokugawa shogunate in 1868, the year of Boshin (the dragon).

13. The characters for *ohizamoto* (by his knees) are glossed with *on soba*, which simply means "by his side." *TSK*, 299.

14. Ibid., 295–96.

15. Ibid., 296.

16. Only samurai were permitted to wear swords in the Tokugawa period, and thus swords were the symbol of the samurai class. In 1876, the Meiji government completely banned the wearing of swords.

17. *TSK*, 296.

18. Ibid., 255.

19. Ibid.

20. Ibid., 264.

21. The only character who "might eventually become an antigovernment terrorist" is Kiriyama Benroku, who, as Jim Reichert pointed out, embodies "male-male sexuality" and is simultaneously designated as "backward" in the social Darwinian scale. For an extensive discussion on how *Tōsei shosei katagi* constructs the character of Kiriyama, see Reichert, *In the Company of Men*, 75–84.

22. *TSK*, 249–50.

23. Ibid., 296.

24. Ibid., 406.

25. Ibid., 297.

26. The success of Tomoyoshi, as a Kaishintō activist and a lawyer, is, like Tomosada's and Miyoshi's, entirely defined within the parameters of the present. In 1876, licenses to practice law began to be issued to those who passed an examination, and party politics began around 1881.

27. *TSK*, 337.

28. The election law that specified such eligibility was passed along with the first constitution in 1889, but these restrictions were known well in advance.

29. *TSK*, 375.

30. Ibid., 265.

31. Ibid.

32. Ibid., 266.

33. Ibid., 267.

34. Ibid., 343.

35. The New Aristocracy Edict (*Kazokurei*), an edict that defined the rights and privileges of aristocrats, was promulgated in 1884. The government set out to secure its power by granting titles to the supporters who later became members of the aristocratic house (*Kizokuin*).

36. The term *yūjo* refers to women of the pleasure quarters, namely, geisha and prostitutes. Whereas a geisha mainly entertains her customers with her artistic skills, such as *shamisen*, chants, and dances, prostitutes sell their bodies. However, as one might expect, it is often impossible to draw a line between these groups of women. Sexual services were certainly not limited to prostitutes. It should also be noted that there were ranks among prostitutes; high-ranking women in well-established licensed prostitution quarters such as Yoshiwara were

cultural icons equipped with artistic skills. These women's customers raised *their* reputations by becoming patrons. For a more extensive discussion on the *yūjo*, see Yoshimi, *Baishō no shakaishi*; Ishii, *Yoshiwara*; Wakita and Hanley, *Jendā no Nihonshi*; Ogi, Kumakura, and Ueno, *Fūzoku/sei*.

37. Despite this similarity, women in this text are never free of their second-ary status. They are always affected by their male partners' rise and fall within the new system of Meiji. In other words, their relationships with men determine their socioeconomic positions. The positions of men and women are thus clearly asymmetrical.

38. *TSK*, 263.

39. Ibid., 378.

40. When Tanoji becomes a geisha and leaves the Komachidas, Kōji tells her not to visit him too often for she is "now registered with the other house" (ibid., 267). Kaodori, before she became a prostitute—at which time she took her cur-rent name—was called Mizuno Tami, which indicates that she was registered with the Mizuno family (ibid., 401).

41. Ibid., 381.

42. Ibid., 265.

43. Otsune meets Miyoshi soon after the Battle of Ueno. Otsune's brother Zenjirō had been having an affair with Miyoshi's mistress, Ohide (who, we later find out, is Kaodori's mother). When the Battle of Ueno broke out, Zenjirō and Ohide had conspired to run away with valuable possessions belonging to Miyoshi. In the midst of the turmoil, Zenjirō and Ohide were separated, and Zenjirō was killed. Otsune found his body a few days later, along with the objects he had stolen from Miyoshi. She decided to return these items to Miyoshi, who praised her highly for her honesty.

44. *TSK*, 400.

45. As evidenced in Narushima Ryūhoku's *Ryūkyō shinshi*, the leaders of the Meiji government who were from Satsuma and Chōshū were criticized for their "barbaric" manners when they went to the refined Yanagibashi. Accordingly, they developed their own entertainment district in Shinbashi.

46. According to Suita Dōshi's *Tokyo gijō*, Sukiyamachi had been ranked sec-ond after Yanagibashi in the Edo period. Inscribed in the artistic practices and appearance of Sukiyamachi geisha were the demeanor and mannerisms of Edo period geisha. Suita Dōshi, *Tokyo gijō* (Tokyo: Dōbunten, 1883).

47. Ibid., 12.

48. *TSK*, 322.

49. Ibid.

50. Ibid., 324.

51. Ibid., 334.

52. Ibid., 352.

53. Ibid., 290.

54. Ibid., 224.

55. The Japanese term used for "close friend" is *dōhō* (同胞), which means "comrade." The word also has the English word *brother* attached to it (rendered in *katakana* scripts) in a form of *rubi*, or glosses.

56. *TSK*, 234.

57. Ibid., 334.

58. *Shōsetsu shinzui*, 159; Twine, *Essence of the Novel*, 97.

59. After the initial rumor that he had become a delinquent, Sanji had locked himself up in his room to devote time to his studies. Unable to turn down Tomoyoshi's invitation, he goes to a teahouse where the celebration is to take place, at which point he accidentally meets Yoshizumi and the conflict ensues. The manner in which Tomoyoshi is removed from the scene indicates that his celebration was a simple mechanism for dragging Sanji out of his seclusion.

60. *TSK*, 236.

61. In contemporary Japanese, *gakusha* refers to "scholar." In the early Meiji period, however, *gakusha* meant "learned men."

62. *Shōsetsu shinzui*, 69; Twine, *Essence of the Novel*, 23–24.

63. The word *idealism* is given in a form of *rubi* to gloss the characters *kakū*.

64. *TSK*, 336.

65. *Yūjo* were all bound with debts to their master or mistress, which needed to be paid off for them to retire from their profession.

66. Of course, Toyotarō gains a different kind of interiority defined by his own knowledge of betrayal; it is one that struggles with the fact that he has relinquished his love.

CHAPTER 6

1. Kornicki, *Reform of Fiction*, 35–37.

2. Such an association between literature and time derives from the compilers' engagement with Taine's *History of English Literature* and Posnett's *Comparative Literature*, the influence of which has been noted by many, including the compilers themselves. See Nakayama, "'Bungakushi' to nashonaritī"; Shinada, *Man'yōhū no hatsumei*; Brownstein, "From *Kokugaku* to *Kokubungaku*"; Suzuki, "Gender and Genre"; Shirane, "Curriculum and Competing Canons"; Yoda, *Gender and National Literature*.

3. Mikami and Takatsu, *Nihon bungakushi*, 5.

4. Haga, *Kokubungakushi jikkō*, 6.

5. Takeshima Hagoromo, *Nihon bungakushi* (Tokyo: Jinbunsha, 1906), 2.

6. Suzuki, "Gender and Genre," 77.

7. See, for example, Ōwada, *Wabungakushi*; Ochiai and Utsumi, *Kokubungakushi kyōkasho*; Ogura, *Kokubungakushi kyōkasho*.

8. Nonacademic journals had published shorter renditions of Meiji literary history earlier. Yanagida Izumi states that Uchida Roan's "Gendai bungaku" (Contemporary Letters) published in *Kokumin no tomo* from November 1891 to January 1892 has the earliest rendition of Meiji literary history. Yanagida, *Meiji no shomotsu*, 141.

9. Ōwada, *Meiji bungakushi* (Tokyo: Hakubunkan, 1894). Reprinted as *Meiji bungakushi* (Tokyo: Nihon tosho sentā, 1982), 95.

10. Haga, *Kokubungakushi jikkō*, 257–58.

11. Shioi Ukō and Takahashi Tatsuo, *Shintai Nihon bungakushi* (Tokyo: Fukyūsha, 1902), 227–28.

12. I must add that there are exceptions. Narrative that merely captures *Shōsetsu shinzui* as a simple event in history continues in some literary histories in the twentieth century: Takahashi Tansui, *Jidai bungakushi* (Tokyo: Kaihatsusha, 1906), and Fujioka, *Kokubungakushi kōwa*, are some such examples.

13. "Meiji no shōsetsu," 261.

14. It also refers to *Shōsetsu shinzui* as a text that called for the "independence of art." Iwaki, *Zōho Meiji bungakushi* (Tokyo: Ikueisha, 1909). Reprinted as *Zōho Meiji bungakushi* (Tokyo: Nihon tosho sentā, 1982), 319.

15. "Bungeishi," 61.

16. Shimamura Hōgetsu, *Meiji bungaku hensenshi kōwa* (Tokyo: Bungaku fukyūkai, 1915). Reprinted in *Meiji shōsetsu bunshō hensenshi, Meiji shōsetsu naiyō hattatsushi, Meiji bungaku hensenshi kōwa* (Tokyo: Nihon tosho sentā, 1982), 10 (hereafter cited as *Meiji bungaku hensenshi kōwa*).

17. *Meiji jidai bunpan*, 67–68.

18. *Bungei hyakka zensho* (Tokyo: Ryūbunkan, 1909). Reprinted in *Bungei shiryō jiten* (Tokyo: Nihon tosho sentā, 2002), 1:690.

19. Ibid., 669.

20. "Bungeishi," 61.

21. "Meiji bundan ni okeru ikuta no kōkei," 13.

22. Ibid., 13–14.

23. *Meiji bungaku hensenshi kōwa*, 20. See also Tayama Katai, "Meiji bungaku no gaikan," *Bunshō sekai*, October 15, 1912.

24. Hibi, *Jiko hyōshō no bungakushi*.

25. Takayama Chogyū, "Biteki seikatsu o ronzu," compiled in *Kindai bungaku hyōron taikei 2: Meijiki II*, ed. Yoshida Seiichi and Asai Kiyoshi (Tokyo: Kadokawa shoten, 1972), 157.

26. I must note, however, that Takayama Chogyū's introduction of Nietzschean philosophy, especially in relation to what became known as "individualism" (*kojin*

shugi), plays a significant role in the enthusiasm for "the self" (*jiko*) and its development at the turn of the century.

27. I owe a great deal to Karatani Kōjin's groundbreaking work, *Nihon kindai bungaku no kigen*, which locates the discovery of landscape around this time. In it, he demonstrates the establishment of a certain semiotic constellation that allows for "reality" to come into being. I seek to supplement his discussion and examine how people practiced such a mode of reading by identifying how readers and writers began to share and exchange common information.

28. Kunikida Doppo, "Yoga sakuhin to jijitsu," in "Jijitsu to sakuhin," *Bunshō sekai*, September 1907, 16.

29. Ibid., 17.

30. Tokuda Shūsei, "E no moderu to shōsetsu no moderu," in "Jijitsu to sakuhin," *Bunshō sekai*, September 1907, 21.

31. As Nakayama Akihiko and others have noted, readers' columns existed long before this time. However, they began to appear on the front page around this time. On *Kokumin shinbun*'s readers' columns, see Kaneko, "Shinbun no naka no dokusha to shōsetsuka."

32. *Kokumin shinbun*, August 6, 1907.

33. Ibid., August 5, 1907.

34. For a brilliant analysis of the role of gossip columns in Tōson's *Haru*, see Nakayama, "'Sakka no shōzō' no saihensei."

35. However, what began as a debate between the naturalists and the moralists later developed into a debate among the naturalists. Shimamura Hōgetsu, Tayama Katai, and Hasegawa Tenkei argued for the separation of art and real life, arguing that even though art is based on real life, art is not something that is acted out. The younger naturalists, such as Iwano Hōmei, however, argued for the unity of art and real life. See Nakayama, "'Geijutsu' no seisei." Moreover, as Nakayama has noted, *shōsetsu*'s artistic status rose around this time as did the reputation of literary writers, which is evident from the fact that many were invited to the *bunten* (an art exhibition sponsored by the Ministry of Education), though Nakayama is quick to point out the still unstable status of writers.

36. See Hibi, *Jiko hyōshō no bungakushi*, 127.

37. Katagami Tengen, "Mikaiketsu no jinsei to shizenshugi," in *Shimamura Hōgetsu, Hasegawa Tenkei, Katagami Tengen, Sōma Gyofūshū, Meiji bungaku zenshū* (Tokyo: Chikuma shobō, 1967), 43:223.

38. Katagami Tengen, "Jiko no tame no bungaku," in *Shimamura Hōgetsu, Hasegawa Tenkei, Katagami Tengen, Sōma Gyofūshū, Meiji bungaku zenshū* (Tokyo: Chikuma shobō, 1967), 43:241.

39. *Meiji jidai bunpan*, 146.

40. Iwaki, *Zōho Meiji bungakushi*, 392.

41. *Bungei hyakka zensho*, 703.

42. Ibid., 665. The general formula that extends from *Shōsetsu shinzui* and *Ukigumo* to naturalism is quite consistent in these literary histories. However, there are exceptions. *Bungei hyakka zensho*, for example, characterizes *Ukigumo* and *Tajō takon*'s psychological depiction as too "logical" (704).

43. Suzuki is quick to note that only in the late 1930s do we see the usage stabilize. Suzuki, *Nihon no "bungaku" gainen*, 271. There are several exceptions here: for example, *Gendai bungei hyōronshū*, a volume of *Nihon gendai bungaku zenshū* published in 1969, includes criticisms dating from 1886. Perhaps the sudden surge of the modern (*kindai*) in the 1930s that Suzuki discusses is better situated within the general trend of (re)discovering Meiji, a discussion to which I will turn shortly.

44. See, for example, Miyajima, *Meiji bungaku jūnikō*, 75–76; Kojima, *Meiji Taishō shin bungaku shikan* (originally published in 1925), 73; Kanai, *Meiji Taishō bungakushi*, 58; Asahi shinbunsha, *Meiji Taishōshi*, 64.

45. Hijikata, "Meiji no bungei hyōron," 210.

46. Kanzaki, "Shajitsu shōsetsu," 199.

47. Shinoda, "Shakai shōsetsu to shakai shugi shōsetsu," 218.

48. See Narita, *Rekishigaku no sutairu*.

49. Yoshino Sakuzō, "'Meiji bunka kenkyūkai' ni tsuite." Quoted in Sekii, "Nihon kindai bungaku kenkyū no kigen," 26.

50. The other members were Miyatake Gaikotsu, Inoue Kazuo, Fujii Jintarō, Ishii Kendō, Ishikawa Iwao, Ono Hideo, and Osatake Takeki.

51. Yoshino, "Meiji bunka no kenkyū ni kokorozaseshi dōki," 103.

52. Narita, *Rekishigaku no sutairu*, 110.

53. Shinoda, "Meiji bungaku kenkyū ni kansuru ichi kōsatsu," 125. Shinoda published *Kindai Nihon bungakushi* in 1932 based on this historical framework.

54. Kanzaki, "Meiji bunshōshiron," 182.

55. Karaki, "Meiji bungaku ni okeru jiga no hattenshi," 45.

56. Honma, "Kibō futatsu mittsu."

57. See Sekii, "Nihon kindai bungaku kenkyū no kigen."

58. See ibid., 31–32.

59. The academic-centered character of the Meiji Literary Circle was in part the reason that it split into two within eight months, and the new group, Meiji Bungaku Danwakai (Discussion League of Meiji Literature), was founded in October 1932. Its primary members were Yanagida Izumi, Kimura Ki, Shinoda Tarō, Kanzaki Kiyoshi, and Hijikata Teiichi; this group also included many critics who eventually led the postwar literary scene, such as Yamamuro Shizuka, Hirano Ken, and Odagiri Hideo.

60. Narita, *Rekishigaku no sutairu*, 52–53.

61. Kobayashi Takiji, "Uyokuteki henkō no shomondai," in *Shōwa hihyō taikei* (Tokyo: Banchō shobō, 1968), 1:203. See also Miyamoto Kenji, "Seiji to geijutsu: seiji no yūisei no mondai" (hereafter cited as "Seiji to geijutsu"), for his discussion on Hayashi Fusao's *Seinen* and the issue of representing the Meiji Restoration in fiction. This is compiled in *Gendai Nihon bungaku ronsōshi*, ed. Hirano Ken, Odagiri Hideo, and Yamamoto Kenkichi (Tokyo: Miraisha, 1957).

62. An interesting parallel should not be overlooked here: at the tumultuous moment marked by the aftermath of the Great Kanto Earthquake, which also overlaps with the change from the Taishō to the Shōwa period, people looked toward Meiji as the beginning of Japanese modernization. The beginning of a new era, the Shōwa period, and a resurrection from the aftermath of the Great Kanto Earthquake coincide. The Meiji period was, in other words, undeniably the "past." Many critics have observed this parallel. See, for example, Narita, *Rekishigaku no sutairu*, 52–53; Komori, "Kigen no gensetsu," 143, 146–47.

63. Asahi shinbunsha, *Meiji Taishōshi*, 43–44.

64. Senuma, "Shinri bungaku no hatten to sono kisū," 85. Here are some other examples: Kojima Tokuya situates *Shōsetsu shinzui* as a work that "discussed the essence of realism (*shajitsu shugi*) that runs through the many *shōsetsu* we have today." Kojima, *Meiji Taishō shin bungaku shikan*, 77. Iwaki Juntarō claims that portrayal of reality (*genjitsu byōsha*) is the common thread of Meiji literature; along with Shōyō's *shōsetsu*, he refers to "realism (*shajitsu*), which defined the writings of Kōyō and his group, Shiki's 'realistic description' (*shasei*), and the reality (*genjitsu*) of works after 1907." It is clear that Iwaki has in mind the naturalist school when he refers to "works after 1907," which he later characterizes as "literature that exposes reality." Iwaki, *Meiji Taishō no kokubungaku* (Tokyo: Seishōdō, 1925). Reprinted as *Meiji Taishō no kokubungaku* (Tokyo: Nihon tosho sentā, 1982), 179, 220.

65. Miyajima, *Meiji bungaku jūnikō*, 91–92. See also Kataoka Yoshikazu's "Meiji kōki no shōsetsu," which characterizes the naturalists' works as having finally "established the *shajitsu shugi* that has been intended but was not easily actualized since Shōyō" (275).

66. Takasu, *Meiji bungakushiron*, 377.

67. See also Karaki, "Meiji bungaku ni okeru jiga no hattenshi"; Kanzaki, "Shajitsu shōsetsu"; Kojima, "Tsubouchi Shōyō kenkyū"; Karaki, "Kindai bungaku to seikatsu no mondai."

68. Kataoka, "Wakaki dokusha ni uttau," 9, and "Shinkankakuha wa kaku shuchō su," 242. The efforts by Itō Sei (1905–69) and Horiguchi Daigaku (1892–1981) to introduce "stream of consciousness" and other modernist techniques were part of such criticism against realism. See Itō, "Shin shinri shugi bungaku"; Horiguchi, "Shōsetsu no shin keishiki to shite no 'naishin dokuhaku.'"

69. Hijikata, "Meiji no bungei hyōron," 208.

70. Aono, "'Shirabeta' geijutsu," 34.

71. Kataoka, "Meiji kōki no shōsetsu," 276.

72. Karaki, "Bungaku to seikatsu," 255.

73. See, for example, Kanzaki Kiyoshi's "Shajitsu shōsetsu": "The new literary historians like to discuss the reasons why bourgeois realism embodied by *Shōsetsu shinzui* and *Ukigumo* did not develop. It goes without saying that Ken'yūsha's realism, which is connected to *Shōsetsu shinzui*'s conservative and base aspects, restricted bourgeois literature to poor realism and stagnant objectivism." Kanzaki, "Shajitsu shōsetsu," 199. See also Kojima's "Tsubouchi Shōyō kenkyū," which situates *Shōsetsu shinzui* as an embodiment of capitalistic liberalism that rejected didacticism as a remnant of the feudalistic past.

74. He and other Marxist critics used *shizenshugi sakka* (naturalist writers) to refer to any bourgeois realist, even when they were not associated with the naturalist movement; these writers included Uno Kōji, Shiga Naoya, and other so-called *geijutsuha* (art-for-art's-sake) writers. Kurahara, "Puroretariya rearizumu e no michi," 118.

75. Note that the criticism against the nonsocial self is not limited to proponents of proletarian literature. Coming to a very different conclusion, Ikuta Chōkō in "Meiji bungaku gaisetsu" also criticizes the lack of social awareness: "Neither the naturalists nor the Shirakaba school had been awakened by modern social consciousness (*kindaiteki shakaiteki ishiki*)." He continues, "True literature will appear when social awareness and class consciousness intermingle with Japanese tradition." Ikuta Chōkō, "Meiji bungaku gaisetsu," *Nihon bungaku kōza* (Tokyo: Shinchōsha, 1927), 5:55, 61. The nationalistic tone is shared by Takasu Yoshijirō, in his *Meiji bungakushiron*; after he situates the naturalists as those who "only portrayed personal environment and forgot to portray the truth of real society," he claims the following: "In short, the literature of the Meiji period in general continued to chase Euro-American literature and developed significantly, but it did not reach the point of producing literature that was unique to Japan. . . . Even if Meiji literature was modeled after Euro-America, it goes without saying that the national character (*kokuminsei*) appeared," suggesting that the Japanese national character could not be tamed by Euro-American trends. Takasu, *Meiji bungakushiron*, 378, 380.

76. I must add here that there was another group of writings that had a tremendous impact upon the discussions, namely, "mass literature" (*taishū bungaku*), which emerged in full force after the Great Kanto Earthquake. The varying discussions on what constitutes art and artistic value were in many ways governed by the existence of mass literature.

77. Kurahara, "Geijutsu undō ni okeru sayoku seisan shugi," 98–99. See also *Bungei sensen*'s article "Shakai shugi bungei undō" (Socialist Literary Movement),

which states, "We must be a socialist before an artist. Socialist literature must first be art. There is no contradiction in these two statements" (84–85).

78. "Seiji to geijutsu," 151.

79. I must add here that he is not against the proletariats; he is arguing against the Marxist intellectuals who try to "paint everything with their ideology." He feels that he must protect literature from the "demonic hand of politics" until the proletariats can properly inherit literature. Minegawa, "Geijutsuha sengen," 176.

80. Ozaki, "Bungei jihyō," in *Bungaku jidai*, May 1931. Reprinted as *Bungaku jidai*, vol. 3, no. 5 (Tokyo: Yumani shobō, 1995), 28. Nakamura Murao also supports such a view by insisting that the value of *shōsetsu* is "exploration of human existence," suggesting that it is a proletarian literary movement that is limited in scope, not realist literature. Nakamura, "Ichi ni mo ni ni mo san ni mo ningen-sei," 22–23.

81. Funahashi, "Geijutsuha no nōdō," 231.

82. Shinoda, "Shakai shōsetsu to shakai shugi shōsetsu," 204.

83. Proletarian literature continued to be published, but clearly lacking the dominance it had in the past decade or so. Many discussions about proletarian literature and *geijutsuha* literature continued, but with less urgency.

84. See Nakamura, "Tenkō sakkaron," 328.

85. Hayashi, "Sakka to shite," 66–67.

86. Kobayashi Takiji, "Dōshi Hayashi Fusao no 'Sakka no tame ni' 'Sakka to shite' soreni taisuru dōshi Kamei Katsuichirō no hihan no hihan," in Hirano Ken, Odagiri Hideo, and Yamamoto Kenkichi, eds., *Gendai Nihon bungaku ronsōshi* (Tokyo: Miraisha, 1957), 2:143.

Glossary

ari no mama ありのまま　As it is or as they are.

bōkan suru 傍観する　To observe.

bonkin 凡近　The ordinary.

bungaku 文学　Now a standard translation of "literature." Prior to its coupling with literature, *bungaku* signified a paradigm of knowledge, especially *kangaku* classics.

bungakushi 文学史　Literary histories or history of letters.

chiiku 智育　Intellectual education; as opposed to *tokuiku* or moral education.

datsu-a 脱亜　De-Asianization.

gakumon 学問　Knowledge or learning.

gakusha 学者　A learned man or scholar.

gense 現世　The present.

gesaku 戯作　Playful writings or a body of writing considered secondary to serious or scholarly texts. The subgenres of *gesaku* include *sharebon* (books of wit and fashion), *kokkeibon* (humorous stories), *ninjōbon* (books of sentiments), *yomihon* (books for reading), *kibyōshi* (yellow-cover books), and *gōkan* (bound books).

gijin 義人　Good and righteous men.

giyū 義勇　Justice and courage.

haishi 稗史　Commoner's history. Derived from the Chinese system of classification in which *haishi* was defined against *seishi* (正史), the first character of which means "official" or "correct," whereas the second denotes "history."

Haishi thus refers to writings of historical events that were not included in official history.

hakuwa shōsetsu 白話小説   "Chinese" vernacular fiction, *baihua xiaoshuo* in Chinese. *Hakuwa* lineage is, however, not necessarily Chinese (= not Japanese), especially after the increase in works of adaptations in Edo Japan.

jidai 時代   The historical; as opposed to the social (*sewa*).

jinbun hatsuiku 人文発育   Human development.

jingi hakkō 仁義八行   Eight Confucian virtues.

jitsugaku 実学   Real or practical knowledge.

jitsuroku 実録   Documentary fiction.

kajin saishi 佳人才子   A beautiful woman and a man of talent.

kanbun 漢文   Sinified Japanese prose.

kangaku 漢学   Typically translated as "Chinese learning." However, whereas classical writings of *kangaku* may have originated in China, the practice of *kangaku* has a long history in Japan, and it is quite misleading to suggest that *kangaku* and its Confucian foundation are Chinese and *not* Japanese.

kanjō shisō 感情思想   Thoughts and feelings.

kanzen chōaku 勧善懲悪   Didacticism or "encourage virtue, castigate vice."

kōa 興亜   Asianism.

kokugaku 国学   Native learning.

Kokubungakka 国文学科   Department of National Letters, founded in 1889.

koshinbun 小新聞   Small newspapers.

Koten Kōshūka 古典講習科   Program for Study in the Classics, founded in 1882.

kyogaku 虚学   False or impractical knowledge.

monogatari 物語   A genre of tales or prose fiction. *Monogatari* is also a nominalized form of the verb *monogataru*, referring to "the act of telling."

mosha 模写   To copy, in contemporary Japanese, which is often taken to mean *shajitsu*, denoting mimetic description.

ninjō fūzoku setai 人情風俗世態   Emotions, customs, and manners.

ōseki 往昔   The bygone past.

ōshinbun 大新聞   Large newspapers.

risshin shusse 立身出世   Success and advancement.

sai 才   Ability necessary for success and advancement, or *risshin shusse*.

sakusha no ishō 作者の意匠   The writer's design.

seiji kōdan 政治講談 Political oration.

seishitsu 性質 A character's disposition, characteristic, or attribute.

sewa 世話 The social; as opposed to the historical (*jidai*).

shajitsu 写実 Mimetic depiction or realism.

shijuku 私塾 Private schools.

shizoku 士族 The former samurai class.

shōsetsu 小説 "Novel" is now the standard translation, but *shōsetsu* was a contested term in the early Meiji period, with signifieds ranging from "trivial writings" to "vernacular fiction."

sodoku 素読 Literally "raw reading," a form of recitation that trained students to declaim and memorize *kangaku* classics through the rhythm and sounds of the sentences, regardless of understanding their content.

sōshi 壮士 Stalwart youth.

taijin gakusha 大人学者 Established and learned men.

tokuiku 徳育 Moral education; as opposed to *chiiku* or intellectual education.

yōgaku 洋学 Western learning.

yomihon 読本 Books for reading.

yūjo 遊女 Women of the pleasure quarters.

zen'aku jasei 善悪邪正 Good/bad and right/wrong.

Works Cited

Anderson, Benedict. *Imagined Communities: Reflections on the Origin and Spread of Nationalism.* New York: Verso, 1991.

"Annan no senpō." *Jiyū shinbun,* June 13, 1883.

Aono Suekichi. "'Shirabeta' geijutsu." In *Gendai bungakuron taikei,* vol. 4, *Puroretaria bungaku,* ed. Nakano Shigeharu and Aono Suekichi. Tokyo: Kawade shobō, 1954.

Asahi shinbunsha, ed. *Meiji Taishōshi: geijutsuhen.* Vol. 5. Tokyo: Asahi shinbunsha, 1931.

Asukai Masamichi. *Meiji taitei.* Tokyo: Kōdansha gakujutsu bunko, 2002.

———. "Miyazaki Muryū no gensō." In *Nihon kindai seishinshi no kenkyū.* Kyoto: Kyoto daigaku gakujutsu shuppankai, 2002.

———. *Nihon no kindai bungaku.* Tokyo: San'ichi shobō, 1961.

———. "Seiji shōsetsu to 'kindai' bungaku." In *Nihon kindai no shuppatsu.* Tokyo: Haniwa shobō, 1973.

Baba Tatsui. "Nairan no gai wa kakumeika no ayamachi ni arazu." *Jiyū shinbun,* July 21–22, 1882.

Bhabha, Homi K. *Location of Culture.* New York: Routledge, 1994.

Bourdieu, Pierre. *The Logic of Practice.* Stanford: Stanford University Press, 1990.

———. *Outline of a Theory of Practice.* Cambridge: Cambridge University Press, 1977.

Brownstein, Michael C. "From *Kokugaku* to *Kokubungaku*: Canon-Formation in the Meiji Period." *Harvard Journal of Asiatic Studies* 47, no. 2 (December 1987): 435–60.

"Bungaku sekai no kinkyō." In *Kindai bungaku hyōron taikei 1: Meijiki I*, ed. Yoshida Seiichi and Asai Kiyoshi. Tokyo: Kadokawa shoten, 1971.

Bungei hyakka zensho. In *Bungei shiryō jiten*, vol. 1. Tokyo: Nihon tosho sentā, 2002.

"Bungeishi." *Taiyō: Hakubunkan rinji zōkan 2*, vol. 15, no. 3 (1909): 1–192.

Caddeau, Patrick W. *Appraising Genji: Literary Criticism and Cultural Anxiety in the Age of the Last Samurai*. New York: State University of New York Press, 2006.

Chakrabarty, Dipesh. Afterword to *Mirror of Modernity: Invented Traditions of Modern Japan*. Ed. Stephen Vlastos. Berkeley: University of California Press, 1998.

Chambers, William, and Robert Chambers. *Chambers' Information for the People*. Philadelphia: J. B. Lippincott, 1855.

"Chōsen hatashite museifu naru ka." *Tokyo nichi nichi shinbun*, August 8, 1882.

"Chōsen ni shissu no gi." *Jiyū shinbun*, October 25–29, 1882.

"Chōsen no hanto utazaru bekarazu." *Yūbin hōchi shinbun*, August 7, 1882.

"Chōsen no henpō." *Jiyū shinbun*, August 1–2, 1882.

"Chōsen o shosuru no seiryaku." *Chōya shinbun*, May 15, 1881.

"Chōsen seiryaku." *Tokyo Yokohama mainichi shinbun*, August 8–13, 16–19, 1882.

Doak, Kevin M. "Civil Society and the Uses of France in Early Meiji Japan." Paper presented at the 50th annual meeting of the Association for Asian Studies, Washington D.C., March 29, 1998.

Dumas, Alexandre. *Memoirs of a Physician*. 2 vols. London: G. Routledge, 1893.

———. *Six Years Later; or, The Taking of the Bastille*. Philadelphia: T. B. Peterson & Brothers, 1875.

"Eitei ga Shinfutsu ni chūsai suruto wa hatashite makoto kana." *Jiyū shinbun*, August 1, 1883.

Fogel, Joshua A. *The Literature of Travel in the Japanese Rediscovery of China, 1862–1945*. Stanford: Stanford University Press, 1996.

Foucault, Michel. *The Archaeology of Knowledge and the Discourse on Language*. New York: Pantheon Books, 1972.

———. *The Order of Things: An Archaeology of the Human Sciences*. New York: Vintage Books, 1973.

Fujii Sadakazu. "Kodai bungaku shiron." In *Iwanami kōza: Nihon bungakushi— bungaku no tanjō yori hasseiki made*, vol. 1. Tokyo: Iwanami shoten 1995.

———. *Nihon "shōsetsu" genshi*. Tokyo: Taishūkan shoten, 1995.

Fujikawa Yoshiyuki. "Hon'yaku bungaku no tenbō." In *Iwanami kōza: Nihon bungakushi—henkakuki no bungaku III*, vol. 11. Tokyo: Iwanami shoten, 1996.

Fujioka Sakutarō. *Kokubungakushi kōwa*. Publisher unknown, 1908.

Fukuzawa Yukichi. "Chōsen dokuritsutō no shokei." In *Fukuzawa Yukichi zenshū*, vol. 10. Tokyo: Iwanami shoten, 1960.

————. "Chōsen no kōsai o ronzu." In *Fukuzawa Yukichi zenshū*, vol. 8. Tokyo: Iwanami shoten, 1960.

————. "Datsu-aron." In *Fukuzawa Yukichi zenshū*, vol. 10. Tokyo: Iwanami shoten, 1960.

————. *Encouragement of Learning*. In *Fukuzawa Yukichi on Education: Selected Works*, ed. and trans. Eiichi Kiyooka. Tokyo: University of Tokyo Press, 1985.

————. *Gakumon no dokuritsu*. In *Fukuzawa Yukichi zenshū*, vol. 5. Tokyo: Iwanami shoten, 1959.

————. *Gakumon no susume*. Tokyo: Iwanami bunko, 1978.

————. "Gyūba Takuzō-kun Chōsen ni iku." In *Fukuzawa Yukichi zenshū*, vol. 8. Tokyo: Iwanami shoten, 1960.

————. "Sensō to nareba hisshō no san ari." In *Fukuzawa Yukichi zenshū*, vol. 10. Tokyo: Iwanami shoten, 1960.

Funahashi Seiichi. "Geijutsuha no nōdō." In *Gendai Nihon bungaku ronsōshi*, vol. 2, ed. Hirano Ken, Odagiri Hideo, and Yamamoto Kenkichi. Tokyo: Miraisha, 1957.

Gaimushō, ed. *Nihon gaikō bunsho*. Vol. 10. Tokyo: Nihon kokusai rengō kyōkai, 1949.

Gluck, Carol. *Japan's Modern Myths: Ideology in the Late Meiji Period*. Princeton, N.J.: Princeton University Press, 1985.

Gotō Masato. "Gimin kenshō o meguru jiyūshugi to fashizumu—Komuro Shinsuke hen *Tōyō minken hyakkaden* ni tsuite." *Ritsumeikan daigaku jinbun kagaku kenkyūjo kiyō* 65 (February 1996): 1–24.

Haga Yaichi. *Kokubungakushi jikkō*. Tokyo: Fuzanbō, 1899.

Hardacre, Helen. "Creating State Shintō: The Great Promulgation Campaign and the New Religions." *Journal of Japanese Studies* 12, no. 1 (Winter 1986): 29–63.

Hashikawa Bunzō. "Fukuzawa Yukichi no Chūgoku bunmeiron." In *Hashikawa Bunzō chosakushū*, vol. 7, *Kindai Nihon to Chūgoku*. Tokyo: Chikuma shobō, 1986.

Hattori Hitoshi. "Saisetsu Bakin no bunshō ishiki—dōjidai no shosō, Sanba to kokugaku to." In *Kyokutei Bakin no bungakuiki*. Tokyo: Wakakusa shobō, 1997.

Hayashi Fusao. "Sakka to shite." In *Kindai bungaku hyōron taikei 7: Shōwaki II*, ed. Takahashi Haruo and Hoshina Masao. Tokyo: Kadokawa shoten, 1972.

Hayashi Motoi. "Kaisetsu." In *Tōyō minken hyakkaden*, by Komuro Shinsuke. Tokyo: Iwanami shoten, 1957.

Hibi Yoshitaka. *Jiko hyōshō no bungakushi: jibun o kaku shōsetsu no tōjō*. Tokyo: Kanrin shobō, 2002.

Hijikata Teiichi. "Meiji no bungei hyōron." In *Nihon bungaku kōza: Meiji Taishōhen*, vol. 12. Tokyo: Kaizōsha, 1934.

Honma Hisao. "Kibō futatsu mittsu—Meiji bunka kenkyūkai e." *Kokumin shinbun*, December 11, 1924.

Horiguchi Daigaku. "Shōsetsu no shin keishiki to shite no 'naishin dokuhaku.'" In *Gendai bungakuron taikei*, vol. 5, *Modanizumu/geijutsuha*. Tokyo: Kawade shobō, 1954.

Ichishima Shunjō. "Meiji bungaku shoki no tsuioku." Afterword in *Shōsetsu shinzui*, by Tsubouchi Shōyō. Tokyo: Tokyōdō, 1926.

Ikuta Chōkō. "Meiji bungaku gaisetsu." In *Nihon bungaku kōza*, vol. 5. Tokyo: Shinchōsha, 1927.

———. *Meiji jidai bunpan*. Tokyo: Hakubunkan, 1907.

"Imada rakutan suru ni oyobazu." *Jiyū no tomoshibi*, January 17, 1885.

Ino Kenji. *Meiji bungakushi*. Vol. 1. Tokyo: Kōdansha, 1985.

"Ippō o higo subekarazu." *Chōya shinbun*, September 16–18, 1884.

Ishida Tadahiko. *Tsubouchi Shōyō kenkyū*. Fukuoka: Kyūshū daigaku shuppankai, 1988.

Ishii Ryōsuke. *Yoshiwara: Edo no yūkaku no jittai*. Tokyo: Chūō Kōronsha, 1969.

Itagaki Taisuke, ed. *Jiyūtōshi*. Vol. 2. Tokyo: Gosharō, 1910.

Itō Sei. "Shin shinri shugi bungaku: shōsetsu no shin keishiki to shite no naishin dokuhaku." In *Gendai bungakuron taikei*, vol. 5, *Modanizumu/geijutsuha*. Tokyo: Kawade shobō, 1954.

Iwaki Juntarō. *Meiji Taishō no kokubungaku*. Tokyo: Nihon tosho sentā, 1982.

———. *Zōho Meiji bungakushi*. Tokyo: Nihon tosho sentā, 1982.

"Kakugo wa yoika." *Jiyū no tomoshibi*, December 29, 1884.

Kamei Hideo. "Gūi to bungakushi—*Shōsetsu shinzui* kenkyū III." *Hokkaidō daigaku bungakubu kiyō* 39, no. 1 (November 1990): 121–72.

———. *Kansei no henkaku*. Tokyo: Kōdansha, 1983.

———. *Meiji bungakushi*. Tokyo: Iwanami shoten, 2000.

———. "Seishi jitsuroku to shōsetsu haishi—*Shōsetsu shinzui* kenkyū II." *Hokkaidō daigaku bungakubu kiyō* 38, no. 3 (March 1990): 121–77.

———. *Shintai, kono fushigi naru mono no bungaku*. Tokyo: Renga shobō shinsha, 1984.

———. *"Shōsetsu"ron: Shōsetsu shinzui to kindai*. Tokyo: Iwanami shoten, 1999.

Kamei Hideo, Komori Yōichi, and Takada Mamoru. "Teidan: Dōjidai to bungaku kenkyū." *Bungaku* 3, no. 2 (April 1992): 44–80.

Kanagaki Robun and Sansantei Arindo. "Chosakudō kakiage." In *Nihon shoki shinbun zenshū*, vol. 40. Tokyo: Perikansha, 1993.

Kanai Kasatarō. *Meiji Taishō bungakushi*. Private printing, 1928.

Kaneko Akio. "Shinbun no naka no dokusha to shōsetsuka—Meiji 40 nen zengo no *Kokumin shinbun* o megutte." *Bungaku* 4, no. 2 (April 1993): 38–49.

Kanzaki Kiyoshi. "Meiji bunshōshiron." In *Meiji bungakushi shūsetsu*. Tokyo: Nihon bungakusha, 1932.

————. "Shajitsu shōsetsu." In *Nihon bungaku kōza: Meiji bungakuhen*, vol. 11. Tokyo: Kaizōsha, 1934.

Karaki Junzō. "Bungaku to seikatsu." In *Showa hihyō taikei*, vol. 1. Tokyo: Banchō shobō, 1968.

————. "Kindai bungaku to seikatsu no mondai." In *Gendai Nihon bungaku zenshū*, vol. 95, *Gendai bungei hyōronshū II*. Tokyo: Chikuma shobō, 1958.

————. "Meiji bungaku ni okeru jiga no hattenshi." In *Meiji bungaku kenkyū*. Tokyo: Seikōkan shoten, 1933.

Karatani Kōjin. *Nihon kindai bungaku no kigen*. Tokyo: Kōdansha, 1980.

Katagami Tengen. "Jiko no tame no bungaku." In *Meiji bungaku zenshū*, vol. 43, *Shimamura Hōgetsu, Hasegawa Tenkei, Katagami Tengen, Sōma Gyofūshū*. Tokyo: Chikuma shobō, 1967.

————. "Mikaiketsu no jinsei to shizenshugi." In *Meiji bungaku zenshū*, vol. 43, *Shimamura Hōgetsu, Hasegawa Tenkei, Katagami Tengen, Sōma Gyofūshū*. Tokyo: Chikuma shobō, 1967.

Kataoka Teppei. "Shinkankakuha wa kaku shuchō su." In *Gendai Nihon bungaku ronsōshi*, vol. 1, ed. Hirano Ken, Odagiri Hideo, and Yamamoto Kenkichi. Tokyo: Miraisha, 1957.

————. "Wakaki dokusha ni uttau." In *Gendai bungakuron taikei*, vol. 5, *Modanizumu/geijutsuha*. Tokyo: Kawade shobō, 1954.

Kataoka Yoshikazu. "Meiji kōki no shōsetsu." In *Meiji bungakushi shūsetsu*. Tokyo: Nihon bungakusha, 1932.

Kawamoto Hideo. *Ōtopoiēshisu: daisan sedai shisutemu*. Tokyo: Seidosha, 1995.

Keene, Donald. *Dawn to the West: Japanese Literature of the Modern Era*. Vol. 1. New York: Holt, Rinehart and Winston, 1984.

Kimura Naoe. *Seinen no tanjō: Meiji Nihon ni okeru seijiteki jissen no tenkan*. Tokyo: Shin'yōsha, 1998.

"Kōa no mondai oyobi tōyō no gensei." *Yūbin hōchi shinbun*, June 6, 1884.

Kobayashi Takiji. "Dōshi Hayashi Fusao no 'Sakka no tame ni' 'Sakka to shite' soreni taisuru dōshi Kamei Katsuichirō no hihan no hihan." In *Gendai Nihon bungaku ronsōshi*, vol. 2, ed. Hirano Ken, Odagiri Hideo, and Yamamoto Kenkichi. Tokyo: Miraisha, 1957.

————. "Uyokuteki henkō no shomondai." In *Shōwa hihyō taikei*, vol. 1. Tokyo: Banchō shobō, 1968.

Kōda Rohan. "Meiji nijūnen zengo no nibunsei." In *Meiji bungaku kaisōshū*, vol. 1, ed. Togawa Shinsuke. Tokyo: Iwanami bunko, 1998.

Kojima Tokuya. *Meiji Taishō shin bungaku shikan*. In *Meiji Taishō bungakushi shūsei*, vol. 8. Tokyo: Nihon tosho sentā, 1982.

————. "Tsubouchi Shōyō kenkyū." In *Meiji bungaku kenkyū*, ed. Fukuda Hisamichi. Tokyo: Seikōkan shoten, 1933.

Kokuritsu kyōiku kenkyūjo, ed. *Nihon kindai kyōiku hyakunenshi.* Vols. 1–4.
Tokyo: Kyōiku shinkō kenkyūkai, 1974.

Komori Yōichi. *Buntai to shite no monogatari.* Tokyo: Chikuma shobō, 1988.

———. "Kigen no gensetsu—Nihon bungaku kenkyū to iu sōchi." In *Naiha suru chi—shintai, kotoba, kenryoku o aminaosu,* ed. Kurihara Akira et al. Tokyo: Tokyo daigaku shuppankai, 2000.

———. *Kōzō to shite no katari.* Tokyo: Shin'yōsha, 1988.

———. *Nihongo no kindai.* Tokyo: Iwanami shoten, 2000.

———. *Posutokoroniaru.* Tokyo: Iwanami shoten, 2001.

Komuro Shinsuke. *Kōa kidan: Murenren. Jiyū shinbun,* April 6–June 18, 1884.

———. *Tōyō minken hyakkaden.* Tokyo: Iwanami shoten, 1957.

Kōno Kensuke. *Shomotsu no kindai: media no bungakushi.* Tokyo: Chikuma shobō, 1999.

Kornicki, Peter. *The Reform of Fiction in Meiji Japan.* London: Ithaca Press, 1982.

Kunikida Doppo. "Yoga sakuhin to jijitsu." In "Jijitsu to sakuhin," *Bunshō sekai* (September 1907): 16–21.

"Kuni kore o sadamuru no gi." *Tokyo nichi nichi shinbun,* February 22–23, 1881.

Kurahara Korehito. "Geijutsu undō ni okeru sayoku seisan shugi." In *Gendai bungakuron taikei,* vol. 4, *Puroretaria bungaku,* ed. Nakano Shigeharu and Aono Suekichi. Tokyo: Kawade shobō, 1954.

———. "Puroretariya rearizumu e no michi." In *Kindai bungaku hyōron taikei 6: Taishōki III Shōwaki I,* ed. Miyoshi Yukio and Sofue Shōji. Tokyo: Kadokawa shoten, 1973.

Kuroki Morifumi. "Kōakai/Ajia kyōkai no katsudō to shisō." In *Kōakai hōkoku/ Ajia kyōkai hōkoku,* vol. 1, ed. Kuroki Morifumi and Masuzawa Akio. Tokyo: Fuji shuppan, 1993.

———. "Kōshin jiken to *Chōya shinbun*—hisenron o chūshin to shite." In *Nashonarizumu no dōtai—Nihon to Ajia,* ed. Tokumoto Masahiro et al. Fukuoka: Kyūshū daigaku shuppankai, 1989.

Kuroki Morifumi and Masuzawa Akio, eds. *Kōakai hōkoku/Ajia kyōkai hōkoku.* Vol. 1. Tokyo: Fuji shuppan, 1993.

Kwon Sok-bong. "Ryōsen shikō ni kansuru ichi kōsatsu." *The Han* 3, nos. 6–7 (June, August 1974): 69–94, 85–101.

Kyokutei Bakin. *Nansō Satomi hakkenden.* 10 vols. Ed. Koike Fujigorō. Tokyo: Iwanami shoten, 1995.

Lee Yeounsuk. *"Kokugo" to iu shisō—kindai Nihon no gengo ninshiki.* Tokyo: Iwanami shoten, 1996.

Liu, Lydia H. *Translingual Practice: Literature, National Culture, and Translated Modernity—China, 1900–1937.* Stanford: Stanford University Press, 1995.

Luhmann, Niklas. *Observations of Modernity*. Stanford: Stanford University Press, 1998.

———. *Social Systems*. Stanford: Stanford University Press, 1995.

Maeda Ai. "Bakin to Tōkoku—kyō o megutte." In *Maeda Ai chosakushū*, vol. 4, *Genkei no Meiji*. Tokyo: Chikuma shobō, 1989.

———. "Gesaku bungaku to *Tōsei shosei katagi*." *Nihon kindai bungaku* 2 (August 1965): 13–23.

———. "Kindai bungaku to katsujiteki sekai." In *Maeda Ai chosakushū*, vol. 2, *Kindai dokusha no seiritsu*. Tokyo: Chikuma shobō, 1989.

———. *Kindai dokusha no seiritsu*. Tokyo: Yūseidō, 1973.

———. *Kindai Nihon no bungaku kūkan: rekishi, kotoba, jōkyō*. Tokyo: Shin'yōsha, 1983.

———. "Meiji rekishi bungaku no genzō—seiji shōsetsu no baai." In *Maeda Ai chosakushū*, vol. 4, *Genkei no Meiji*. Tokyo: Chikuma shobō, 1989.

———. "Meiji shoki gesaku shuppan no dōkō—kinsei shuppan kikō no kaitai." In *Maeda Ai chosakushū*, vol. 2, *Kindai dokusha no seiritsu*. Tokyo: Chikuma shobō, 1989.

———. "Ondoku kara mokudoku e." In *Maeda Ai chosakushū*, vol. 2, *Kindai dokusha no seiritsu*. Tokyo: Chikuma shobō, 1989.

Marran, Christine L. "The Allure of the Poison-Woman in Modern Japanese Literature." Ph.D. diss., University of Washington, 1998.

Masamune Hakuchō. "Mukashi no nikki." *Kindai bungaku* 1, no. 1 (January 1946): 12–14.

Matsumura Shun'suke. *Kaimei shōsetsu: Harusame bunko*. In *Meiji bungaku zenshū*, vol. 1, *Meiji kaikaki bungakushū 1*. Tokyo: Chikuma shobō, 1966.

Matsuoka Kiichi. *Jiyū shinbun o yomu: Jiyūtō ni totte no jiyū minken undō*. Nagoya: Yunite, 1992.

"Meiji bundan ni okeru ikuta no kōkei." *Bunshō sekai* 7, no. 14 (October 15, 1912): 12–128.

"Meiji hon'yaku bungaku nenpyō." In *Meiji bungaku zenshū*, vol. 7, *Meiji hon'yaku bungakushū*. Tokyo: Chikuma shobō, 1972.

"Meiji 13 nen shūkai jōrei." In *Nihon kindai shisō taikei*, vol. 11, *Genron to media*, ed. Matsumoto Sannosuke and Yamamuro Shin'ichi. Tokyo: Iwanami shoten, 1990.

Mertz, John Pierre. *Novel Japan: Spaces of Nationhood in Early Meiji Narrative, 1870–88*. Ann Arbor: Center for Japanese Studies, University of Michigan, 2003.

Mikami Sanji and Takatsu Kuwasaburō. *Nihon bungakushi*. Tokyo: Nihon tosho sentā, 1982.

Minegawa Hiroshi. "Geijutsuha sengen." In *Gendai bungakuron taikei*, vol. 5, *Modanizumu/geijutsuha*. Tokyo: Kawade shobō, 1954.

Miyajima Shinsaburō. *Meiji bungaku jūnikō.* Tokyo: Shinshidansha, 1925.

Miyamoto Kenji. "Seiji to geijutsu: seiji no yūisei no mondai." In *Gendai Nihon bungaku ronsōshi,* vol. 2, ed. Hirano Ken, Odagiri Hideo, and Yamamoto Kenkichi. Tokyo: Miraisha, 1957.

Miyazaki Muryū. *Jiyū no kachidoki. Jiyū shinbun,* January 18–21, 1883.

———. *Jiyū no kachidoki.* In *Meiji bungaku zenshū,* vol. 5, *Meiji seiji shōsetsushū* 1. Tokyo: Chikuma shobō, 1966.

Motoda Eifu. "Kyōgaku seishi." In *Nihon kindai shisō taikei,* vol. 6, *Kyōiku no taikei,* ed. Yamazumi Masami. Tokyo: Iwanami shoten, 1990.

Nakamura Masanao. *Saigoku risshihen.* Tokyo: Kōdansha, 1981.

Nakamura Mitsuo. "Tenkō sakkaron." In *Showa hihyō taikei,* vol. 1. Tokyo: Banchō shobō, 1968.

Nakamura Murao. "Ichi ni mo ni ni mo san ni mo ningensei." In *Bungaku jidai* 3, no. 5: 22–23. Tokyo: Yumani shobō, 1995.

Nakamura Yukihiko. "Gesakuron." In *Nakamura Yukihiko chojutsushū,* vol. 8. Tokyo: Chūō kōronsha, 1982.

Nakayama Akihiko. "'Bungakushi' to nashonaritī—waisetsu, Nihonjin, bunka bōeiron." *Kindai chi no seiritsu 1890–1910 nendai.* In *Iwanami kōza: Kindai Nihon no bunkashi,* vol. 3. Tokyo: Iwanami shoten, 2002.

———. "'Geijutsu' no seisei—'bijutsu' to 'bungaku' no ba oyobi Hōgetsu, Katai, Tenkei." *Nihon kindai bungaku* 61 (October 1999): 14–28.

———. "'Sakka no shōzō' no saihensei—*Yomiuri shinbun* o chūshin to suru bungei goshippuran, shōsokuran no yakuwari." *Bungaku* 4, no. 2 (April 1993): 24–37.

Narita Ryūichi. *Rekishigaku no sutairu: shigakushi to sono shūhen.* Tokyo: Azekura shobō, 2001.

Narushima Ryūhoku. "Ōshū kiji: Karyū shunwa daigen." Preface to *Ōshū kiji: Karyū shunwa,* trans. Oda Jun'ichirō. In *Meiji bungaku zenshū,* vol. 7, *Meiji hon'yaku bungakushū.* Tokyo: Chikuma shobō, 1972.

———. *Ryūkyō shinshi.* In *Meiji bungaku zenshū,* vol. 4, *Narushima Ryūhoku, Hattori Bushō, Kurimoto Ryōunshū.* Tokyo: Chikuma shobō, 1969.

"Nihonhei no buryoku o unai ni shimesu beshi." *Jiyū shinbun,* December 27, 1884.

Nishi Amane. *Hyakugaku renkan.* In *Nishi Amane zenshū,* vol. 4. Tokyo: Munetaka shobō, 1981.

"Nisshin no kankei." *Jiyū shinbun,* November 3, 1883.

Noguchi Takehiko. *Shōsetsu: ichigo no jiten.* Tokyo: Sanseidō, 1996.

Ochi Haruo. *Kindai bungaku seiritsuki no kenkyū.* Tokyo: Iwanami shoten, 1984.

Ochiai Naobumi and Utsumi Kōzō. *Kokubungakushi kyōkasho.* Tokyo: Meiji shoin, 1903.

Ogi Shinzō, Kumakura Isao, and Ueno Chizuko, eds. *Fūzoku/sei.* In *Nihon kindai shisō taikei,* vol. 23. Tokyo: Iwanami shoten, 1990

Ogura Hiroshi. *Kokubungakushi kyōkasho.* Tokyo: Kōbunsha, 1904.

Okada, Richard H. *Figures of Resistance: Language, Poetry, and Narrating in the Tale of Genji and Other Mid-Heian Texts.* Durham, N.C.: Duke University Press, 1991.

Okitsu Kaname. *Meiji kaikaki bungaku no kenkyū.* Tokyo: Ōfūsha, 1968.

———. *Meiji shinbun kotohajime: "bunmei kaika" no jānarizumu.* Tokyo: Taishūkan shoten, 1997.

Ono Azusa. "Gaikō o ronzu." *Tōyō ronsaku.* In *Ono Azusa zenshū,* vol. 4. Tokyo: Waseda daigaku shuppanbu, 1981.

———. "Shuku kaikō." In *Waseda daigaku hyakunenshi,* vol. 1, ed. Waseda daigaku daigakushi henshūjo. Tokyo: Waseda daigaku shuppanbu, 1978.

Osa Shizue. *Kindai Nihon to kokugo nashonarizumu.* Tokyo: Yoshikawa kōbunkan, 1998.

"Ōshū no taisei o ronjite Futsushin jiken no kyokusei o danzu." *Yūbin hōchi shinbun,* September 18, 20, 1884.

Ōwada Tateki. *Meiji bungakushi.* Tokyo: Nihon tosho sentā, 1982.

———. *Wabungakushi.* Tokyo: Hakubunkan, 1892.

Ozaki Gakudō. "Kokusaihō wa Shina to Chōsen to o ninshiki sezu." *Yūbin hōchi shinbun,* December 18, 1884.

———. "Shina to tatakau no rigai o ronzu." In *Ozaki Gakudō zenshū,* vol. 2. Tokyo: Kōronsha, 1956.

Ozaki Shirō. "Bungei jihyō." In *Bungaku jidai* 3, no. 5: 28–31. Tokyo: Yumani shobō, 1995.

Posnett, Hutcheson Macaulay. *Comparative Literature.* New York: D. Appleton, 1886.

Reichert, Jim. *In the Company of Men: Representations of Male-Male Sexuality in Meiji Literature.* Stanford: Stanford University Press, 2006.

Rokoku kyomutō jijō. Trans. Nishikawa Tsūtetsu. Tokyo: Kurita Shintarō, 1882.

Rokoku kyomutō no yurai. Ed. Andō Kyūjirō. Osaka: Andō Kyūjirō, 1882.

"Rō narukana sensei seifu no ken." *Jiyū shinbun,* June 26, 1883.

Saitō Mareshi. *Kanbunmyaku no kindai: Shinmatsu = Meiji no bungakuken.* Nagoya: Nagoya daigaku shuppankai, 2005.

Sakai Naoki. "Jobun." *Toreishīsu* 1 (2000): 2–10.

Sakai, Naoki. *Translation and Subjectivity—"On Japan" and Cultural Nationalism.* Minneapolis: University of Minnesota Press, 1997.

Sakazaki Shiran. "Shōsetsu haishi no honbun o ronzu." In *Kindai bungaku hyōron taikei 1: Meijiki 1,* ed. Yoshida Seiichi and Asai Kiyoshi. Tokyo: Kadokawa shoten, 1971.

Sakurada Momoe. *Nishi no umi chishio no saarashi.* In *Meiji bungaku zenshū,* vol. 5, *Meiji seiji shōsetsushū 1.* Tokyo: Chikuma shobō, 1966.

"Satekosona." *Jiyū no tomoshibi*, January 15, 1885.

"Seiji ni kansuru haishi shōsetsu no hitsuyō naru o ronzu." In *Kindai bungaku hyōron taikei 1: Meijiki 1*, ed. Yoshida Seiichi and Asai Kiyoshi. Tokyo: Kadokawa shoten, 1971.

Sekii Mitsuo. "Nihon kindai bungaku kenkyū no kigen—Meiji bunka kenkyūkai toenpon." *Nihon bungaku* 43, no. 3 (March 1994).

Senuma Shigeki. "Shinri bungaku no hatten to sono kisū." In *Gendai Nihon bungaku zenshū*, vol. 95, *Gendai bungei hyōronshū II*. Tokyo: Chikuma shobō, 1958.

"Shakaishugi bungei undō." In *Kindai bungaku hyōron taikei 6: Taishōki III Shōwaki I*, ed. Miyoshi Yukio and Sofue Shōji. Tokyo: Kadokawa shoten, 1973.

Shibahara Takuji. "Taigaikan to nashonarizumu." In *Nihon kindai shisō taikei*, vol. 12, *Taigaikan*, ed. Shibahara Takuji, Ikai Takaaki, and Ikeda Masahiro. Tokyo: Iwanami shoten, 1988.

Shimamura Hōgetsu. *Meiji bungaku hensenshi kōwa*. In *Meiji shōsetsu bunshō hensenshi, Meiji shōsetsu naiyō hattatsushi, Meiji bungaku hensenshi kōwa*. Tokyo: Nihon tosho sentā, 1982.

Shinada Yoshikazu. *Man'yōshū no hatsumei: kokumin kokka to bunka sōchi to shite no koten*. Tokyo: Shin'yōsha, 2001.

"Shina no haiboku wa Nihon no sachi nari." *Tokyo Yokohama mainichi shinbun*, August 29–30, 1884.

"Shinfutsu no wa." *Jiyū shinbun*, May 17, 1884.

"Shinkoku heisei." *Jiyū shinbun*, October 16–25, 1883.

Shinoda Tarō. "Meiji bungaku kenkyū ni kansuru ichi kōsatsu." In *Meiji bungakushi shūsetsu*. Tokyo: Nihon bungakusha, 1932.

———. "Shakai shōsetsu to shakai shugi shōsetsu." In *Nihon bungaku kōza: Meiji bungakuhen*, vol. 11. Tokyo: Kaizōsha, 1934.

Shioi Ukō and Takahashi Tatsuo. *Shintai Nihon bungakushi*. Tokyo: Fukyūsha, 1902.

Shirane, Haruo. "Curriculum and Competing Canons." In *Inventing the Classics: Modernity, National Identity, and Japanese Literature*, ed. Haruo Shirane and Tomi Suzuki. Stanford: Stanford University Press, 2000.

———. "'Kokubungaku' no keisei." In *Iwanami Kōza: Bungaku*, vol. 13, *Neishon o koete*, ed. Komori Yōichi et al. Tokyo: Iwanami shoten, 2003.

"Shōgakkō kyōin kokoroe." In *Nihon kindai shisō taikei*, vol. 6, *Kyōiku no taikei*, ed. Yamazumi Masami. Tokyo: Iwanami shoten, 1990.

Shō Rō. "Datsu-a nyū-ō o mezasu kindai Nihon no Ajia ninshiki." In *Sabetsu to sensō—ningen keiseishi no kansei*, ed. Matsuura Tsutomu and Watanabe Kayoko. Tokyo: Akashi shoten, 1999.

Smiles, Samuel. *Self-Help*. New York: A. L. Burt, 19—.

Suita Dōshi. *Tokyo gijō*. Tokyo: Dōbunten, 1883.

Suzuki Sadami. *Nihon no "bungaku" gainen*. Tokyo: Sakuhinsha, 1998.

Suzuki, Tomi. "Gender and Genre: Modern Literary Histories and Women's Diary Literature." In *Inventing the Classics: Modernity, National Identity, and Japanese Literature*, ed. Haruo Shirane and Tomi Suzuki. Stanford: Stanford University Press, 2000.

———. *Narrating the Self: Fictions of Japanese Modernity*. Stanford: Stanford University Press, 1996.

Taine, Hippolyte. *History of English Literature*. Trans. Henri Van Laun. New York: Worthington, 1889.

Takabatake Ransen. *Kōsetsu kono tegashiwa*. In *Meiji bungaku zenshū*, vol. 2, *Meiji kaikaki bungakushū 2*. Tokyo: Chikuma shobō, 1967.

Takada Mamoru. *Hakkenden no sekai: denki roman no fukken*. Tokyo: Chūkō shinsho, 1980.

Takahashi Tansui. *Jidai bungakushi*. Tokyo: Kaihatsusha, 1906.

Takasu Yoshijirō. *Meiji bungakushiron*. Tokyo: Nihon hyōronsha, 1934.

Takayama Chogyū. "Biteki seikatsu o ronzu." In *Kindai bungaku hyōron taikei 2: Meijiki II*, ed. Yoshida Seiichi and Asai Kiyoshi. Tokyo: Kadokawa shoten, 1972.

———. "Meiji no shōsetsu." In *Nihon gendai bungaku zenshū*, vol. 8, *Saitō Ryokuu, Ishibashi Ningetsu, Takayama Chogyū, Uchida Roanshū*. Tokyo: Kōdansha, 1967.

Takemori Ten'yū. "'Henka' 'hensen' to iu koto—*Tōsei shosei katagi* o megutte." *Kokubungaku kaishaku to kanshō* 45, no. 3 (March 1980): 31–41. π

Takeshima Hagoromo. *Nihon bungakushi*. Tokyo: Jinbunsha, 1906.

Takeuchi Yō. *Gakureki kizoku no eikō to zasetsu*. In *Nihon no kindai*, vol. 12. Tokyo: Chūō kōron shinsha, 1999.

"Takeyari tazusaete undōkai." In *Nihon kindai shisō taikei*, vol. 21, *Minshū undō*, ed. Yasumaru Yoshio and Fukaya Katsumi. Tokyo: Iwanami shoten, 1989.

Tayama Katai. "Meiji bungaku no gaikan." *Bunshō sekai* (October 15, 1912): 2–11.

Tōkai Sanshi. *Kajin no kigū*. In *Meiji bungaku zenshū*, vol. 6, *Meiji seiji shōsetsushū 2*. Tokyo: Chikuma shobō, 1967.

Tokuda Shūsei. "E no moderu to shōsetsu no moderu." In "Jijitsu to sakuhin," *Bunshō sekai* (September 1907): 21–24.

Tokutomi (Roka) Kenjirō. *Footprints in the Snow*. Trans. Kenneth Strong. New York: Pegasus, 1970.

———. *Omoide no ki*. Tokyo: Min'yūsha shuppan, 1901.

Tokutomi Sohō. "Kinrai ryūkō no seiji shōsetsu o hyōsu." In *Kokumin no tomo*, vol. 1. Tokyo: Meiji bunken, 1966.

———. "Nisshikan jiken ni kansuru no iken." In *Nihon kindai shisō taikei*, vol. 12,

Taigaikan, ed. Shibahara Takuji, Ikai Takaaki, and Ikeda Masahiro. Tokyo: Iwanami shoten, 1988.

———. "Osaka no goku." In *Kokumin no tomo*, vol. 1. Tokyo: Meiji bunken, 1966.

Tomasi, Massimiliano. *Rhetoric in Modern Japan: Western Influences on the Development of Narrative and Oratorical Style*. Honolulu: University Of Hawai'i Press, 2004.

"Tōyō no kiun." *Chōya shinbun*, April 13, 1884.

"Tōyō renkōron." *Yūbin hōchi shinbun*, November 19, 1879.

"Tōyō shokoku no keisei." *Tokyo Yokohama mainichi shinbun*, June 27–28, 1879.

"Tōyō shokoku wa bankoku kōhō no rieki o bunshu sezu." *Tokyo Yokohama mainichi shinbun*, October 10, 1884.

Tsubouchi Shōyō. *The Essence of the Novel*. Trans. Nanette Twine. *Occasional Papers* 11. Queensland: Department of Japanese, University of Queensland, 1981.

———. "Kaioku mandan." In *Shōyō senshū*, vol. 12, ed. Shōyō kyōkai. Tokyo: Daiichi shobō, 1977.

———. "Kyokutei Bakin." In *Shōyō senshū*, vol. 12, ed. Shōyō kyōkai. Tokyo: Daiichi shobō, 1977.

———. "Shōsetsu o ronjite shosei katagi no shui ni oyobu." In *Kindai bungaku hyōron taikei 1: Meijiki 1*, ed. Yoshida Seiichi and Asai Kiyoshi. Tokyo: Kadokawa shoten, 1971..

———. *Shōsetsu shinzui*. Tokyo: Iwanami bunko, 1936.

———. *Shōsetsu shinzui*. Tokyo: Nihon kindai bungakkan, 1979.

———. *Shōsetsu shinzui*. In *Meiji bungaku zenshū*, vol. 16, *Tsubouchi Shōyōshū*. Tokyo: Chikuma shobō, 1969.

———. *Shōsetsu shinzui*. In *Nihon kindai bungaku taikei*, vol. 3, *Tsubouchi Shōyōshū*. Tokyo: Kadokawa shoten, 1974.

———. *Tōsei shosei katagi*. In *Nihon kindai bungaku taikei*, vol. 3, *Tsubouchi Shōyōshū*. Tokyo: Kadokawa shoten, 1974.

Uchida Roan. "Jogaku zasshi no shōsetsuron." In *Meiji bungaku zenshū*, vol. 24, *Uchida Roanshū*. Tokyo: Chikuma shobō, 1978.

Udagawa Bunkai, ed. *Tenmei sōdō: Fushimi gimin den*. Kyoto: Shinshindō, 1883.

Ueda Kazutoshi. "Kokugogaku no sōseiki." *Kokugo to kokubungaku* (August 1934): 1131–38.

"Waga hō no Shina ni taisuru seiryaku ikan." *Chōya shinbun*, December 21, 23 1884.

"Wagakuni ga Shinfutsu ni taisuru no seiryaku." *Jiyū shinbun*, June 19–24, 1883.

"Wagakuni ni jiyū no shushi o hanshoku suru ichi shudan wa haishi gikyoku tō no tagui o kairyō suru ni ari." In *Kindai bungaku taikei 1: Meijiki 1*, vol. 1, ed. Yoshida Seiichi and Asai Kiyoshi. Tokyo: Kadokawa shoten, 1971.

Wakita Haruko and S. B. Hanley, eds. *Jendā no Nihonshi—shutai to hyōgen shigoto to seikatsu.* Vol. 2. Tokyo: Tokyo daigaku shuppankai, 1994–95.

Walthall, Ann. Introduction to *Peasant Uprisings in Japan: A Critical Anthology of Peasant Histories.* Ed. and trans. Ann Walthall. Chicago: University of Chicago Press, 1991.

Waseda daigaku daigakushi henshūjo, ed. *Waseda daigaku hyakunenshi.* Vol. 1. Tokyo: Waseda daigaku shuppanbu, 1978.

Yamada Shunji. "Bōkan suru katarite no haikei—Tsubouchi Shōyō *Tōsei shosei katagi.*" *Kokubungaku kaishaku to kanshō* 56, no. 4 (April 1991): 39–45.

———. "*Tōsei shosei katagi* ni okeru 'sakusha' no ichi: ninjōbon o kagami to shite." *Nihon bungaku* 40, no. 1 (January 1991): 1–13.

Yamada Yūsaku. "Jobun—bungakushi no kōzu." In *Kindai bungaku I*, ed. Yamada Yūsaku. Tokyo: Gakujutsu tosho shuppansha, 1990.

———. "*Tōsei shosei katagi*—katarite o megutte." In *Nihon no kindai shōsetsu: sakuhinron no genzai*, vol. 1, ed. Miyoshi Yukio. Tokyo: Tokyo daigaku shuppankai, 1986.

Yamamoto Taketoshi. *Kindai Nihon no shinbun dokushasō.* Tokyo: Hōsei daigaku shuppankyoku, 1981.

———. *Shinbun to minshū: Nihongata shinbun no keisei katei.* Tokyo: Kinokuniya shoten, 1994.

Yamamuro Shin'ichi. *Shisō kadai to shite no Ajia: kijiku, rensa, tōki.* Tokyo: Iwanami shoten, 2001.

Yamazumi Masami. "Kaisetsu." In *Nihon kindai shisō taikei*, vol. 6, *Kyōiku no taikei*, ed. Yamazumi Masami. Tokyo: Iwanami shoten, 1990.

"Yamu o ezunba Futsukoku to dōmei subeshi." *Tokyo Yokohama mainichi shinbun*, January 14, 1885.

Yanagida Izumi. *Meiji no shomotsu, Meiji no hito.* Tokyo: Tōgensha, 1963.

———. "Seiji kōdan kotohajime." In *Zuihitsu Meiji bungaku*, vol. 1. Tokyo: Shunjūsha, 1938.

———. *Seiji shōsetsu kenkyū I.* In *Meiji bungaku kenkyū*, vol. 8. Tokyo: Shunjūsha, 1967.

———. *Shōsetsu shinzui no kenkyū.* In *Meiji bungaku kenkyū*, vol. 2. Tokyo: Shunjūsha, 1966.

Yasuda Toshiaki. *Teikoku Nihon no gengo hensei.* Tokyo: Seori shobō, 1997.

Yasukawa Jun'nosuke. *Fukuzawa Yukichi no Ajia ninshiki—Nihon kindaishizō o torae kaesu.* Tokyo: Kōbunken, 2000.

———. "Nisshin sensō to Ajia besshi shisō—Nihon kindaishizō no minaoshi." In *Sabetsu to sensō—ningen keiseishi no kansei*, ed. Matsuura Tsutomu and Watanabe Kayoko. Tokyo: Akashi shoten, 1999.

Yoda, Tomiko. *Gender and National Literature: Heian Texts in the Constructions of Japanese Modernity.* Durham, N.C.: Duke University Press, 2004.

Yoshimi Kaneko. *Baishō no shakaishi.* Tokyo: Yūzankaku shuppan, 1984.

Yoshino Sakuzō. "Meiji bunka no kenkyū ni kokorozaseshi dōki." In *Yoshino Sakuzō senshū*, vol. 11. Tokyo: Iwanami shoten, 1995.

Index